NAVAJO LAND, NAVAJO CULTURE

Also by Robert S. McPherson

The Journey of Navajo Oshley: An Autobiography and Life History (Logan, Utah, 2000)

River Flowing from the Sunrise: An Environmental History of the Lower San Juan, with James Aton (Logan, Utah, 2000)

Together: The Building of a Community College (San Juan, Utah, 1997)

A History of San Juan County: In the Palm of Time (Salt Lake City, 1995)

Sacred Land, Sacred View: Navajo Perceptions of the Four Corners Region (Provo, Utah, 1992)

The Northern Navajo Frontier, 1860–1900: Expansion through Adversity (Albuquerque, 1988)

Navajo Land, Navajo Culture

THE UTAH EXPERIENCE IN THE TWENTIETH CENTURY

Robert S. McPherson

UNIVERSITY OF OKLAHOMA PRESS : NORMAN

Publication of this book was made possible in part by generous support from the Charles Redd Center for Western Studies.

Earlier versions of several chapters have been published previously. "Naalyéhé Bá Hooghan, 'House of Merchandise': Navajo Trading Posts as an Institution of Cultural Change, 1900–1930" and "From Dezba to 'John': The Changing Role of Navajo Women in Southeastern Utah," reprinted from *American Indian Culture and Research Journal*, vol. 16, no. 1 and vol. 18, no. 3, respectively, by permission of the American Indian Studies Center, UCLA. © 1992, 1994 Regents of the University of California. "Poverty, Politics, and Petroleum: The Utah Navajo and the Aneth Oil Field," coauthored with David A. Wolff, reprinted from *American Indian Quarterly*, vol. 21, no. 3 (summer 1997), by permission of the University of Nebraska Press. Copyright © 1998 University of Nebraska Press, "History Repeats Itself: Navajo Livestock Reduction in Southeastern Utah, 1933–1946," reprinted from *American Indian Quarterly*, vol. 22, nos. 1 & 2 (spring 1998), by permission of the University of Nebraska Press. Copyright © 1999 University of Nebraska Press.

Library of Congress Cataloging-in-Publication Data

McPherson, Robert S., 1947–
    Navajo land, Navajo culture : the Utah experience in the Twentieth Century / Robert S. McPherson.
        p. cm.
    Includes bibliographical references and index.
    ISBN 978-0-8061-3410-9 (paper)
        1. Navajo Indians—History—Sources. 2. Navajo Indians—Land tenure. 3. Navajo Indians—Economic conditions. 4. Oral tradition—Utah. 5. Land settlement patterns—Utah—History—20th century. 6. Social adjustment—Utah—History—20th century. 7. Utah—Politics and government. 8. Utah—Economic conditions. 9. Utah—Social life and customs. I. Title: Utah experience in the Twentieth Century. II. Title.

E99.N3 M5158 2001
979.1'004972—dc21   2001023405

This paper in this book meets the guidelines for permanence and durability of the Committee on Production Guidelines for Book Longevity of the Council on Library Resources, Inc.

To Betsy and the children

CONTENTS

ILLUSTRATIONS

PHOTOGRAPHS

MAP

PREFACE

Southeastern Utah, nestled in the Four Corners, where Utah, Arizona, Colorado, and New Mexico meet, is a land of contrast. The topography speaks of difference: a half-hour drive can take one to the desert, another half hour to an alpine setting, still another to the rolling sagebrush plains and red rock canyons characteristic of the Colorado Plateau. The dramatic beauty lends itself to a variety of interpretations as well as uses.

Various cultures and subcultures—Navajos, Utes, Paiutes, Hispanics, and Anglos—have used and interpreted the land. Arriving at different times with different political, economic, and cultural agendas, these peoples have worked out a colorful, though not always cooperative, past. Conflict and change have been as much a part of this experience as have friendship, trust, and sharing. To find perfection in any one group is unrealistic, just as it is difficult to find a particular piece of land that is satisfactory to everyone. Contrast is a basic spice of the history in this region.

In writing about this history, one encounters both pleasures and pitfalls. It is intensely informative as a microcosm of culture and race relations. The region's prehistoric Anasazi ruins and tales of Ute, Navajo, pioneer, and cowboy experiences pique the imagination. In some respects this period in the region's history—primarily the nineteenth century—overpowers the seemingly less dramatic twentieth century. Readers fascinated by the earlier period may fall into one-sided, comfortable stereotypes of the Indian as either the noble red man or the antagonist to "progress."

What follows is an economic history of the Navajos living in south-eastern Utah during the twentieth century. But it is more than that: it is a glimpse into the past, informed when possible by a Navajo cultural perspective derived from oral history. The Navajos' story moves far beyond the role of the antagonist or the cliché of blanket-weaving, sheepherding nomads of the desert. Their history is dynamic and far reaching. One of the major currents running through this work is that these people were deeply involved in carving out their own destiny and adapted readily to "progress" when it was perceived as beneficial. This is not to suggest that everything happened just the way the Navajos planned or desired. In fact, as the dominant culture had an increasing effect on the People, they made some dramatic shifts to accommodate the needs of time and place. Yet the Navajos were anything but passive. Their story, told with their help, is one of adaptation to evolving circumstances tied to the land.

There is also a risk in telling this story. Today, more than ever before, writing American Indian history can be an undertaking fraught with danger. At a time when such buzzwords as "politically correct" and "culturally sensitive" are part of the everyday lexicon, should a white man even be expected to venture onto this sacred turf? But it is unrealistic to expect that Indians alone will or even should write all of their history. It is imperative that their perspective is included. Good history has to inform, to provide a variety of perspectives. Certainly the past can provide numerous examples of history from a white perspective—an intellectual "manifest destiny" approach that rides roughshod over the peoples and cultures that did not share the same values or circumstances as those putting pen to paper. The result: "ethnocentrism writ large."

Now the pendulum of sensitivity has swung sufficiently in the other direction. Some strident voices demand that only American Indians have the right and obligation to tell their own history. While most historians agree in part with this sentiment, the problem rests in the word *only*. For some white historians, the sins of the past—both of omission and commission—have returned to plague even the best-intentioned writer. One becomes wary, acutely sensitive to the feelings of Indian people who are now both subject and recipient and proprietors of their past.

Historically, it was the Navajos' oral tradition that preserved this past. These stories and teachings still hold a strength, beauty, and perspective that must be used in retelling the history of past generations. The written record, although rooted in a different perception and medium, provides another glimpse of the same picture. Both views are necessary, though neither one, even when combined, provides a total reality.

This book is a history of the Navajos and how they, their culture, and their economy changed. But there are many books and a plethora of articles that discuss these topics. How is this one different? A number of authors have chosen to write about the Navajos and the livestock economy. For instance, Louise Lamphere's *To Run After Them: Cultural and Social Bases of Cooperation in a Navajo Community* and Klara B. Kelley's *Navajo Land Use: An Ethnoarchaeological Study* are two works that examine Navajo relations with the land and economic forces. Both are well-documented, technical studies that quantify Navajo economic activity to establish patterns of land use and social relations. Both authors undertook lengthy fieldwork with the Navajos, who provided substantial detail from which their analyses are derived. But one cannot miss the form of presentation of the material: it is the voice of academia. This is neither a plus nor a minus, but it lends itself to an often-heard criticism leveled by Navajo people that anthropological works can be difficult to understand from a Navajo perspective. While the information may be accurate, the Navajo voice is lost.

Different from these two works are Kent Gilbreath's *Red Capitalism: An Analysis of the Navajo Economy* and Philip Reno's *Mother Earth, Father Sky, and Economic Development*. While the latter title suggests a Navajo perception of the land and the economy derived therefrom, both books look at coal, oil, uranium, water, and forests in a purely monetary sense. Financing businesses and the growth of entrepreneurs is Gilbreath's concern, while Reno analyzes costs and benefits and the development of products. The voice of supply and demand and the stock exchange ring much louder than those of the elders, who strongly influenced economic activities in traditional Navajo society. This, again, is not to say that these books, representing a particular approach and genre, do not have their place. But they reflect the thinking of the dominant culture and not traditional Navajo beliefs.

Sam Bingham and Janet Bingham's approach in *Between Sacred Mountains: Navajo Stories and Lessons from the Land* is closer to the one I employ. Their work grew out of a four-year project in the Rock Point Community School in which students, parents, and community members shared their thoughts and experiences about the land and people, their history and future. The Navajo voice is heard throughout, mixed with that of social science (history, anthropology, economics, etc.). The book is successful in bridging the chasm between academia and the Navajo elder.

Navajo Land, Navajo Culture is a further attempt to join the view of the social scientist with that of the Navajo. I have spent many hours listening to Navajo people tell their history, some of which is at wide variance with published accounts. The chapter on livestock reduction in the 1930s is a good example, wherein the Navajos compare this traumatic episode to that of the Long Walk and incarceration at Fort Sumner in the 1860s. The connection between these two events is theirs and is one not often made by social scientists. Other chapters re-create the feelings and rationale for everything from bartering at a trading post to acting in John Ford movies and from experiencing technological change brought by the automobile to working with a burgeoning tourist industry. I hope I have succeeded in giving a clear presentation of at least part of the Navajo elders' perspective.

As a white man outside of the culture, I am acutely aware of the difficulty of translating accurately the words and feelings in the way the speaker intended. Once something is written in black ink on a white page, the words become cold and subject to misinterpretation. For instance, as elders talked about the introduction of the car into Navajo society, they would laugh, finding pleasure in recounting the different ideas circulating about this strange phenomenon. I have tried to communicate this sense of wonder and amusement.

There is of course another voice in these pages, that of the historian. A few of the chapters examine issues that may feel uncomfortable and contrary to what is expected. It is popular today to point out, with sharpened word, the wrongs of the past (and there were many of them) perpetrated by the white man. There is a never-ending need to accord fair treatment and respect to all people and cultures. At the same time, one should not avert one's gaze from actions that may raise eyebrows and questions. Take the chapter on traditional deer hunting, for instance. Historians who examine the written record will find substantial correspondence concerning off-reservation Navajo and Ute hunting parties in the Four Corners region. What does one do with this information? I have tried to explain what could have happened using both sides of the cultural ledger. The intent was neither to open old wounds nor to add fuel to political issues of today but to come to a cultural explanation in a historical context. Although the topic is controversial, I hope the treatment is balanced.

Another problem arises in using the vocabulary of the dominant culture. There are many words that do not translate directly from Navajo into English. There are also words that have a connotation different from their denotation and so give a sense not intended by the writer. The word *myth* is an example. Many American Indian writers find this term offensive because it suggests something that is not true, a mere fable, of no consequence. Philosophers and anthropologists such as Joseph Campbell and Victor Turner have studied myths and explained that these teachings provide the charter for a culture, answer deep, significant questions concerning the general human experience, and are indispensable in providing rules and values in an otherwise chaotic world. Every culture has them, even though some stories may not be recognized as such. When the term "myth" is used, however, the old, pejorative attitude still clings to it. Unfortunately, there is no other word in the English language that can serve as a substitute. I use "myth" here to refer to a narrative that is sacred and true to those who believe in it. No pejorative connotation is intended.

Other words that may be problematic are *supernatural*, here defined simply as having more than a natural, physical power that is connected to deity, and *traditional*, used here to refer simply to a series of patterns established in the past. For those living in the twentieth century, "tradition" means the lifestyle of those raised in the time when livestock served as the basis of the economy and Navajo religious values provided a core philosophy for understanding the world. Chronologically, one might point to the 1920s as a representative period, before livestock reduction, Christianity, the Native American Church, and the wage economy made serious inroads into the culture. One must also recognize that change is a constant, that a people never "stand still," and so this definition of tradition serves more as a reference point in time than as a fixed rule or lifestyle.

Perhaps the most important thing I hope will come from this book is an appreciation for the complexity of the history of the Utah Navajos and the customary values they bring to their daily lives. They are a contemplative yet fun-loving people who have much to offer us as we move into the twenty-first century. Their history provides the soil from which future generations will grow. For those not yet born, the cultural soil of the twentieth century is filled with lessons that enrich. There is much to be proud of.

ACKNOWLEDGMENTS

Anyone who has thumbed through even a few pages of this book has seen the heavy dependence upon Navajo oral history. Indeed, the single most important element that makes this an interesting contribution to the plethora of books already in existence is the Navajo voice juxtaposed with that of the social scientist. The People's perspective shapes this narrative and gives expression for their greatest concern: sharing the past with future generations. I hope their desire to tell their story is fulfilled. Therefore, it is with great appreciation that I recognize the contribution made by the Utah Navajos, with permission from the tribe, to the writing of this history.

There are always those who rise above the rest in bringing a work to fruition. Marilyn Holiday and Baxter Benally have been crucial guides through the interview process as they traveled, translated, and taught along the way. Early mornings on the road, the hours spent visiting homes, and the time perched on the tailgate of a pickup truck filled our days. The return home at sunset or later adds to memories and feelings of accomplishment. Marilyn's and Baxter's steadiness throughout have made this work possible.

Two organizations were also particularly helpful. The Utah Humanities Council provided much of the funding to pay those who were interviewed, as well as those who translated and typed the interviews. The support of the Council, which is composed of professionals who care, was timely and crucial. The College of Eastern Utah–San Juan Campus provided transportation, a sabbatical leave, and the intangible encouragement necessary to accomplish the task. Both groups were indispensable.

There were others. The Navajo Nation Museum assisted with photographs, the Navajo Nation's Archives granted access to the J. Lee Correll Collection, the federal government's Denver Records Center made available its holdings, and the Charles Redd Center for Western Studies (Brigham Young University) provided supplementary funding. Both Brigham Young University and the University of Utah opened various archival collections for my use.

On a more personal note, I appreciate the encouragement that Betsy, my wife, has always given. My children have been understanding and supportive throughout and encouraged Dad to follow his interests. These are priceless gifts.

I have tried to represent the topics in this book fairly and sensitively. If there are inaccuracies, I take full responsibility. My one goal has been to write a history that is representative of the Utah Navajos' experience from their perspective. If I have succeeded, it is because of their help.

NAVAJO LAND, NAVAJO CULTURE

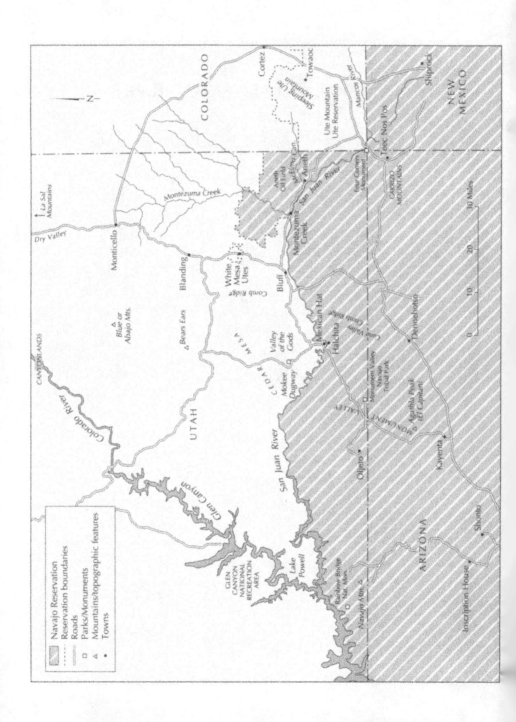

CHAPTER ONE

PROLOGUE TO THE PRESENT

Setting the Stage for the Twentieth Century

Ada Black sat on the edge of her worn couch looking directly at us. With brown eyes fixed, her thin voice rising and falling, she sketched images from the past. Blue veins ran beneath the skin of her hands and wrists like lines on a map, marking her seventy-four years of life that October day in 1991. Ada's cotton dress, the bandanna that covered her gray hair, and her scuffed leather shoes spoke of the physical poverty that she had faced most of her life. But she was rich in other things. Her wealth was stored in her heart and mind, rooted in the teachings of the Diné—the People.

Marilyn Holiday, a close Navajo friend, and I were there to learn. The tribe had granted us permission to gather information on the Utah Navajos' experience in preparation for writing a county history for the state's centennial, which was to be celebrated in 1996. The interview ranged far and wide as topics concerning uranium mining, the movie industry, family relations, and cultural patterns spilled from Ada's mind. Her life at Navajo Mountain and in Monument Valley had been full, and she shared it freely. The experiences had been varied, yet they were typical for a Navajo woman who had grown up in the 1920s and 1930s, in what is today considered "traditional" culture. But there was one theme that threaded through her monologue: the land and the gods who created, developed, and infused it with power. It served as the starting and ending point between which everything else was bound. This was central to Ada's understanding of everything that the white man's world calls history. Underlying the events of the past was an explanation rooted in spirituality, a view that is far different from that which is expected or even tolerated in most academic circles as a causative force. God(s)-centered history is usually not accepted by scholars, because this type of cause and effect is not traceable, the results are not reproducible, and the "proof" is based on a value system rooted in belief, not fact. Such a view was foreign to Ada, who felt not a ripple of misgiving. She invested her time in faith, not doubt; her world was one of respect for the sacred, unshakable in its understanding.

As we sat on her couch, the fall sunshine streamed through an east-facing window, warming the room. Ada began relating events in her life that were representative of what many Utah Navajos had experienced. The core of her beliefs shone through as she began:

> This earth is our mother and is the place we first cry. Our first sounds are made on it. . . . We rest on it. On it we are growing. The darkness covers us to tell us to sleep and rest. It is here we make offerings. Both mother earth and the darkness have offerings. The sun that goes across the sky has offerings. It is the same for the moon; it also shines light for us. It is like this. So all the things have offerings. We use this as a shield to live by. With this protection, we experience no harm. . . . I am telling you all that I know.[1]

Ada thus briefly outlined a major concept underlying the Navajo perception of many events in the twentieth century. Understanding the history of the Utah Navajo is as much a religious undertaking as it is an economic, historical, or anthropological experience. Her history, and that of thousands of Navajos like her, had its beginning with the gods and a creative period long before this world as we know it was fashioned. The holy beings created everything spiritually before it was formed physically. They provided patterns of thought and well-being, implanting them in the hearts and minds of both animate and inanimate creations. In the three or four previous worlds beneath this one, animals acted like humans, the gods established types of relationships between different creatures, objects were given powers to both help and harm, and Navajo culture and thought received its foundation.[2] In short, the gods initiated the elements of the universe in a series of evolutionary steps that went from simple to complex and from spiritual to physical.

Not all was perfect. Each world was abandoned because the People and the creatures inhabiting it failed to adhere to the guidelines established by the holy beings. Separation, destruction, and death followed. For instance, in the last world beneath this one, Coyote, the trickster, stole a water baby, angering the spirit within the waters and causing them to rise and flood the land. People and animals fled across the shrinking landmass until they found a hollow reed through which they escaped into this world. Eventually, Coyote returned the stolen water baby and set about on a new series of escapades.

When the Diné finally reached this, the fifth or glistening world, they emerged either in the La Plata Mountains of Colorado or in the Navajo Dam area near present-day Farmington, New Mexico, and started their wanderings to the Pacific Ocean. The People, animals, and holy beings interacted freely in a landscape made sacred through thought and deed. The gods placed four sacred mountains—Blanca (east), Mount Taylor (south), San Francisco Peaks (west), and Hesperus (north)—to form a boundary around Navajo land and provide powers of blessing and protection. The Diné began a series of migrations that scattered them in various directions across the land and gave rise to a system of more than sixty matrilineal clans. A large number of these are still present, defining family and kinship bonds of cohesion.[3]

Perhaps one of the most important events during this mythological period was the birth of twin boys named Monster Slayer and Born for Water. Their father was Sun Bearer and their mother Changing Woman, important Navajo deities. The boys were conceived through supernatural means during a time when human-eating monsters roamed Navajo land. Changing Woman tried her best to shelter the boys from harm, but they eventually took it upon themselves to leave the safety of home to obtain supernatural help from their father. Following a series of adventures, they traveled to the sky and were tested to ensure they were actually the sons of Sun Bearer. With the help of supernatural beings, the Twins triumphed in their tests, obtained weapons such as arrows made of lightning and sunbeams, then returned to earth to do battle.

The monsters were no match for the weapons and wits of the young men. Once defeated, the body parts of these foes were sliced off and thrown in different directions, and they are now seen spread throughout the land. To the Navajos who have been taught these events, the land serves as a rich mnemonic device, reminding them of the time when the holy beings struggled to make the earth safe for the People. It is sacred, made holy by the spiritual events that have occurred on it.[4]

From these stories and teachings spring a complex series of cere-monies used to heal and protect the Navajo from both physical and supernatural harm. Most of these chantways fall into three categories: Holy Way rituals that are directed by the gods to attract good and restore health; Evil Way rituals that exorcise ghosts, malevolent spirits, and the effects of witchcraft; and Life Way rituals that treat injuries from accidents.[5] All of the Navajo ceremonies help shape the worldview of the people and speak to those beliefs that make them unique.

Archaeologists and anthropologists have a different view of the ori-gin of the Navajo. Unlike the Numic-speaking Utes and Paiutes who live as neighbors in the Utah portion of Navajo country, the People derive from the Athabascan language stock. A large body of literature argues an origin and chronological sequence that ties the Navajo to ancestral lands in present-day northwestern Canada and Alaska around the time of Christ. Using a technique called glottochronology to meas-ure language change between groups over time, anthropologists have determined that linguistic differences between Navajos and other Atha-bascan speakers indicate tribal divergences. For instance, the Hupas, now living in California, separated from the Navajos about 1,100 years ago; the Kutchin and the Beaver groups in Canada, 890 and 690 years ago respectively; the Jicarilla and San Carlos Apaches, 300 years ago; and the Chiricahua Apaches, 170 years ago. If these dates are relatively accurate, the Navajos separated from their ancestral stock roughly 1,000 years ago.[6] Because there are many variables that enter into language change, not all scholars agree with these figures, but they help to pro-vide an understanding of differences among groups.

Another concern is how the People traveled to their present location. A number of explanations offer a variety of routes: down the west coast and then into the Southwest, through the Rocky Mountains to use a cold climate technology, down the eastern side of the Rocky Mountains, or a combination of these routes. Most scholars now agree on the more west-erly passage.[7] Clyde Kluckhohn, a respected scholar of Navajo culture, believes the Navajos' forefathers could have been in the Southwest by

A.D. 1000, while David M. Brugge, a noted anthropologist, says that "by 1300 the Apacheans [Athabascan speakers] must have been close to the northern periphery of the Anasazi region."[8] If mythology is an indicator of events, the Navajos had extensive contacts with the Anasazi, as outlined in their rich body of lore.[9]

Others do not agree that the Navajos were in the Southwest that early, although the dates of occupation are being pushed back from the long-accepted A.D. 1500. For instance, recent excavations north of Farmington, New Mexico, and just south of the Colorado state line have yielded twelve sites with twenty-three radiocarbon dates that predate the 1500s, the earliest going back to the 1300s. Because of this new information, "it appears likely that the Navajo were in the Four Corners region by at least A.D. 1400. . . . The period of time between the last Anasazi occupations north of the San Juan River and the earliest Navajo sites is now only about a century, suggesting the possibility that future research may establish contemporaneity between the two cultures."[10] This is particularly important, since the region producing these early dates is considered by the Navajos to be the area of their oldest habitation once they emerged from the worlds beneath this one.

Recognized Navajo archaeological remains in southeastern Utah are from a much later time. The earliest-dated Navajo structure is in White Canyon, with a tree-ring date of A.D. 1620. Five other dates exist for the Navajo Mountain area, going back to the last quarter of the 1700s; and sixteen dates, ranging between 1700 and 1800, come from Butler Wash, Montezuma Creek, White Canyon, and the Bears Ears.[11]

Spanish documents first referred to the Navajos in the early 1630s.[12] For the next two centuries, Spanish and, later, Mexican writers chronicled their struggles with these bands of "wild" Indians. The Navajos raided Hispanic and Pueblo groups alike, stealing livestock and crops, capturing women and children, and killing or harassing those who pursued them. Adoption of the horse, gun, and evolving tactics enhanced Navajo military power; their economy subsequently changed with the introduction of sheep, goats, and cattle. Social and political practices altered as a result of a growing slave trade and shifting alliances, all of which created a dynamic frontier. By 1675 the Navajos and their northern neighbors, the Utes, were well mounted and aggressively pursuing the Spanish and their sedentary Indian allies.

Navajos abandoned their homes, similar to this male hogan, during the "Fearing Time." Not until the end of hostilities and the Treaty of 1868 did the Navajos begin to reclaim land and resources lost through warfare. Photo from Milton Snow Collection, NE8-46, Navajo Nation Museum.

A brief sketch based on fragmentary Spanish and Mexican reports of this fluid situation shows how fickle the antagonists could become. The early relationship between the Navajos and Utes and the Spanish was characterized by jockeying for position to gain the upper hand militarily. The Spanish and their Pueblo allies were stationary, profitable targets for mobile forces who descended at random from a canyon and desert wilderness. Although the Spanish took hundreds of Navajos captive and used them either as domestic servants or as slaves in the silver mines of Zacatecas, Mexico, there were still too many enemies operating in fragmented bands to force the Indians to the bargaining table. Throughout the 1600s Spanish power ebbed and flowed. Friction with "wild" Indians, like the Navajos, caused the government periodically to send expeditions north in pursuit of raiders. Imprecise geographic references make it difficult to determine how far these forces penetrated into the Four Corners region, but the record is clear that the Navajos and other hostile tribes served as an unintentional lure, drawing their enemies into new lands. Southeastern Utah became increasingly familiar terrain to these first Euro-Americans.

In 1720 the Spanish hit on the plan of turning the Utes and Comanches against the Navajos and achieved this with telling effect. For the next fifty years the Spanish enjoyed an uneasy peace with their archrivals. By 1754 the Navajos abandoned what they considered their homelands—called Dinétah—in northern New Mexico and took up residence farther south in places removed from the Utes.

Therefore, it is not surprising that when Fray Francisco Atanasio Dominguez and Fray Silvestre Velez de Escalante traveled into southeastern Utah in 1776 they encountered no Navajos. They recognized the San Juan River (or, as they called it, the Navajo River) as the northern boundary of this tribe and the southern boundary of the Utes yet reported no Athabascan presence.[13] Of Utes and Paiutes, there were plenty.

Relations among the Navajo and the Spanish and their allies remained unsettled right up to the time of official Spanish withdrawal from North America in 1821. When the Mexican government assumed control over the vast area known today as the American Southwest, it was ill prepared for what it encountered. The Navajos and other tribes increased raids on Mexican and Pueblo settlements along the Rio Grande and believed themselves impervious to retaliatory attacks. Mexican forces were generally smaller in number, poorly equipped, and unprepared for the long-range warfare necessary to bring their enemies to meaningful peace talks. Punitive raids by the Mexicans were as much slaving expeditions for economic purposes as they were military measures of frontier policy. Hostility only increased.

The Mexican reaction was misguided frustration. Like their Spanish predecessors, they sent out expeditions to attack the Navajos. These forays were almost totally ineffective; the invasions did little except to intensify the Indians' raiding efforts. For instance, in June 1823 José Antonio Vizcarra set out from Santa Fe with fifteen hundred men to punish some Navajo recalcitrants and bring them to the peace table. Vizcarra skirmished his way through the Chuska Mountains of northern New Mexico to the Hopi mesas in Arizona, then headed north toward Utah. Near the present site of Cow Springs Trading Post, Arizona, Vizcarra attacked two Paiute camps, "believing they were Navajos; for having taken up arms, there was no one to warn [him] they were Paiutes."[14]

Vizcarra's men killed four warriors and captured seven slaves, the soldiers basing their actions on the rationale that the Indians possessed goats—"which only the Navajos have." He released the Paiutes after they corrected this mistaken impression. A day later Vizcarra had a running fight with Navajos fleeing before him. He captured livestock—87 cattle and more than 400 sheep and goats—but lost 5 horses and inflicted no casualties. The soldiers slept that night near Oljeto Creek, within the boundaries of San Juan County, Utah.[15]

A separate column of men under Colonel Don Francisco Salazar headed toward the confluence of the Colorado and San Juan Rivers in search of the Navajos. Like Vizcarra, they attacked a group of Paiutes, later were convinced of their mistake, and freed them. Salazar then trudged east to Laguna Creek near Kayenta, where he crossed a fresh livestock trail heading toward the Bears Ears, a well-known topographic formation in Utah. The next day he followed the trail, then eventually turned south to Chinle Wash. He skirmished all day with Navajos who had begun "harassing the party, hoping to impede the march; they continued the harassment, striking a flank and drawing back, causing the soldiers to chase them."[16] By August 18 he had rejoined the main expedition under Vizcarra and departed for Santa Fe.

A Navajo account of this incident or one similar to it tells of how Mexicans chased the Navajos to the mouth of Copper Canyon in southeastern Utah. The Indians fled across the San Juan River with their livestock, then headed toward its confluence with the Colorado River. The soldiers in the meantime gathered all the livestock they could find and moved toward El Capitan in Monument Valley, skirmishing as they went. Navajos fired into their camp at night, killing five men, who were then buried at El Capitan. They stampeded and recaptured half the stock near Teec Nos Pos and fought a pitched battle in which thirteen more Mexicans were killed without the loss of a single Navajo. According to the person recounting this incident at the turn of the century, bones still lay around the site, "the trees nearby were still full of arrows, and handfuls [of arrowheads] could be picked up on the ground, with part of the Mexicans' saddles."[17] A similar fate awaited other expeditions into northern Navajo lands. By the time the Americans took control of the Southwest in 1848, the Mexicans were no doubt ready to hand over responsibility for fighting the Navajos. The U.S. Army, a larger organization with greater resources than the Mexican army, wisely returned to the earlier Spanish policy of encouraging Indian to fight Indian.

In the 1850s the fragile peace existing between the Navajos and the Utes, with the encouragement of the Anglo-Americans, began to disintegrate.[18] What could have been a fairly even contest of power started to turn against the Navajos. In addition to increased warfare with U.S. troops, drought and early frosts caused the failure of the 1857 corn harvest. The Navajos realized that the San Juan River and its tributaries provided a major planting area for crops, and if hostilities increased, use of this region could be denied them by the Utes.

The government chose to capitalize on these tensions and used a variety of forces to defeat the Navajos. In addition to conventional military units, which followed plans devised in part by Christopher "Kit" Carson, the government received help from Indian tribes angered by the Navajos, from Mexicans interested in obtaining more slaves for labor, and from white people who wanted to neutralize a long-standing foe.[19]

Presiding over this assortment of forces was General James H. Carleton, who charged his troops with bringing the Navajos to Fort Sumner on the Pecos River in east-central New Mexico. As the warfare intensified, American Indian and Anglo groups fanned out in search of an elusive enemy, forcing many Navajos to flee in every direction to the periphery of their lands.

As a result, Navajo enslavement boomed as never before, with Rio Arriba, Abiquiu, and Taos serving as markets for Mexicans to purchase their human merchandise. By January 1862 at least six hundred Navajo women and children were held captive in New Mexico through a system described as "worse than African slavery." The number of unreported slaves can only be guessed; however, by 1865 Carleton estimated that at least three thousand were living in Mexican households.[20]

The experience of Manuelito, one of the last Navajo war chiefs to surrender, provides a good example of the tremendous pressure placed on the People during this period of history called by the Navajos the "Fearing Time." Manuelito, born near the Bears Ears in southeastern Utah, at this point was living along the Little Colorado River. His success in war made him a symbol of Navajo resistance that the military wanted to crush. By 1864 he had watched the decimation of his tribe and heard rumors of how the People fared in captivity, fearing that if he surrendered, he and his followers would be massacred.

Still, Manuelito continuously asked Navajos whom he trusted about conditions at Fort Sumner. In February 1865 he told one such friend and messenger that "he intended to die where he was, that he was not stealing, that he could always be found . . . and did not intend to run away."[21] The interpreter told the military that Manuelito's band, under the control of six wealthy men, had approximately 600 horses, 3,000 sheep, 30 warriors, and 100 women, children, and elders.

Carleton gave Manuelito an option. Either he could surrender and keep his livestock or the Utes would find him, enslave his family, and take everything he owned. A group of chiefs from Fort Sumner visited Manuelito to deliver the ultimatum, but he told them not "to use up horse flesh or time in trying to persuade him." Less than a month later, Herrera Grande, one of these chiefs, met Manuelito at Zuni and returned with him to his camp. He noticed that a recent Ute raid had reduced the leader's band by half, and now there were only fifty horses and forty sheep. Manuelito said, "Here is all I have in the world. See what a trifling amount. You see how poor they are. My children are eating roots." His horses were too weak to make the trip, but if his people remained, they might lose their lives. The women wept at the thought of staying there, but Manuelito refused to leave his lands, bounded by the sacred rivers and mountains, and felt that there was now little to lose. Herrera left, saying, "I have done all I could for your benefit; I have given you the best advice. I now leave you as if your grave were already made."[22]

When Carleton heard this report, he ordered that Manuelito should be captured, placed in irons, and, if need be, killed out of mercy for those he controlled. Members of Manuelito's band started to trickle in to military posts, and Herrera received word that he could bring in Manuelito's sister and family. Less than a year later, a captive said that the Utes had dispersed Manuelito's group and that the war chief was living with his brother, surviving by hunting and eating buried corn that he traded with the Hopis. Two months previous, Utes had attacked his band while he was absent. Most of the men were killed by Cabeza Blanca.

> The Ute Chief took survivors and a large number of women and children with him to his own country. . . . A number were killed by

the Utes on their way thither . . . [but] a treaty was made by the remnant of the band with the Utes, who told them . . . that [the military] intended to keep them in confinement, and that it was better for them to live in amity with them [the Utes] and in freedom.[23]

In spite of this peace, Manuelito turned himself in to the army. In September 1866 he surrendered at Fort Wingate along with his twenty-three-member following. He was impoverished, had lost partial use of his left arm from a wound received from the Hopis, and had little to eat. An agent summarized Manuelito's experience: "[S]tarvation induced a surrender where a million dollars in money had failed to ensure success to the numerous military attempts to capture this celebrated chief and his band."[24]

Evidence of the enemies' effectiveness can also be found in Navajo oral tradition. Even today, the older people tell stories passed down in their families of the trauma visited on them by native and Euro-American incursions. While not all of the tales concern Utes—some are about Mexicans, Apaches, and Pueblo groups—many follow much the same pattern and establish both heroes and villains. Many elicit the teaching of values as much as the perception of history.

Manuelito, for instance, is said to have been an especially good fighter. One man tells of how Manuelito wore a mask on the back of his head, could shoot arrows as he ran backward, and fooled the enemy as to the direction he was traveling. He also had his people capture eagles to feather their arrows, saying, "We will not be killed poorly; we will be considered dangerous." Each man carried arrows dipped in snake venom, and according to the Navajos, when they wounded an enemy, the body quickly swelled and died.[25]

The central focus of many of these narratives rests in a flight to freedom, and as in most Navajo mythology, the emphasis is on travel through a specific geographic region. One woman told of meeting a bear that guided, protected, and fed her on the journey. The animal indicated when she should eat, and when another bear approached the pair, the protector killed it. An owl befriended a woman who asked it to lead her down a steep canyon wall. By hooting at intervals, the bird directed her on a safe route. Later, a dove led her to water.[26] Many of these animals appear in Navajo mythology, serving as either protectors or helpers.

During this period of conflict with the Utes and the Mexicans, the Navajos called on all the supernatural power available to them.

The number of Navajos at Fort Sumner eventually swelled to more than eight thousand, estimated by some contemporary sources as approximately two-thirds of the total Navajo population.[27] Those remaining at large, hid in the hinterlands, avoiding contact with unsympathetic outsiders. Southeastern Utah and northern Arizona served as a gathering place for some of the Navajos looking for a sanctuary from the pressures of war. Navajo oral tradition is rich in stories of battles, slave raids, and flights into the wilderness.[28] One of the most detailed accounts, as told by his son, Hashkéniinii Begay, in 1939, concerns a leader named Hashkéniinii who lived in the Kayenta–Monument Valley area in the early 1860s. The Utes and U.S. soldiers, part of Kit Carson's efforts to round up the Navajos, arrived in late summer "when the heads of grass were full" and started "grabbing them [Navajos] off like rabbits, a few here and a few there, . . . anywhere they could be found."[29]

The soldiers freed a few of their captives so that they might urge others to surrender. To this offer Hashkéniinii replied, "I was born and have lived in this country and I will die in it. I will not come in, even if I am killed by the Utes." He and his family, seventeen people in all, gathered twenty sheep, three horses, and a muzzle-loading rifle, then set out for Navajo Mountain, traveling mostly at night. They watched the soldiers' and Utes' movements by day and their campfires by night, even after the two groups parted company in search of fresh prey. Hashkéniinii drove his livestock and pushed his people unmercifully (earning his name, which means "Giving Out Anger"), foraged for food, and drank water trapped in rock basins and crevices until they arrived on the east side of Navajo Mountain. His wife feared the Utes more than the soldiers, yet she begged her husband to stop this ceaseless traveling. He did. The family took up residence within the protective confines of the canyons and slopes of the mountain. To this day, Navajo Mountain is considered a shield, a place of protection, and is noted for the performance of ceremonies that serve a similar function.[30]

At first Hashkéniinii believed his was the only group that escaped, but he later learned that other families and individuals, such as Dághaa' Sikaad living in the Kaibeto area, K'aayeełii near the Bears Ears, and

Spane Shank in the Navajo Mountain region, had also found refuge. In fact, according to a report in October 1864,

> less than one-half the tribe has surrendered. . . . [It] is the opinion of those best informed as to their resources that it will take years to entirely subdue and remove them, as those still running at large are well mounted, well armed, have stock to live upon, and are the bravest and most warlike of the tribe.[31]

Hashkéniinni stated that he was aware of at least one hundred people in the Black Mesa area who had escaped and that much of the livestock was never rounded up until he collected a herd of sheep that would grow to more than one thousand head by the time the Navajos were released from Fort Sumner in 1868.

The Navajos at Fort Sumner were anxious to return to their homelands. Disease, malnutrition, physical abuse, a foreign environment, and enemy slave raids had all taken their toll. The People offered prayers and ceremonies, asking the holy beings to help deliver them from a fate that many considered worse than death. On May 28, 1868, William Tecumseh Sherman signed a treaty with the Navajos, allowing them to return to a square reservation sitting astride the New Mexico–Arizona border. Just before their release Sherman warned, "[I]f you go to your own country, the Utes will be the nearest Indians to you; you must not trouble the Utes and the Utes must not trouble you. . . . You must not permit any of your young men to go to the Ute or Apache country to steal."[32]

This advice was hardly necessary. Following a few sporadic raids for women and livestock in 1868, the Utes became more peaceful, although agents reported that for the next few years large Navajo populations avoided living too close to the San Juan region. The friction of the previous war had burned an indelible scar into the memories of the Navajos— a scar that has continued to this day through their oral traditions. The Utes had earned their Navajo name Nóóda'i, "The Enemies You Continually Fight With."

The Navajos returned home, pushing beyond the small area designated as their new boundaries, in search of water for agriculture and grass for livestock. Those Navajos who had never surrendered encountered a small trickle of others willing to move closer to the Utes' domain.

Soon the numbers grew as natural increase of population and livestock spread throughout the core reservation lands already claimed.

At the same time that southeastern Utah became more appealing to Navajo livestock owners, the People met the early stages of Mormon and non-Mormon homesteading—white settlers attracted to the area by the waters of the San Juan River. Only the Utes could justify a strong aboriginal claim to the area, but the two most active groups in the region—Navajos and Anglos—were farmers dependent on water for crops and grazing lands for livestock. For approximately fifty years both sides competed for ownership and control; unlike many scenarios acted out elsewhere in the American West, here the American Indian occasionally triumphed.

This period was marked by petty and not-so-petty strife. Livestock, land, and trading posts were the catalysts for conflict. Letters requesting military assistance flowed from the San Juan as unlicensed trading post owners complained about the actions of their customers, as cattlemen watched Navajo livestock feed on the public domain, and as Navajo families settled north of their reservation boundaries. Resources acted as magnets, drawing people farther from established homes and creating headaches for agents, settlers, and Indians alike. Even government policy indirectly encouraged Indians to take up individual allotments on the public domain. [33]

When President Chester A. Arthur, through an executive order in 1884, provided all of the lands in Utah south of the San Juan River to the Navajos, it was hoped that this would quell the competition for territory with settlers. In reality, the order recognized an accomplished fact, that the Navajos had expanded far beyond the 1868 reservation borders. Now there was a clearly defined boundary—the San Juan River—that allowed no room for misunderstanding. Or so it seemed. What President Arthur and some of the local agents had not foreseen was that the expanding Navajo population, the growing herds of livestock, and the discovery of precious metals eight years later would drastically change the situation.

In 1892 white men were eyeing lands west of 110 degrees longitude. This territory, later known as the Paiute Strip, generally encompassed the area of Monument Valley, Navajo Mountain, and the lower part of the San Juan and Colorado Rivers before their waters crossed the Utah-

Arizona state line. Interest by whites in prospecting this land went back to the early 1880s; by 1892 mining concerns had created sufficient pressure to ensure that the government would return the lands of the Paiute Strip to the public domain.[34] This action came none too soon. Starting in December 1892, a large influx of miners descended on the banks of the San Juan in search of rumored deposits of flake or flour gold.[35] At the end of January 1893 an estimated three thousand miners were panning, shoveling, scraping, and burrowing into the banks and bars along the San Juan.[36] As with most get-rich-quick schemes, the boom in San Juan did not take long to bust. By March 1893 most of the miners had left for richer diggings in western Colorado.

To the Navajos this was just another example of the white man's madness. The loss of this rough country, peripheral to major areas of the livestock industry, was a setback to a relatively small number of Indians, yet they still protested the mining on the south side of the river by destroying claim markers, scattering horses and burros, and generally intimidating the interlopers.[37] Eventually, interest in the Paiute Strip faded.

In 1895 Howard Ray Antes, an independent Methodist missionary and self-styled Indian advocate, settled in Aneth. He and his wife, Eva, established the Navajo Faith Mission to bring succor to the Navajos during the height of the depression. He built his first home of logs but soon started construction on a much larger, more elaborate sandstone structure. By 1904 Antes's site boasted a large house, a smaller school building, and surrounding farmlands and orchards located on the river's floodplain.[38] How much actual preaching he did to the few white and numerous Indian people in the area is questionable, but the Navajos named him Hastiin Damįįgo, "Sunday Man."

The minister also became the spokesman for the Navajos living in the Aneth region as they confronted Anglo livestock owners interested in public grasslands. Antes assumed the responsibility of writing passes "on the authority of the Commissioner of Indian Affairs and the Secretary of the Interior of the United States" for Navajos wishing to graze livestock on the north side of the river.[39] Local cattle and sheep owners as well as the county government were irate, as the Navajos paid no taxes and had their own reservation lands.[40]

Antes next seized the opportunity to end the conflict over rangelands. Government surveys conducted through the region in 1899, along with the increased interest in ditch building for agricultural purposes, fostered the idea that perhaps the lands along the north side of the river should become a permanent part of the reservation. As a solution to the problems of self-sufficiency for a burgeoning population, advocates pointed out that "land along the river can be irrigated and put under a state of cultivation far cheaper per acre than any other part of the reservation."[41]

There was also growing interest in establishing some type of agency to maintain economic and political control in this far-flung corner of the Navajo Reservation. Problems over land, water, trade, hunting, and government responsibility underscored the need for the Four Corners region to have someone who could deal with issues before they became inflamed. In 1903 subagent William T. Shelton founded the Shiprock Agency in New Mexico, adding one more voice of change on behalf of the Navajo.

The time was right. Antes, with Shelton's blessing, wrote a letter on April 10, 1904, to President Theodore Roosevelt, asking for an enlargement of the reservation. These lands in the Aneth–Montezuma Creek area were the first that Navajos requested north of the river. After some initial revisions because of survey problems, President Roosevelt signed Executive Order 324A on May 15, 1905, creating that portion of the reservation. Known today as the Aneth area, these lands encompass the region beginning at the mouth of Montezuma Creek, east to the Colorado state line, south along the state boundary, then down the San Juan River to Montezuma Creek. Lands previously claimed or settled were excluded from the reservation.[42]

By 1906 Indian agents were again raising the cry for more reservation lands to decrease the tension between settlers and, this time, Paiutes and Utes. The San Juan Band Paiutes, numbering fewer than one hundred, had forged ties with the Utes and some Navajos. Members of this Paiute and Ute faction had become so troublesome to the area's white settlers that the Paiute Strip was offered as a place for these Indians to locate on a more permanent basis. A government special investigator suggested the lands west of 110 degrees longitude "be again withdrawn from public entry and set apart as a reservation for Indian use, specifying particularly the San Juan Paiutes and including other Paiute Indians of southern Utah who have not been provided for otherwise."[43] In 1908, when withdrawal of the lands from the public domain became a reality, the Paiutes may have had their name placed on the tract, but it was primarily the Navajos who used it.

Approximately a year later, prospectors began filing petitions for access to minerals and oil located on the withdrawn lands. Neither the Northern Navajo Agency in Shiprock nor the Western Navajo Agency in Tuba City, Arizona, was anxious to oversee this area, because it was unsurveyed, extremely isolated, and technically belonged to the Paiutes, whose agency was in distant southwestern Utah. By default, the Western Navajo Agency took the reins of control, but its agents made visits only when necessary. Justification for this was based on the travels of the Paiute people residing around Navajo Mountain, who frequented Tuba City for help, as did the Navajos living on the Strip.[44]

By 1921 new economic forces called for a new determination of the land's status. Paradise Oil and Refining Company, Monumental Oil Company, and traders such as John Wetherill and Clyde Colville from Kayenta sought the right to locate and pump petroleum from the land, which they believed was vacant.[45] Indeed, the Monumental Oil Company was already drilling just east of the 110th meridian, and Mormon cattlemen were illegally ranging five hundred animals on the Strip. The Bureau of Indian Affairs (BIA) acquiesced and in 1922 released the 600,000 acres back to the public domain without consulting the Navajos.

That was in July. Three months later, as word of the transaction filtered down to the Navajos, petitions to make the Strip part of the reservation again began to arrive in Washington. At center stage was Elsie Holiday, a twenty-one-year-old, full-blooded Navajo graduate from the Sherman Institute in California. As a local spokesperson for her people, she drew up four petitions, attached 134 signatures, and fired them off to the commissioner of Indian affairs, the secretary of the interior, the Indian Rights Association, and interested agents. Holiday argued that Monument Valley Navajos had lost some of their best rangelands and water holes with the stroke of a pen, that ancestors and relatives were buried there, that an unclear boundary line would lead to increased range conflicts, and that the Navajos were willing to relinquish any claims to oil and mineral rights in return for grazing privileges. The white men's cattle had already gotten mixed in with Navajo livestock, and some of the owners were masquerading as government men, telling the Navajos to leave and tearing down and burning fences and corrals.[46]

Five years later the tribal government in Window Rock was still expressing the same sentiments. Council members from the Monument Valley area believed that soon there would be no more lands available for tribal acquisition and that this particular parcel was "by far better grazing or farming land than the average lands of the Western Navajo Reservation."[47] Between 1930 and 1932 a series of meetings in Blanding drew state and federal government officials, members of the Navajo Tribal Council, Navajo and Ute agents, and stockmen from both sides of the San Juan to the bargaining table. The desire for control of two major ranges—the Aneth Extension and the Paiute Strip—encouraged each side to compromise in an attempt to reach a fair agreement and stop the incessant fingerpointing. On July 15, 1932, committee members reached a final settlement that became law six months later, on January 19, 1933. Those representing the white interests agreed that the Paiute Strip and the Aneth Extension would become part of the Navajo Reservation. In return, the American Indians and their advocates agreed to relinquish their right to establish individual homesteads in San Juan County north of the tribal boundaries, although the forty-four pending claims would be honored. The BIA insured that Navajo lands, where appropriate, would be fenced, that the Indians would abide by state game laws when hunting off the reservation, and wandering livestock that crossed boundaries would be handled according to published livestock rules.

Thus the experiences of the nineteenth century and the first quarter of the twentieth century offered an important backdrop against which future events would be staged. Hunting, farming, the livestock industry, mining, and tourism were all tied to the landscape, a dramatic country on which this region's history would be played out. At the turn of the century, the Navajos of southeastern Utah had survived the trauma of Fort Sumner, expanded their reservation to the north, and enjoyed a culture still very much intact. No doubt there had been changes, a few of which were forced but most of which were adopted selectively. The twentieth century, however, witnessed an increased tempo in this process. The traditional culture that had evolved over time would require rapid adjustments, as the isolation of the Four Corners region made way for increased contact and dependence on the more dominant white culture. The land was still the central focus, but it would be used in a way that the Navajo could not have anticipated.

CHAPTER TWO

NAVAJO AND UTE DEER HUNTING

Consecration versus Desecration

In this day of environmental sensitivity, the general public often views American Indians as the ecologist's ecologists. Stemming from the nineteenth century's notion of the noble savage and the all-wise sage of the woods, these ideas blossomed in the 1960s, 1970s, and 1980s as society looked for symbols with which to confront increasing mechanization, urbanization, and complexity. For example, an advertisement developed in the 1970s showed Iron Eyes Cody (part Cree, part Cherokee) paddling a canoe across a polluted, garbage-strewn lake. The tears streaming down his cheek as he surveyed the scene were as much tears for the simplicity of the past as they were a comment about today.

Some social scientists have argued that there was sometimes a wide gap between this stereotype and reality.[1] Studies of Indians living in the northeastern and southeastern United States, as well as a large body of work on tribes in northern Canada, have painted a far different image of the Indian as ecologist. Historians point out the intense nature of Indian land use and many of the problems created by the cultural views that directed this use.

A prominent example of this genre is Calvin Martin's *Keepers of the Game*, published in 1978.[2] Martin argues that eastern Canadian Indians decimated the beaver population in the seventeenth century. This occurred not only for economic purposes but, more important, because the Indian believed that the animals had renounced their spiritual obligations to prevent sickness and death caused by disease. Given this breach of trust, the Indians set aside their normal hunting taboos and practices, went to war against the animals, and freely harvested (almost to the point of extinction) the beaver. Martin insists that "[t]he fur-to-trade-goods exchange, although it exacerbated this spiritual decay, was thus more a symptom than its cause."[3]

A firestorm of protest and a blizzard of new research argued against Martin's thesis, resulting three years later in *Indians, Animals and the Fur Trade*, edited by Shepherd Krech III.[4] In it, scholars looked at cultural dynamics during various historical periods and in various geographic locations, trying to explain why the Indian seemed to abandon traditional, religiously fostered practices to charge pell-mell into the disastrous results of a market economy. Although all the contributors to the volume agreed to disagree with Martin, many of their own ideas were in conflict. No single solution proved acceptable to everyone, but what emerged was a better understanding of the complexity of pinning down an answer using an ethnohistorical approach.

My purpose here is to shed a different light, this time in the Southwest, on a similar phenomenon. During the late nineteenth and early twentieth century, there were a flurry of reports that suggested the deer herds of the Four Corners region were being decimated. Indian agents, the newspapers, and private and public correspondence told of Navajo and Ute hunting parties scouring the land for deer hides. These Indians were said to be slaughtering large numbers of animals, which aroused such a hue and cry that future game hunting policies and treaty rights were affected. Did this slaughter occur, and if so, why? Was the role of the deer in Navajo and Ute culture, at this point, solely economic, or were there religious considerations that encouraged or discouraged mass hunting? And what part did the white man play in either helping or hindering the growth or destruction of the deer herds in this region? Discussion of these questions, with some tentative answers, again reveals the complexity of understanding cultural dynamics in this historical context.

To the Navajo the deer is a sacred animal. Known in ceremonial terms as "The Youthful Chief of the White Patch," the deer is considered kin to antelope and elk.[5] During the time of the myths, two holy beings, Black God (Haashch'ééshzhiní) and Talking God (Haashch'ééłti'í), created the game animals. The gods traveled a southern and a northern route, placing the animals in different locations on or near Navajo lands suitable to their way of life. The deer were to live in the mountains and eat the plants there, many of which were considered by the Navajo to be medicinal. When one ate deer meat, the curative powers from plant and animal worked together to heal.

Because deer lived in the mountains, they were also said to be protected by thunder and lightning. Their antlers held supernatural power that had to be respected by leaving them in the wild, away from the home, the domain of women and children. Deer also helped to determine the amount of rain in an area. When it was dry, these animals cried to the holy beings, who sent soaking rains to the earth.[6]

Before the animals wandered off to their special haunts, Talking God and Black God gave instructions. The holy beings explained the relationship between the hunter and the hunted and told the animals under what conditions they were expected to give up their lives. The gods told the deer, "Talking God will be master of all. . . . In days to come when Earth People petition Talking God, when they pray to him, and Talking God consents to give you to the Earth People, . . . then only shall Earth People kill and eat you. . . . If one has prayed to these [holy beings] and one has held a sing to them, only then will one kill deer such as one desires."[7] The deer were happy with this arrangement and promised to live and die as the gods had instructed.

Deer hunting myths contain rules that define success in the chase and subsequent good health, or, if these rules are not practiced, promise failure, crippling disease, or death. A brief examination of these teachings illustrates how hunting stressed success in a supernatural sense far and above the importance of technique and the actual kill. The myths tell how the gods instructed the first hunters to learn the hunting songs "so that they will be able to kill any kind [of deer] they wish." The hunters were also told not to speak ill of deer because these animals could hear a person over a mountain; that the different parts of a dressed deer must be treated with respect; that Talking God and Black God controlled them and knew when a deer was cleaned and skinned in the proper way; and that if the Navajos hunted properly, they would always have enough meat to eat.[8]

Placing turquoise under a young cedar tree or breaking off four branches and pointing the tips to the east can also attract game. When hunters take these actions, the deer cannot hide and must honor the human's wish. But if the hunter does something wrong, then the deer can bound out of his presence by the sheet lightning found on its left leg. "Even if there is a steep hill or a slippery surface, [the deer] will disappear from sight in the blinking of an eye, and will turn into . . . bushes, rocks, [or] dead trees, which are left behind."[9]

Proper treatment led to success. Cecil Parrish, a Navajo living in Monument Valley, recalls an old medicine man named Hastiin Tso who was famous for his control of the weather and other natural elements. Parrish remembers how he went hunting with Hastiin Tso on a number of occasions and the effect the medicine man had on the deer:

> Even though the deer were easily frightened creatures, he would talk to them and they would not be scared away. They would walk around our camp and we would kill them. I asked him what sacred name he used. He said he did it through Talking God because these were his creatures. He said, "I ask him for the deer and he gives them to me." This is what he did in front of me. The elders used to do this a long time ago. They would ask for them [deer] and they were given. The elders were probably asking the owner of these deer, just as we would ask for things. They knew the right words to do this.[10]

The experience of a man named Left Handed illustrates the problem of not knowing the appropriate ritual formulas. In his account, he and another man separated from a larger party on an extended hunt. The partners found a place with many deer that they were able to approach, but no matter how many times they shot, not a single animal fell. The deer frolicked about but did not run away, and in fact they seemed to come closer with every shot. Left Handed reported, "[By evening,] we made them so tame . . . they were around us like burros."[11] Finally, one was killed after the hunters used every method, from leaning their rifle against a tree to shooting standing up and sitting down. The reason for their dismal success was that they did not know a single song or prayer associated with hunting.

The sacredness of the act of hunting was emphasized in the songs used to prepare for the ritual of taking life. A part of one song says, "In the dark the large buck is calling. . . . It is calling for the black bow. . . . It is calling for the yellow feathered arrow. . . . From above arrows struck the big buck. . . . At a holy place this has happened."[12] A Navajo hunter continued to renew his ritual power before, during, and after the hunt. Sweat baths, songs, prayers, and instructions from the hunting leader reminded the participants of their responsibilities.

In the northern part of the reservation, once they crossed the San Juan River, the Navajo hunters' whole demeanor changed. They often communicated through wolf, coyote, or owl calls, talked of killing and bloodshed (a practice normally taboo around the domain of the home), built a circular hunting camp according to prescribed ritual, and prepared themselves and their weapons through sacred procedures. Buck Navajo, a medicine man, said that the coyote, wolf, crow, and mountain lion were all hunters and friends of Navajo hunters. The crow cries ahead and tells the hunter where the game is located. By following prescribed practices, many traditional Navajos believed they were spiritually changed and could accomplish more than was ordinarily possible.[13]

The first deer seen by the group was to be killed lest it warn the others to depart. Once this was accomplished, the hunters raced to the dead animal, turned its head toward the camp, and said, "May others like you follow; may you bewitch many others."[14] In preparing the deer, the intestines in the forward part of the body cavity were removed first in order to "cause the rest of the deer to retrace their steps again when they are flushed and run away."[15] The hunters placed the head and horns under a tree with plants, leaves, and branches that the deer enjoyed, so that it could transform into another deer. Turquoise was often left as an offering with the head, which "called" for the precious stones in order to create another animal.[16] It also protected the hunter from the ill effects of lameness and loss of hearing or sight.[17]

A medicine man explained, "While you are butchering the deer, it will be standing there watching you. From then on, it is in harmony and is happy as it leaves."[18] Another man mentioned that returning hunters were forbidden to cross south of the San Juan River without cutting off the skin and legs of their game, because if this were not done, many foreign people would come into Navajo territory and take over the land. He concluded by saying, "Evidently this has happened because we have done the forbidden."[19]

Even some seemingly unrelated actions were proscribed by taboos. Hunters performed bodily functions in a hole, on a bush, or in the trunk of a tree so that, like the urine, the game would not run off. They could not shoot at crows, wolves, or coyotes because these animals helped to locate game and were invited to feast on the remains. The Navajo leader also warned the Bear People of the ensuing hunt so that these animals could leave. Hunters did not point with their fingers or use the words "far away" because the deer would hear, laugh, and disappear.[20]

The holy beings told the hunters that as long as proper respect was shown, "[w]e will not hide the deer from you, for they are your livestock, your food. We will place them in front of you."[21] But if proper procedures were not followed, then the game suffered, reported to the other animals its mistreatment, and encouraged the creatures to flee, for "no game would want to be killed by a man who was careless."[22]

Navajo Oshley, a longtime Navajo resident of southeastern Utah, told of a hunting party that had been doing well. As the men departed from camp one morning, they left one man behind to watch the gear and prepare food for the hunters' return. He was cautioned not to eat anything, but he eventually weakened and did. A crow flying overhead spied him in the act and cawed, "He ate. He ate." The leader of the hunting party heard the cry, returned with his men to the camp, confronted the man, who admitted his guilt, and then performed another ceremony to purify the group before setting out again. Oshley ended by saying, "Hunting is very sacred and very real."[23]

Myths teach the consequences of disobedience. Talking God told the first hunters that if they did not use songs and prayers, they would not kill a single deer because he would "determine in his mind to withdraw the game."[24] At one point, Mountain Lion, Wolf, and some of the Earth People became convinced that the holy beings did not care and so flagrantly disobeyed instructions. The gods decided to withdraw the animals because "what was forbidden they have done . . . [and] nothing is holy to them."[25] Black God called the animals to his mountain home so that "[w]herever game had been plentiful, not one was left roaming."[26]

The hunters returned home without success, mystified as to why there were no more deer. Eventually, the Earth People repented and the animals came back—but only after the gods gave the deer a sharpened sense of smell to increase the difficulty of killing them. The holy beings cautioned the hunters once more that the only way the animals could be taken was by keeping holy the songs, prayers, and sacred name associated with their prey. By doing so, one could "kill according to his desires."[27]

The Navajos did not draw a distinction between killing bucks, does, and fawns. In some myths fawns were said to have the most supernatural power and were the "bosses" over the more mature animals. A hunter could die just from hearing its cry, or turn into a "sloppy" person "with phlegm running down his nose" if he was not careful.[28] Body parts used from does included the udders, marrow, and tripe. Fawns provided skins for medicine bags, and curdled milk from their stomachs was used to make cheese. Meat from any of these animals could be wasted without angering the gods as long as the hunter followed proper skinning and butchering practices.[29] Therefore, respect was not based on total utilization as much as from following a prescribed formula. Access to game was based on adhering to spiritual beliefs not necessarily congruent with biological laws of cause and effect.

Ute hunting practices parallel those of the Navajo. Although not nearly as much has been written about the Southern Ute view of taking deer, there is enough to say with certainty that it was not taken lightly and was dependent on religious values. Deer were sacred to the Utes, comparable to the importance of the buffalo to the Plains Indian. Clothes, tepees, food, and much of their equipment were heavily dependent on this animal. Unlike the Navajos, who depended primarily on sheep and goats, the Utes saw the deer as a central part of their lives.

The Utes' movement to the mountains in the summer and the lower canyon systems in the winter followed the same migration patterns as the deer. Groups of five or six families joined to hunt and gather in the late spring and fall hunts. Each of these bands would have a leader who was selected because he made wise decisions about where to obtain food and how to keep the group out of trouble. A spiritual leader understood the supernatural powers associated with the land and how to best appeal to them. He went to the "power points," or places where supernatural powers resided, during the season of use and on behalf of his group prayed and left an offering to ask for help.[30] The leader harnessed control of this power and used it on behalf of his people, although it could be helpful or dangerous in the hands of its user. The power could also dissipate through overuse.[31] Individual prayer by the members of the band was also practiced but not at the sacred site used by the shaman.

Thus the world was much more than just a physical realm placed here to sustain life. It was a gift from the Creator of All Life, Sinawav, and imbued with spiritual powers. Deer hunting was just one aspect of this sacred view. Recently, a Ute elder responded to questions about deer hunting by saying that the killing and cleaning of the deer and the prayers that were offered had been established by the "ancestors." The correct way to skin, clean, and care for the deer was circumscribed by traditional values; a portion of the meat was offered to the four directions "to feed everybody—the Universe"; and all must be done with prayer.[32] Another person mentioned that after a deer was killed, a part of this prayer asked, "May I always kill a big one."[33] This perspective placed hunting squarely in the sacred realm.

Yet when one turns to the historical record, the issue becomes confused. Late-nineteenth-century southeastern Utah and the Four Corners region in general provide a specific time and place to illustrate this confusion. This area was one of the last to be settled by whites, saw heavy use by Navajos and Utes, and produced a substantial number of pertinent accounts concerning incidents that occurred between the 1880s and the early 1900s. Scientific studies and reports of game wardens did not appear until later, but eyewitness accounts, when taken collectively, provide a rich source of information with which to study, from a white perspective, the impact of Native American hunting.

Although southeastern Utah north of the San Juan River was mostly public domain outside established reservations, the Weeminuche Band of the Southern Utes considered it theirs. This is not to suggest that there were not some Navajo people living in and using this area and that Navajo mythology did not recognize many of the land features in its teachings. Small bands of Navajos either visited or took up residence there as early as the late 1700s, but it was not until the mid-1880s, as the reservation expanded north, that larger populations entered to stay.[34] By this time the Utes and their close relatives, the San Juan Band Paiutes, and some Navajos were already there, hunting deer. All three groups were equally well armed with repeating rifles.

When the Southern Utes and Navajos each received their reservations in 1868, the treaties stipulated that they would "retain the right to hunt on any unoccupied lands contiguous to the reservation, so long as the large game may range thereon in such numbers as to justify the chase."[35]

The Indians took advantage of this opportunity as neither group could survive solely on its livestock or agricultural production. The deer herds on the Navajo Reservation had been assiduously hunted, causing the men to go farther and farther afield.[36] By the 1880s the Utes' reservation had shrunk from roughly a third of Colorado to a land area only 15 miles wide and 110 miles long in some of the most desolate territory in the southwestern corner of the state. Few alternatives, other than off-reservation hunting, allowed the Indians the opportunity to obtain wild game.

When bands of Navajos and Utes left their reservations to hunt, they soon encountered the cattlemen who grazed their herds in the same places and at the same time of year. Grass, forbs, brush, and water were most plentiful on the mountains, so it was not long before Indian agents received blistering correspondence from the stockmen, spelling out Indian activities. Edmund Carlisle, owner of the huge Kansas and New Mexico Land and Cattle Company, informed the Southern Ute agent in 1884 that a group of Indians had left the reservation with written permission from a local trader. According to Carlisle, they had been setting fire to the timberlands on the south side of Blue Mountain in San Juan County, Utah, causing severe damage, and had killed not only deer but also cattle. The livestock owners wanted soldiers sent to control the Utes and "other Indians." More letters followed, indicating that this hunting group, consisting of forty Southern Utes and the same number of Navajos, was heading west to continue the hunt.[37] Cowboys and citizens alike threatened to form groups to attack the Indians, and although no organized posse moved against them, anger and frustration continued to mount.[38]

The next few years showed little improvement. In 1885 one man complained that hunger had forced half of the Southern Utes off the reservation, burning grass and killing cattle, and that he dared not hunt for fear of being killed. The following year the people of Moab recounted how the Utes bullied them while passing through on a hunting expedition that had netted "several thousand deer [killed] simply for their hides."[39] The townspeople swore that if the Utes and their friends did not leave, the whites would handle the situation in their own way.

Anglos, however, were not the only ones concerned about the herds. Southern Utes from Colorado entered southeastern Utah with the express purpose of rounding up the deer like cattle and either killing or driving them closer to their reservation. The Southern Utes and Paiutes already living in Utah were greatly angered by this attempt to remove game from their territory. The first of three annual hunts started in 1884, with an estimated three hundred Indians killing deer by the hundreds and drifting thousands of others to the south and east of the La Sal Mountains. According to one Anglo report, there were so many carcasses left rotting that cattle and horses would no longer range in those areas.[40]

The drives in 1885 and 1886 added more fuel to the fires of resentment between Colorado and Utah Utes, not to mention the settlers. A petition signed by sixty-four men from McElmo Canyon, located west of the Ute Reservation, complained that the Indians would not allow the whites to kill game, while other reports claimed that more than two hundred Utes "armed to the teeth" were hunting on the Blue and La Sal Mountains.[41] Spring and summer saw new groups of Indians setting out for the hunt. One party returned in July with "lots of buckskins"; another forty people set out in August with seventy-five to one hundred horses to help pack the meat and hides back home. At the same time, eighty Utes went north and killed over two hundred deer. Many of these deer were fawns whose skin sold for only twenty-five cents each. Only a tenth of the meat was taken. White settlers, again, complained bitterly about this wanton destruction.[42]

By 1889 events had reached a boiling point. That September, the commissioner of Indian affairs, T. J. Morgan, wrote to Ute agent Charles Bartholomew directing him not to allow the Southern Utes to hunt off their reservation even though earlier treaties granted this right.[43] As the newspapers cried for control, many Indians had already left for the hunt. One article, titled "Send the Soldiers," told how Navajos and Utes were "killing game and alarming the people." The Ute agent sent runners to the principal chiefs, asking about their kinsmen. He was told that most were at home, that they had not been and were not now involved in hunting for skins only, and that the cattlemen had generated these reports to control the range.[44] Bartholomew agreed with his chiefs' point of view. He sent a notice to the papers explaining the Indians' position and said he was making every effort to recall stray groups.[45]

To settle the conflicting reports, the military sent Second Lieutenant George Williams to Blue Mountain in December 1889. Although Williams saw no Indian hunters, he estimated that two hundred to three hundred Navajos and Utes had been hunting there but had returned to their reservations. The Indians, he reported, had "killed a good many deer as is shown by the number of hides they have sold to the trader."[46] The twelve families living in Monticello, at the base of the mountain, reported that the Utes hunted for hides and meat, the Navajos primarily for hides. The trader, Mons Peterson, felt the latter sold more green hides than the Utes because of superior horses and hunting techniques. Many of the cowmen complained that with all of the Indians chasing through the woods, the livestock had grown wild and harder to herd.

Williams also reported that too many Indian groups were hunting in the same territory. Traditionally, Navajos and Utes did not get along with each other, and rubbing shoulders while armed in the isolation of the mountains could lead to an explosive situation. Although no conflict actually erupted between them, there was friction between the Colorado Utes and the Utah Utes. Hatch, from Utah, got into an argument with Cowboy, from Colorado, while camped at Peters Spring near Monticello. During a friendly card game, Hatch verbally attacked the Southern Utes for their useless slaughter of the deer herds in Utah. Cowboy went on the defense, became angered, shot Hatch, and the two camps separated. A vicious fight between two of the women ensued in Monticello while the men dismounted and prepared for a shoot-out amid the settlers' cabins and stores. Cooler heads prevailed, and both groups went their way, leaving a vivid reminder of the importance of the deer herds to all Indian peoples.[47]

In the 1890s increased pressures on the Utes by their agents and an expanding Navajo population intensified the competition for and use of resources. Dozens of individuals from Grand and San Juan Counties signed petitions complaining about Indian hunting practices and depredations on livestock. They still mentioned Ute activities, but the Navajos now stood center stage in the drama of pursuing the herds.[48] The Ute agent took the opportunity to show that his charges were really on the reservation and that much of the hunting was being done by Navajos but that the blame was still placed on the Utes. He even sent a letter to the Navajos and their agent saying that the Utes and their white neighbors complained about Navajos killing game both on and north of the Ute Reservation. He commanded that they leave with all of their live-

Traditional Navajo and Ute hunting was invested as much with religious practices as with economic and governmental concerns. These Southern Utes crossing
the Los Pinos River typify the well-armed hunting groups of the late nineteenth
century. Photo by Horace Poley, the Denver Public Library, Western History
Collection.

stock and no longer make the Utes' land their headquarters for killing
cattle and hunting deer.[49]

Others expressed concerns about the Navajos living outside their
reservation. Citizens of Spar City, Colorado, complained that a party of
twelve Navajos killed seven elk and thirty deer, leaving the carcasses to
"rot and fester in the sun." The settlers blamed the Navajo agent for
allowing the "red pests" to leave their lands. In 1893 the governor of
Colorado wrote to President Grover Cleveland complaining about groups
of one hundred to one hundred fifty Navajos and Utes in the same general area, who left their reservations because of lack of rations and pro-
ceeded to destroy bucks, does, and fawns. When the deer "congregated
at certain times of the year [they were] attacked in full force," leaving
the game wardens helpless when confronted with such large numbers
of Indians.[50]

Bartholomew once again denied that the Utes were involved. He pointed out that he rarely gave passes to Utes for off-reservation hunting, that his people were all present and accounted for, that he knew of large Navajo foraging parties operating in the area, and that his charges were faithful to the United States, kept the game laws, and were ready to serve as a force for good against the "Navajo menace."[51]

Just how much of a "menace" were the Navajos to the game herds? Indian accounts of the number of deer killed are sketchy, but they do exist. In fall 1890 Old Mexican, a Navajo from the Montezuma Creek–Aneth area, tells of hunting with a group of relatives on Blue Mountain for thirty-three days, during which they killed a total of seventy bucks and does. A few days after his return home, he left again with a party of three. They hunted only for skins and killed sixty-seven more animals. He personally had twenty-two hides, twelve of which he sold to a trader at fifty cents apiece. Ten years later he could have sold two hides at the Aneth post for $7.00 but chose to sell them in Crystal, New Mexico, farther inside the reservation, for $30.75.[52] Supply-and-demand economics operated at the counters of the trading posts.

This last point is important. Hunting for hides was not an accepted practice in traditional Navajo and Ute teachings. Both cultures had spiritual laws regarding the taking of game, but they did not address issues raised by a foreign capitalist system. The sanctions applied in a traditional setting were spiritual but not focused on herd reproduction and maintenance. Hunting solely for hides was an outgrowth of an economy that provided desirable goods in exchange for materials the market demanded. Traders accepted whatever would sell, and they were not necessarily concerned about what took place beyond the confines of their posts.

There are other examples from the same geographic area and time period that show how the religious system of the American Indians did not address the same concerns expressed by the white man. For instance, Left Handed hunted with a party of eleven men over a week's time; the group killed seventy-one animals. The leader said it was time to stop because the men were getting tired. Some time later Left Handed and three other men hunted for nine days and killed sixteen deer. The amount of time spent by each group depended on their success. The leader of this party, when asked how long they would hunt, replied, "It all depends on how the deer will be. If we can't get anything, then we'll just turn around and come back. If we kill some, and if we keep on killing some, then we will stay until we think we can't get anymore."[53]

Another eyewitness account tells of how the leader of a hunting party sent four men down a canyon, where they built blinds and waited for the remaining six participants to flush deer into them. The drive started at sunrise, and before long the riders heard shots in the distance. By the time they reached the concealed shooters, most of the firing had stopped. "There were slaughtered deer all around them. . . . We killed so many deer that we spent the rest of the day skinning them."[54] Assuming these scenes were enacted at other times and places, one can see the effect on the herds.

Decimation of game animals was not confined to the Southwest. By 1894 the Shoshone and Bannock, as well as white hunters, had been whittling away at the deer and elk populations. Similar reports came from Idaho, Wyoming, Montana, northern Utah, and the Dakotas but were especially prevalent around Yellowstone Park, where visitors complained of gruesome sights. A Supreme Court decision pertaining to the Wyoming-Bannock case stated that the Indians now had to abide by the game laws of the state or territory in which they hunted and that agents could issue passes for travel off the reservation but that the Indians could not hunt while en route. According to the government, "The slaughter of wild animals in vast numbers for hides only and the abandonment of carcasses . . . is as much a violation of the treaty as an absolute prohibition on the part of the United States against the exercise of such privilege."[55]

Reports continued to flow into the BIA, but this time from the Winslow and Grand Canyon area of Arizona, where tourism and settlement were on the rise. To summarize a large volume of correspondence, starting in 1895, reports of Navajos and Hopis slaughtering game started to pour in. A party of fifty hunters might move into the Mogollon Mountains and start encircling the deer while others moved windward, fired the grass, and drove the animals into the rifle sights of those waiting. One party of thirty-two Navajos reportedly killed 376 deer and 115 turkeys between November 1894 and the beginning of January 1895. A witness claimed that the Indians' favorite time to hunt was when the does were dropping their young because they were easy to approach.[56]

In response to his query, the commissioner of Indian affairs received an answer from the agent stating that only one pass had been issued to six people during this time. As usual, the agent believed these reports were groundless.[57] Forest rangers, however, started enumerating the depredations in the timberlands of the Grand Canyon, asking that the government keep the "wild and inappreciable Indian" off the reserve so the herds could restock. The Navajo agent, George W. Hayzlett, called in the chiefs and clearly explained where their people should not go, sent police after the supposed culprits, and learned that his men could not find any Navajos off the reservation. There was no evidence that "a hundred Indians in line" armed with the "latest magazine rifles" had been there with "175 pack animals loaded with deer and bear meat."[58] Hayzlett vociferously denied any wrongdoing.

Agent Hayzlett, however, would find it increasingly difficult to hold this position. On November 17, 1900, Forest Supervisor George Langenberg reported two hundred Navajos and White Mountain Apaches setting fire to the grass and timber and slaughtering deer. The commissioner of Indian affairs contacted both agents, who had already sent police to the Grand Canyon area to drive the Indians back to their respective reserves. Hayzlett, in defense, said he had issued no passes, had attended dances and meetings to explain the situation, and believed only thirty to forty off-reservation Navajos were actually involved and that they had killed only thirty-five deer.[59]

A few months later new reports surfaced concerning Navajos ranging their flocks and killing game in the Grand Canyon forests. The agent realized they had "raised nothing scarcely for two years and hunger and fear of losing their flocks by starvation may have induced them to take chances and go in violation of all orders."[60] Clemency, he felt, was the best policy. The police sent to return the transients to the reservation found no one, while locals blamed the stockmen for raising a false cry. The next fall there were reports of nineteen Navajos and three Hopis hunting illegally. This time the Navajo agent blamed a trader for hiring these Indians as well as Paiutes to do the killing for him. Regardless of who did it, the reported two hundred deer harvested provided one more claim of heavy herd loss.[61]

After 1900 complaints continued to be lodged, but less frequently. The Franciscan fathers at Saint Michaels, Arizona, wrote at this time, "Owing to wanton slaughter and increasing settlement, game is not very plentiful, but, notwithstanding the game laws to the contrary, hunting parties often make raids and kill deer merely for the hide and sinew."[62] Traders, agents, game wardens, forest rangers, and others who influenced the Navajos made increasing efforts to keep them on the reservation. By 1910 only sporadic correspondence tells of an occasional hunting party on the public domain. No doubt miners, cowboys, farmers, and an assortment of white travelers in the forests also took their share of illegal deer, but the heavy pressure on the deer herds was over. Forest Service estimates indicate that in 1917 there were only 250 deer in the La Sals and 100 in the Blue Mountain area; in 1921, 275; in 1925, 725; and in 1930, 1,225.[63]

In assessing the impact of hunting pressure, one is forced to rely primarily on anecdotal information, as no extensive studies on deer population were conducted at this time in southeastern Utah. William Riley Hurst came to Blanding in 1911 and remembers how scarce the deer were on the mountain and in the juniper-pinyon forests at its base. He helped his father run a sawmill and graze horses on the slopes of Blue Mountain and saw no deer during the 1910s and 1920s. Around 1916 some boys running a trapline came across a deer track and told some of their friends, who after school rode out to see this unusual phenomenon.[64]

Another man said that when he was a boy during this same period and was out riding with his dad, they spooked a small herd of animals across the canyon from them. They thought the animals were coyotes, until they reached the tracks and his father recognized them for what they were. He was "very much surprised because he'd never seen or heard of deer like that in this area."[65] Cowboys also told of occasional sightings, while some Navajos and Utes still hunted with limited success.

In 1927 a group of white men organized a hunt using saddle and pack horses to find deer on Blue Mountain and Elk Ridge. Ten days later they returned with one buck, which they "unselfishly cut up and divided with the residents of Monticello. Never did so little go so far."[66] One can infer from this event that the group of men included a fair representation of the local citizenry, because they shared the proceeds with the town, and also that it must have been a rarity to have deer meat, because of the way it was distributed. Starting in the 1930s the herds returned, and by the 1940s there was an overabundance of animals roaming in ever-increasing herds.[67]

This same pattern appears to be true of the deer along the Grand Canyon and Mogollon Rim. In 1900 elk were extinct, "antelope were hanging on by a thread, . . . wild turkeys were almost totally eliminated," black-tailed deer were on the wane, Sonora deer were nearly extinct, and only the whitetail seemed to be "holding their own."[68] Aldo Leopold, a leading ecologist concerned with "land ethics," estimated, based on samplings done in about 1915 in New Mexico, that of an original deer population of 200,000, only about 10,000 still survived. That same year hunters killed 656 deer in an area of 13,000 square miles.[69]

To blame the depletion of the herds solely on overhunting by Indians is simplistic. That Indians had an impact on the herds cannot be denied. That the white community was quick to report any "wrongs" perpetrated by the Indians also cannot be denied. And exaggeration in reporting occurrences must be considered. Still, the herds were greatly decreased and the written record clearly pointed to the Indians. The intent here is not to lay blame at any particular group's feet but rather to understand the dynamics of what took place and why. There were many factors that affected the deer population, the complexity of which can only be touched on here. Among the factors that influence the number of deer are predation, forage, diseases, accidents, habitat, water, weather, and fires. Each herd responds differently to these variables.

Today, for instance, on Blue Mountain and the La Sals the average ratio of fawns born to does is 73:100 and 70:100 respectively. In wet years, this figure may jump to a high of 80; and in dry years, a low of 50 to 60 fawns. When the ratio drops to 50:100 fawns, the population is barely maintaining; when it drops below this figure, it is in decline.[70] The key concern, then, is "population threshold," that is, what it takes to maintain a viable, flourishing herd.

Weather influenced not only the size of the herds but also the patterns of Indians' lives. Much of the correspondence concerning Indian hunting was written in November and December, the rutting season, when deer were fattest.[71] As winter approached, the animals drifted south to lower elevations, preceded by the Indians and cowmen, who used the canyon system below for their homes and to pasture their livestock.[72] Hunting continued even after man and beast had descended to the juniper- and pinyon-forested mesas between the mountains and the San Juan River, so that there was constant pressure on the herds.

Another pressure was predation. Mountain lions kill as many bucks as does in the canyon country of southeastern Utah, because the males winter in this rough terrain of ledges, caves, and narrow defiles—prime habitat for lions. Coyotes, in contrast, kill mostly fawns, but like the lions, they are opportunists, taking a meal wherever it is found. If a herd is healthy, predation is not a major factor, but when the animals are weakened and struggling, scavengers can play an increasingly significant role.[73] A systematic government program to alleviate these predators did not evolve until after the deer herds had been depleted; thus their impact, as the herds felt heavy hunting pressures, would have been magnified.

The white man also greatly affected the deer population. Cattle, sheep, and deer are direct competitors for grasses and forbs during certain times of the year. In the spring deer eat young grass shoots but soon revert to eating their staple, browse. Unless a region is feeling the effects of a severe drought, this grazing has little impact on how much grass is actually available, and in some instances, grass may come in more fully because the competing vegetation is eaten.

In understanding what transpired in the last quarter of the nineteenth and first quarter of the twentieth century, one must look to the livestock industry. This is a complex story that cannot be told in detail here, but a brief sketch reveals an important pattern.

The rangelands on the mountains and in the canyons were hotly contested by Anglo and Indian stockmen. In general, the dominant livestock companies in southeastern Utah were owned by large cattle outfits who used the inexpensive grass of the public domain. In 1887 Francis Hammond, a leading Mormon stockman, estimated that there were then 50,000 sheep and 8,000 to 10,000 cattle grazing the ranges of San Juan County.[74] Ten months later the Mormon-owned sheep herds had doubled.[75] In addition, three major cattle companies owned by non-Mormons pastured stock around Blue Mountain and the La Sals. These groups averaged between 20,000 and 30,000 animals each, but these figures do not include the estimated 100,000 cattle brought in from Colorado for winter graze and to take advantage of lower taxes.[76] Although the estimates may be disputed and there is no exact count of livestock, there is no question that the infusion of these herds and flocks had a large impact on the deer.

The historical record testifies to this. After the Utes "traded" grazing rights on the La Sal Mountains for a paltry sum, one settler commented, "[T]he way that mountain was eaten up by cattle and sheep from the day of that treaty . . . probably made the old Indian's head swim and he perhaps found difficulty in recognizing it as the same verdant forest where he hunted deer and hid from pursuers."[77] This view is corroborated by the Indians. A Paiute living with the Utes in this area summarized the problem as he told his grievances to a young white man:

> He [Posey] was somewhat concerned about preservation of the land. He told me, and Mancos Jim told me a time or two before, how the country had been when Posey was a boy. And their expression was something like the grass would grow up to the belly of the ponies. He said there was lots of grass and lots of deer and there was hunting. . . . They [cattle] ate up all the grass, . . . and as a result of this, there was pretty poor feed for the Indian ponies and deer. The deer population was very low, and so the Indian felt like this justified them every once in a while in killing a cow, a steer, or something of that sort.[78]

This invasion of cattle could only mean disaster for the deer. The hooves of cattle and sheep, along with the animals' foraging for grass, changed the ecosystem. The grass's root system would have been crushed and altered so that brush gained control of the open space, preventing the grass's regrowth.[79] Also, the hooves of the livestock tended to compact the soil, making runoff and erosion more prevalent, decreasing the opportunity for plant seeds to germinate, and increasing the amount of trampled vegetation. In the mountains of southeastern Utah, germination is critical. The issue quickly becomes, not the amount of winter range, as it is in northern Utah where snows are heavier, but rather what happens to the summer range. The water, grass, forbs, and brush of this range provide the key to survival.

Another factor in this equation is the white man's attitude toward hunting and game management. Although cattle and deer do not compete heavily for the same types of food, any hint of deer sharing the rangeland was viewed by cattlemen as unacceptable competition. William Hurst recalls how some cowboys felt:

They hated deer. Old Jacob Adams was the foreman of the Scorup
and Summerville Cattle Company. . . . He gave all of his cowboys
a 30-30 rifle, furnished them bullets, and told them to kill every
deer they saw. This was his instructions. He said, "Shoot them in
the guts and when they turn, shoot them in the ass." That was old
Jacob's theory. He was a big cattle man and he wanted every one
of them [deer] annihilated. That was pretty much the attitude of all
cattle men in the area.[80]

This Wild West attitude was not curbed until there was tighter government control, spawned by Progressive political reform and an increasing ecological awareness. But in southeastern Utah it would take decades
for this thinking to be implemented.

Perhaps the key role that grass played in the plight of the deer can
help us to understand what was happening to the American Indian.
Many of the reports of Indians slaughtering deer come from white
sources. Certainly the reports were not all fabricated, but just as certainly, they fit a general trend. A major issue of this time and place was
to keep Indians on their reservations, away from white communities
and the resources found on the public domain. There were major political battles and minor physical skirmishes fought throughout this period,
as entrepreneurs on one side pitted themselves against Indians and
agents on the other. Getting Washington's attention or stirring up resentment against the Utes or Navajos could pay dividends when political
decisions were made. The issue of hunting was just one more opportunity to move toward the more economically important goal of obtaining
grass for the livestock industry.[81]

As one pieces together the complex puzzle of range and herd management, a clearer picture of why the deer herds diminished comes into
focus. Pressures for rangeland increased during the 1880s, as thousands
of cattle, sheep, and horses ate the vegetation. The deer, like the Indians,
watched much of their land and larder disappear. Add to this a drought
that lasted ten years, from 1887 to 1897, the role of predators on a weakened herd, the unrecorded effects of diseases transferred from cattle to
deer, the hunting pressures of both Indian and Anglo groups, an insensitive market economy, and an absence of traditional values to meet the
shifting needs of the time, and one begins to understand the extent of
the factors affecting the deer herds.[82]

One cannot lay the blame of the depleted deer herds totally at the feet of the Indian. Still, Indians had a substantial impact on the deer population. Culturally, both Navajos and Utes saw no harm in hunting does and fawns as well as bucks. According to contemporary reports, cattlemen shared this view. During a normal hunt, 60 or 70 percent of the male deer can be killed off. As males mate with more than one female, a herd can remain viable with this kill ratio.[83] But when the breeding stock—does and fawns—goes into decline, the herd moves toward the point where it cannot reproduce sufficiently to replace the rate of attrition. Extinction can then become a reality.

Hunters often take the biggest, strongest deer, upsetting the scheme of natural selection whereby the weak and sickly are the first to be culled from the herd. Navajo and Ute songs and prayers reinforce the idea that the "big buck" is the one to fall prey to the hunter's arrow.[84] The young and weak are left, easy prey for coyotes and wolves.

Did the Navajo and Ute hunters of the late 1800s and early 1900s understand these factors? Perhaps in part. For them, hunting was as much a religious event as it was a practical harvesting activity. To look at the decimation of the herds and insist it happened solely for economic reasons is to miss the point that ritual, prayers, songs, and rules circumscribed much of the Navajos' daily activity. Their culture was changing, but it was not in upheaval. It was not until the 1930s and livestock reduction that their dependence on the market economy became fixed beyond their control. In the case of the Utes and the impoverished circumstances on their reservations, desperation came much earlier.

According to the religious beliefs held by both Navajos and Utes, replacement of the deer occurred on a supernatural, mystical level.[85] For instance, when Navajos succeeded in killing deer, it was because Black God and Talking God released them for that purpose. The holy beings and the animals worked in concert to provide food and skins for those who used proper ritualistic respect. A medicine man explained it this way:

> Before the hunters leave at dawn, they pack their guns and speak to the holy being, Talking God, asking for a big deer to kill that day. Talking God owns all these wild animals, so one has to ask for it before he can kill one. Black God and Talking God rule over these particular animals. They give you the deer, just like someone would give you their sheep. That is why we have to be very careful in how

we butcher and fix the meat. Once we kill the deer, we have to release its spirit back to the "owners" so as to "form" into another deer. This will continue on forever and the deer will never become extinct.[86]

Indeed, where as Calvin Martin suggested that the Cree killed beaver because the two "societies" were at war with each other, just the opposite could be said of the Navajo and the deer. The animal relinquished its life because it was at peace and harmony with its slayer. If this were not so, no deer would appear to the hunter.

As is the case among adherents to any system of beliefs, there undoubtedly were those who viewed the religious aspect of hunting as tangential to the act. How many Navajos felt this way will never be known, but because the Navajo belief system was still intact, without substantial white acculturation yet evident, it seems safe to assume that many Navajos accepted traditional beliefs.

What did the Navajos think when there were few deer left? No doubt the answer would have been a religious one. Most likely, the deer disappeared because some hunters had not followed the proper ceremony. Today, older Navajos still blame problems on lack of respect for these animals. John Holiday, a medicine man from Monument Valley, after telling about the proper care and cleaning of game, said, "Not even two deer ribs were left together before crossing the [San Juan] River. That was how our forefathers used to hunt. Today, nobody cares how they do it. It is no wonder everything has gone wrong. It is obvious that this is where it all started. It is as if a dam broke and all things broke loose."[87] Another medicine man, Claus Chee Sonny, gave similar testimony: "Regarding all the hunting rules of which we have been told: What we were advised not to do, some people did. Many things are not right with us because of this."[88] Thus the Navajo perception of events is based on a religious explanation of physical events in a finite world.

Now, more than ever, it is important to understand both sides of the same world—the physical and the spiritual. The Navajo experience disregarded many of the tangible effects of hunting, while today some white and Navajo hunters emphasize obtaining meat and trophy antlers over the fact that an animal is surrendering its life for another creature to live. To avoid excesses on both accounts, hunters must integrate spiritual, ethical values with a realistic, suitable game management program. Failure to do so will leave the two controlling powers—Talking God and the U.S. government—wondering where their animals have gone.

CHAPTER THREE

GOVERNMENT FARMERS AND THE NAVAJOS

The San Juan Experience, 1892–1933

The Southwest is known for its arid climate, dramatic beauty, and turbulent weather. To its inhabitants who wrest a living from the land, the region's unpredictability, especially in terms of its water supply, provides one of its greatest challenges. The Colorado Plateau in general, and the Four Corners area specifically, is no exception. The San Juan River is the only major, continuously flowing source of water in the northern part of the Navajo Reservation. It courses through Colorado and New Mexico and then crosses into Utah near the Four Corners. Melting snows in the spring and intense thunderstorms in the summer and autumn cause the river to rise and fall sharply. As the moisture pours off the San Juan and Sleeping Ute Mountains in Colorado and the La Sal and Blue Mountains in Utah, dozens of tributaries feed into the river to swell the tide that scours the banks and tears at the floodplains.

Perhaps one of the most graphic examples of this phenomenon was recorded in fall 1941. Between September 9 and October 14, the San Juan River changed from a placid, shallow stream 3 feet deep and 125 feet wide, flowing at 635 cubic feet per second, to a raging torrent 25 feet deep and 240 feet wide, gushing at 59,600 cubic feet per second.[1] The river ravaged hitherto protected floodplains. Only the highest banks contained the water. Few of the irrigation facilities and bridges survived the onslaught. The abrasive action of the streambed's load widened and deepened the channel as the suspended matter swept down the river, depositing its refuse when the waters receded. Eventually part of the streambed filled back as the river brought in new sand, silt, and rocks, but it took years to replace what had been removed so quickly.

Dependence on a river like the San Juan had significant implications. Until the government constructed dams and flood control devices, the river had its way. It could be destructive, but it could also be benevolent, bringing its life-giving waters and organic material to those who came to its banks. The Anasazi used the river and its tributaries for two types of farming practices, pot and flood irrigation. The Navajos, but not the Utes, followed suit and located their farms along the river. Although the mean annual rainfall, eight inches in the Aneth area, was less than on other parts of the reservation, the river provided a continuous source of water, while its lower elevation, 4,700 feet, provided a 161-day growing season.[2]

Pot irrigation was inconvenient. Carrying the water to the field was time consuming yet more predictable than dry farming techniques that depended on the moisture in the soil and summer showers to keep the crops alive. Flood irrigation was often more dependable. Navajos cleared and prepared their farms in April. Ditches from the river snaked across the floodplain, taking advantage of the natural slope in the land and direction of flow of the river. The Indians dammed arroyos and worked the water over the fields in a process repeated once or twice during the summer.[3]

Alluvial fans extending from the mouths of intermittent or continuously flowing canyon streams such as Recapture, McCracken, Montezuma, Allen, and McElmo Creeks on the north side of the river and Desert, Lone Mountain, and Tsitah Creeks on the south, encouraged settlements and farming. Irrigation systems were easier to put in at these places because the banks were lower, the soil was rich, and the water was less turbulent.

Planting began in early May and continued through the first part of July, when the "first fruits of the slim yucca burst open." The Navajos planted corn, then melons, then squash, and finally beans, based on the length of the maturation period. The gardener placed from five to fifteen seeds together; those seeds that did not germinate were said to have been "eaten" by those that did. Men used a digging stick to make a hole four to six inches deep as women followed behind and placed the seeds.[4]

Because livestock was an even more important part of their economy, the Navajos spent a lot of time away from the plots planted on the river, returning to weed and water as necessary. Sometimes women, old people, and children stayed behind to tend the crops.

This generalized pattern shifted according to specific conditions. Friction with Ute neighbors, demands of the livestock industry, shifting boundaries of the reservation, and a growing population base exerted pressures in different geographic directions. The overall effect was to expand outward from the heart of the reservation and across its boundaries. White farmers and stockmen on the north side of the San Juan claimed that the public domain belonged to them, since the Indians had their own lands.

Navajo agents did not agree. In the late nineteenth and early twentieth century the government still wrestled with the idea of removing Indians from reservation status and pulling them into mainstream American society as farmers and mechanics. The Dawes Act of 1887 was designed to do just that in other parts of the United States. For the Navajos, however, the reservation not only stayed intact but expanded, and relatively few individuals took up allotments.

By 1892 government officials decided to build on the already established Navajo pattern of livestock and agriculture. The commissioner of Indian affairs, T. J. Morgan, suggested a long-term approach to solving the problem of feeding and controlling the growing Navajo population. First, he believed the reservation should be carefully mapped with an eye for springs, water holes, and streams that could provide water for farms and livestock. Next, a system of dams, wells, windmills, and other water-procuring devices should be integrated into a program to make the Navajos self-sufficient. And finally, every effort should be made to make Indian lands productive so that Navajos would not compete and fight with the white man.[5]

The commissioner charged the army with the task. Lieutenant Odon Gurovitz surveyed the south side of the San Juan and recommended that 260 acres near Bluff be turned into farmlands and that the local Mormons supervise the project.[6] This was ironic in that the last thing the Latter-day Saints wanted was to attract more Navajos into an area where conflict with Utes and Navajos had already netted some bitter years of strife. Still, the river, a constant source of water, could not be

Taken at the mouth of Paiute Canyon near Navajo Mountain, this 1926 photo shows the fruits of Navajo horticulture in a desert land. Photo from H. D. Miser Collection, #615, U.S. Geological Survey.

overlooked, especially since James Francis, a government farmer stationed in Fruitland, New Mexico, was already enjoying some limited success.

In 1893 agent E. H. Plummer begged for money to develop the possibilities. He argued that farm improvements would be the carrot needed to lure the Navajos home; according to some estimates, one-third of the population was then living outside the reservation boundaries.[7] Plows, scrapers, wagons, and seed would be further inducements, and with three or four additional government farmers scattered in strategic locations where Navajos clustered, the south side of the river would act as a magnet to draw and fix the transient population.[8]

Constant Williams, who replaced Plummer as Navajo agent, continued to call for farming on the San Juan. On December 11, 1894, he went to Bluff, where he found the Indians "pitiable" because of crop failures over the previous two or three years.[9] It was surprising, however, that Williams could go to Bluff and suggest that large-scale farming was a viable means of livelihood there, given the community's struggle to maintain itself through agriculture. Indeed, by this time the Mormons had shifted to dependence on raising livestock, and many had settled away from the San Juan where water could be more easily controlled.

It is useful to pause and examine the Mormon experience in the region, which had started in 1880 and continuously faltered and failed up to this time. The settlers' difficult struggle against the San Juan was a prelude to what the Navajos would encounter in a few short years. When a large contingent of Mormons settled in Bluff, they immediately began to plow ditches and prepare for spring planting. Community cooperation and organization characterized this first year, but the ditches were unsatisfactory for a group of people who wanted to move beyond subsistence agriculture.

By 1881 a new canal, costing from $12 to $50 a rod, needed to be dug.[10] The headgate of the canal was located four miles above the town and passed over a long stretch of slickrock. The builders hauled logs, brush, rocks, and earth to construct the riprap channel that extended out into the river to funnel the water. Three such walls would help to control the water and allow it to be turned out onto individual fields. Men cut cottonwood logs from the river's banks, with an estimated one thousand to be woven into the framework to hold tons of rocks and dirt. To encour-

age cooperation, the leaders sold stock in the new ditch, and church officials rebaptized some people as a commitment to the undertaking.

All winter long the men toiled. When April arrived and, with it,
thoughts of spring planting, the workers turned the water down the
ditch and watched it disappear through the porous walls of riprap. As
the spaces filled with sediment, the water inched its way to the fields
close to town. In May the river gnawed away at the top of the ditch. The
water then started to recede, so the workers used shovels to deepen a
course for it to follow, and the crops succeeded.

The next year problems intensified. Banks broke, ditches filled with
sand, crops withered, taxes increased to support the effort, and stock-
holders appointed new leaders to save their economy. During the flood
of 1884, the river carved up the canal, tore out the headgate, and covered
what remained with sand.[11]

Discouraged settlers suggested that the community move from the
river and use a more placid source of water. They considered moving to
Yellow Jacket Canyon until they learned that its owners wanted $30,000
for the land. F. A. Hammond, a newly arrived Mormon leader, decided
that the initially anticipated twenty miles of floodplain farmland would
never materialize, as he saw only 300 acres being farmed successfully.
He turned to the livestock industry and encouraged others to do likewise. Bluff blossomed as it shifted its attention away from the brown,
roiling waters of the San Juan. Forty years after this farming project
started, at an estimated total cost of $150,000 to $200,000, only 175 acres
were still under cultivation and the ditch no longer existed.[12]

So when Constant Williams stood on the banks of the San Juan and
insisted that its waters would be the economic salvation of the Navajos,
one wonders to whom he had talked, as history prepared to repeat itself.
Because the one farmer stationed at Fruitland could not help all of the
Navajos, Williams requested another for the Bluff region. No one was
found to fill the position, so the government handed out seed and farm
tools only to Navajos living along the upper San Juan.

Most of these farming projects were small-scale, individual efforts.[13]
George M. Butler, superintendent of irrigation, had constructed several
ditches on other parts of the reservation, the closest one to Aneth being
the Carrizo Creek Ditch. Sandoval, a local leader from the lower San
Juan, rode one hundred miles to Fort Defiance during the winter of 1896

to solicit help in reclaiming some of the "fine tracts of land" located near his home. Butler recommended a survey of possible locations.[14]

Little rainfall, cold springs, and early frosts continued to discourage the hardiest farmers, but government agents still called for surveys and ditches. In 1901 irrigation inspectors estimated that one-third of all the Navajos could prosper on the San Juan if they just had enough ditches.[15] In 1902 Samuel Shoemaker, supervisor of ditch construction near Fruit-land, received orders from agent George Hayzlett to start a major ditch in the vicinity of Bluff. Shoemaker paid Navajo laborers a dollar a day as the ground thawed and work began. The agent supplied shovels, axes, mattocks, grubbing hoes, augurs, wrenches, hatchets, crowbars, and drills that he hoped would "soon make a mile of ditch in that part of the country."[16]

Hayzlett looked at lands above Bluff in the Aneth–Mancos Creek area, where farming would be "far cheaper per acre than any other part of the reservation." The Navajos there had repeatedly asked for help in creating ditches, and now that the Shiprock agency brought government help, in the person of William T. Shelton, closer, their wishes could become a reality.[17]

Shelton analyzed the situation. He noted that Navajos often constructed ditches that washed out easily at the first high water because they lacked headgates and protective barriers. There was one exception in the Four Corners area, at the junction of Mancos Creek with the San Juan. Eight men labored to build a two-hundred-yard-long, twelve-foot-deep ditch to bring water to fifty acres on a three-hundred-acre tract. Shovels and picks moved the soil, but the Indians had to carry rocks by hand for a quarter mile to build the riprapping. The agent believed that it was worth the $500 in labor to build but that "it [would] no doubt go out at the first high water, not being properly protected."[18] Government farmers could provide necessary guidance to save the ditches and also to irrigate four times the area.

Shelton looked at the Aneth region next. He realized that Navajos had successfully farmed with a number of small ditches around the mouth of McElmo Canyon. Old Mexican, a Navajo who had worked both the mouths of Montezuma Creek and of McElmo Canyon, provides a detailed account of this experience. He tells of taking six days to dig a ditch a mile long to his field. Some passersby stopped to criticize his efforts, teasing that "all the people say water never runs up hill," but he persisted because the soil was good "to raise anything [he] wanted there."[19] It took six days to flood the level field, but by harvest time the corn grew over his head.

Shelton understood the importance of such successes. Armed with $3,000 for irrigation projects in 1905, he appointed another farmer, James M. Holley, to supervise Navajo agriculture and livestock operations. Holley was no stranger to the area. He had come to Aneth in 1899 to open a trading post. During those six years, he had been vocal in alerting government officials about the conflict over grazing lands between white and Navajo stockmen and had even asked for a position helping the Indians.[20]

Once appointed, Holley worked closely with Shelton, but his impact on the Navajos as a government farmer was more important. Old Mexican again provides one of the most detailed accounts of what Holley tried to accomplish. One of his first tasks was to identify the best Navajo workers. The most deserving received tools such as scythes, scrapers, pitchforks, hoes, and saws as rewards for following the government program. Holley hoped to teach through example the benefit of prosperous farms. Thus when Old Mexican harvested his foot-high hayfield, obtaining a stack "eight steps wide and sixteen steps long, and higher than a hogan," the government farmer chose him for additional tasks and leadership opportunities.[21]

Holley marshaled community support for a number of projects. He built a riprap protective barrier to prevent the river from eating away at the top of the Navajos' irrigation ditches. He started road construction to join Aneth to the Four Corners and paid his labor in farm tools, some of which were very enticing. Forty-five days' labor could net a worker a wagon, five days a scraper, and one day a shovel, ax, saw, or other tool. If a person organized a group of men and helped to feed them, the time needed to earn the reward decreased by half. Take for example, the experience of one crew. Slow had a wagon, but he wanted another. He was put in charge of a group of men who, when they arrived at the work site, slaughtered a cow and horse for food. In seven days the crew had earned a wagon for Slow.[22]

Four positive results came from this type of labor. The road improved transportation between Aneth and Shiprock; the Navajos worked as a team, creating community cohesion; the dispersal of tools ensured greater agricultural success; and the Navajos looked more and more to Holley and Shelton for advice, leadership, and equipment. In fact, Shiprock today is still known to older Navajos by the name they gave to Shelton years ago: Naat'áani Nez, "Tall Leader."

Another important project that Holley started was the construction of the government station, located on the terrace below the Aneth Trading Post. Joseph Heffernan bought the store from Holley after Shelton cautioned the farmer that being a trader and a government employee was incompatible.

In fall 1906 Holley organized Navajo laborers and set to work. They made adobe bricks from the soil of the San Juan, cement and lumber came from Shiprock, and Holley provided the floor plan. Construction started in the winter. The bricklayer told Old Mexican to heat the water for the cement and keep him supplied with rocks and adobe. In two days the foundation was completed and in twenty days the bricks laid. For his labor, Old Mexican received $20. That same year Holley built a barn for livestock and the bales of hay and alfalfa he had reaped from his own irrigated fields. The flood of 1933 eventually swept both structures downriver.[23]

The government farmer became increasingly prominent as a focal point of the community. In most areas of the reservation, the trading post was the center of community activity, but the government farmer, assuming that his personality and attitude were acceptable, served as a bridge between white and Navajo society, between official policy and Navajo practices.

Holley performed conscientious service in this respect. His roles ran the gamut from calming family fights to smoothing over a military confrontation and from freighting goods to controlling the river. A few brief examples illustrate his effectiveness. Old Mexican had a problem with his wives mixing with other men. Eventually he threw his hands in the air and turned to making money by hauling supplies. Holley stepped in and told him, "Go back and support your children. . . . [S]ome day one of your children might starve to death or freeze to death. . . . They would put you in jail."[24] Holley also served as a lawyer when a traveling judge heard the case of another man who had a similar problem. The man's wife, at various times, had nine husbands; Holley urged official separation, which the judge granted.

Holley requested a Navajo policeman for the Aneth area to settle domestic disturbances and, more important, to gather children for the Shiprock boarding school as it neared completion. To persuade Old Mexican to take the job, Shelton and Holley gave him a scraper, a double-tree (a crossbar on a wagon for harnessing horses), a shovel, other tools, a grinding stone, one spool of smooth fence wire, and boards for a headgate. Shelton told him, "The reason I am giving you all of this stuff is because I heard Holley talking about you. He said you were a hard worker."[25] Old Mexican certainly appreciated the free goods but postponed as long as possible the decision to become a policeman. "I'll have to tell my folks and the other people before I say anything," he hedged. Eventually he declined the offer, insisting that the Navajos were "pretty hard and ornery."[26] Holley had to go elsewhere for help.

In Shelton's estimation one of the most "ornery" Navajos was a medicine man named Ba'ililii. He lived within a few miles of the government station and did all he could to disrupt Shelton's and Holley's plans. In 1905 Pit-ze-cote, a cohort of Ba'ililii, raped a number of Navajo girls, one of whom was Hattie. One morning as Hattie went out to gather in the horses, Pit-ze-cote approached her, grabbed her horse's reins, pulled her to the ground, bound her arms, and assaulted her. She was sick for months after the incident. Shelton sent Pit-ze-cote to jail at Fort Defiance, which angered his friend Ba'ililii. The medicine man held a sing and schemed with others to free Pit-ze-cote. He reasoned that if he could capture Shelton he could force his friend's release, and, surprisingly, he went to Holley for help with the abduction. The farmer refused but offered to go to Shiprock and talk with the agent. Black Horse and Polly, two friends of Ba'ililii, wanted to take sixty armed men to the agency and, if nothing else, intimidate the rape victims into testifying on behalf of the prisoner. Shelton sent the girls to Farmington, however, and little more came of the incident, which proved to be only one of many involving this group of Navajos.[27]

Ba'ililii and his following avoided having anything to do with the government: they refused to send their children to school, refused to dip their sheep, and married and divorced whomever they wished. Through

Holley, Shelton issued ewes and lambs to the Navajos in the Aneth district. Ba'ililii sold his and bought whiskey with the proceeds. He insisted he had done no wrong, that the government had no control over him, and that he would remain unrepentant.

Sandoval, a Navajo policeman from Shiprock, visited him and told him that if he were not careful, Shelton would take away his "medicine-work," referring to his powerful ceremonial abilities. Then Shelton would round up all his children and put them in school. This conversation ended with Ba'ililii saying that he was not scared: "We all have to die anyway. We don't live forever."[28] On the morning of October 28, 1907, he faced Shelton and Captain Harry O. Williard in a confrontation that resulted in two dead Navajos and the incarceration for two years of Ba'ililii and eight others at Fort Huachuca.

Holley's work as a farmer continued. Scabies, ticks, and lice infested the Navajo sheep, so he placed dipping vats at the mouths of McElmo, Montezuma Creek, and Recapture Canyons. At first the Navajos believed this medicine killed the sheep rather than helped them. Although Shelton did his best to explain the benefits, the Indians remained unconvinced. Old Mexican, showing the faith he had in Holley, suggested the group go to talk to him. The farmer must have been convincing because larger and larger herds of livestock descended on the dipping stations.[29]

By fall 1908 Holley resigned his government post and returned to the life of a trader. J. H. Locke replaced him. Although he lacked Holley's ability to speak Navajo, the Navajos felt "the new farmer [was] kind to the Indians and [gave] them good advice."[30] Locke did not stay long, however; a little over a year later, he was replaced by W. O. Hodgson.

Shelton called a number of Navajos from the Aneth area to Shiprock to find out what they needed. They requested help with their ditches, so the agent pointed to Hodgson, saying, "This fellow will do the work," and then told the Indians to collect a large group of people to get the project under way. The Navajos were paid a dollar a day for chopping trees and two dollars for hauling rocks and brush in their wagons. Hodgson had $400 set aside for the project. Fenceposts and wire served as the framework for the breakwater. The Navajos planted them in the shape of a triangle in which they piled brush and rocks. Two weeks later, eight of these structures were finished, but so was the money. The riverbank was only temporarily saved; by the next spring the water washed all the work downstream.[31]

Hodgson decided to build another ditch elsewhere. He believed that if he dug it deep enough, the water would flow more easily. Old Mexican cautioned against this plan, but Hodgson insisted that within twenty paces the water would be flowing over the land. After the workers finished the ditch, the farmer ordered the headgates opened, but the water never went much beyond the entrance to the field. He commanded the workers to dig farther and achieved the same results. Hodgson then turned to Old Mexican in exasperation and said, "Work it your way. You know more about it. Work it just as you like." And he did. The Navajos tied seven bundles of brush together, lined the bank with them, then spent three days piling rocks on top. He constructed a dam in front of the old ditch and forced the water over the dam and onto the land. His only comment at its completion was, "This Hodgson doesn't know what he is talking about."[32]

If Hodgson was unskilled as a farmer, there were other ways that he could encourage agriculture. On October 20 and 21, 1909, Shelton and the additional farmers instituted an event that continues to this day, the annual Shiprock Fair. The festivities sprang from two months of planning by farmers and traders alike. The fair was heralded by the *Farmington Enterprise* as marking a "new era of progress of the Southwest" and viewed by the locals as the peak of Shelton's six-year effort to remove the "ignorance and superstition of a barbarous people."[33]

In spite of their "barbarity," the Navajos made a "creditable" showing with 290 exhibits, each containing from five to sixty articles. Categories included blankets, silver jewelry, buffalo robes, beadwork, horses, cows, sheep, goats, and a wide array of farm produce. On the top of the produce list were corn, potatoes, pumpkins, squash, beans, watermelons, wheat, oats, alfalfa, apples, and peaches. Judges awarded first- to fourth-place prizes for each category, the rewards ranging from double harnesses, disc harrows, corn drills, and cook stoves to hoes, shovels, and mattocks. There were even prizes for the prettiest and cleanest Navajo babies, the proud mothers receiving a fifty-pound sack of flour.[34] Although the descriptions in the newspapers and some of the fair events were highly paternalistic, they provided an opportunity for the white community to view their Indian neighbors as moving along the path the white man considered "progress." For the Navajos, the event was a chance to socialize and compete for prizes.

The fair drew contestants from more than seventy miles away. There were horse races, footraces, tugs of war, dances, relays, and a Night Chant ceremony. On the final day, after the judging was over, Shelton had the contestants line up to receive their awards. Old Mexican entered watermelons, muskmelons, squash, beets, carrots, sugar beets, and turnips; his wife entered a rug. When he left Shiprock, he had among his prizes a harness, a steel plow, and a single horse cultivator.[35] Over the years, the fair grew in importance as a place of social exchange and as a tool to encourage high-quality agricultural produce.

However, in fall 1911 disaster struck. As people flocked to Shiprock for the fair, heavy rains bogged down the wagons and made it difficult to set up displays. Participants watched the river rise, flood its banks, and fill the fairgrounds. A reservoir upstream broke, adding to the torrent that worked away at the adobe walls of homes, the school, and adjacent facilities. The new Shiprock bridge toppled as the people moved onto the hills nearby, but not until the water started to recede did the onlookers realize the extent of the damage to the school facilities, farms, and orchards.

When the Navajos returned to the lower San Juan, they found their gardens and ditches obliterated and the ground covered with gravel. Many of the good sites no longer were worth farming.[36] The water had even worked at the foundation of the government station, making the house unsafe to live in. Hodgson withdrew to Shiprock until repairs made the structure safe once again, but by then he had developed heart trouble, left the Indian Service, and moved to Phoenix, Arizona.[37]

After the flood, life took up where it had left off. The next year Shelton reported that Navajos had built small irrigation ditches from Farmington to Bluff, a distance of more than one hundred miles. He also pointed out that farms were rarely located near good grazing lands for sheep. Some Indians traveled up to thirty miles to get back to the river to weed and water crops.[38]

In 1914 Herbert Redshaw, the new government farmer, arrived in Aneth. He had taken a roundabout route to get there. Born in Longford, Derbyshire, England, on April 8, 1863, by the age of twelve Redshaw was already captivated by his uncle's tales of land and wealth in America. He worked at odd jobs for two years to earn his passage, and at the ripe age of fourteen he traveled to Parsons, Kansas. There he received only a lukewarm welcome from his surprised uncle. In the following years, he wrangled cattle in Texas and Arizona, farmed bottomlands in Kansas, and married Ella Mead Pratt, who died in 1907 after bearing him seven children. Three years later he joined the Indian Service in Colorado, where he worked at the Grand Junction Indian School as a dairyman. He then transferred to Shiprock for two years until Shelton sent him to Aneth as the government farmer. He remained there until his retirement eighteen years later, in 1931.[39]

Family members describe Redshaw as a "typical old Englishman." He stood over six feet tall, had steel gray eyes, and sported a mustache. His large feet and hands and rawboned build gave him a commanding presence. He wore bib overalls and a broad-brimmed hat, and a corncob pipe filled with George Washington tobacco jutted from his lower jaw. One man quipped that it took more matches than tobacco to keep the pipe operating.[40]

To the Navajos, he was T'áábíích'įidii. An exact translation of this name is difficult, but an approximation is "His Own Devil." The Indians did not apply this epithet with rancor. Redshaw moved slowly, swaying slightly as he methodically swung his arms; His Indian name gives the feeling that he moved like a dead man returned to life. Another possible derivation of his name was his habit of cussing out those who made mistakes on the job with the words, "Go to the devil."[41] Whatever its origin, the name is now applied to the Aneth Chapter, the place that Redshaw struggled to develop.

Much of Redshaw's life at Aneth was filled with the day-to-day tasks of farming along the river. He lived in the government station surrounded by forty acres of alfalfa fields and gardens, many of which Indians planted and maintained. At harvest time he divided the produce among needy Navajos. His red barn and red fences became a landmark to travelers, and his irrigation system proved ingenious. Redshaw not only used the water from McElmo Creek, but, when it started to decrease, he also drew from the San Juan. His main ditch was four feet wide and two feet deep with a main headgate that returned much of the water directly to the river and a smaller stream to flood his fields. By using this system, he alleviated the problem of silt buildup. Redshaw encouraged families to settle nearby as he made the government station a center of activity. He held community meetings under the cottonwood trees along the banks of the river and encouraged the Navajos to settle on the floodplain.[42]

Redsaw dreamed of damming the San Juan River. He hoped to institute his plan near the Four Corners and eventually build another dam at the mouth of McElmo Creek. The proposed structure would be as high as the surrounding hills, with irrigation ditches paralleling both sides of the river. This would alleviate much of the danger of floodplain agriculture, which by now was becoming increasingly popular, as Navajos farmed every available space along the river. Unfortunately, government shortages of funds and enthusiasm precluded the undertaking.[43]

Although Redshaw did not realize his dream, he diligently taught Navajos what he considered the proper method of agriculture. He spoke enough of their language to get by, but for formal occasions he used Eddie Neskaaii from Shiprock as his translator. Harvey Oliver, a Navajo who worked for Redshaw for five years, explained his teaching style: "He would look at it [the garden plot]. He did not just walk around, but he told us how to put watermelon seeds in the ground by counting them. Count the corn or the onions, this is what he said. There were distances between each onion that you should be aware of. He told me to learn all of this."[44] Oliver did learn, and by the end of his work with Redshaw, his salary had increased from $1 to $5 a day. This did not include his carrying the mail to the Ismay Trading Post for $10 a round trip.

Older Navajos today still talk about how Redshaw had one of the first automobiles in the Aneth area. Among other things, it served as the only motorized "school bus" that each fall brought the children to the Shiprock boarding school. The process started with a census number on a metal tag that he hung around the children's necks. Sometimes he provided English names, ensured they received immunizations, and filled the agent's requests for students. Then the farmer squeezed as many as he could into his black government Ford, cranked up the engine, and chugged across the reservation, making the number of trips necessary to get all of the pupils to Shiprock. He also visited the children periodically during the school year and brought them home in the spring. Whether coming or going, it was not a free ride. Many of the children remember having to stop along the way and shovel dirt into the potholes and gullies that dotted the road.[45] Redshaw seldom missed an opportunity to improve the country and teach a lesson about work.

Sometimes, however, Redshaw was the one who learned a lesson. He often took a couple of Navajo men with him when he drove the reservation roads. More often than not he would get stuck in sandy washes or muddy ruts, so he had the Indians get out to push the vehicle free. The Navajos chuckled about fooling Redshaw by getting behind the car as if they were really trying to release it when, in reality, they were doing nothing. Eventually the government farmer caught on to the prank and carried a fifty-foot rope with a handle that had gloves nailed on it for pulling. He attached the rope to the front so that there was no mistake about who was not working.[46]

Around this same time (the early 1920s), Redshaw succeeded in having twenty-five families settled along an irrigation canal that supplied water from the mouth of McElmo Creek.[47] He also kept track of the sheep dipping done in the spring, although for Evan W. Estep, superintendent of the Shiprock Agency, Redshaw was not efficient enough. After telling how sheep dipping was progressing on other parts of the reservation, Estep commented that "Abba Chinda," "Slow Devil" as he translated it, was not ready and had left for Monticello just as a supervisor from Shiprock arrived. The agent threatened that if a quarantine was imposed, Redshaw would be blamed and that "no one ever knew Redshaw to do anything just when it ought to be done or when the other fellow wanted him to do it." Estep was anxious "to go down there and cuss him out right," but he also added that this farmer was a "good man, . . . likely the best I could get in that out of the way place, but he does get on my nerves at times, and no mistake."[48]

Yet Redshaw played a vital role in many of the conflicts that took place during the 1920s. One of the first involved John Hunt, or "Little Mexican," a trader at the Aneth post. In 1919 Jimmy Boatman's son, a twenty-three-year-old Navajo, entered the store, intimidated a young boy behind the counter, and took a pair of overalls. Hunt came out of the back room and seized the pants; a scuffle ensued. The trader slapped the Navajo a few times, wrenched the pants loose, threw him out of the store, and watched him stalk away. A few days later the Navajo died, and the people of Aneth believed the trader was responsible. They talked of a hanging, so Redshaw called the community together and all day long reasoned with the crowd under the cottonwoods. Feelings smoldered until a trial was held in Monticello. Hunt obtained the services of a lawyer from Moab, Knox Patterson, and Joe Tanner and Charles Ashcroft, traders from along the San Juan, served as interpreters for Navajo witnesses. Some of the Indians complained that Tanner was a good friend of Hunt's, and so Ashcroft assumed the primary duties of interpreter.

Meanwhile Tanner went to Aneth and uncovered the crucial fact that two days before the altercation the Navajo man had fallen off a horse and had laid unconscious for half a day. The court directed a doctor to exhume the body; the official notified the judge that the victim did indeed have a previous injury and had died from a blood clot, a condition exacerbated by the fight. The court reduced the charge to assault and battery and fined Hunt $200, after which he moved his trading operations to Bluff's old co-op store. As government agent, farmer, and temporary investigator, Redshaw was glad to see the episode end.[49]

Another conflict centered around range rights. Cattlemen and sheepherders vied for lands near the northern part of the reservation, with some of the ranchers slipping over the boundaries onto Indian lands. As there were no fences, Redshaw told the Indians to herd the animals back onto the public domain, which did not sit well with the stockmen. Many of the whites thought talk of law and authority a bluff, especially the younger men who lacked "the fair attitude of the old-timers." Redshaw pleaded for immediate government action.[50]

The agent agreed with Redshaw's evaluation and added that some of the stockmen had been involved for years in stealing Indian cattle and making a handsome profit from the sales. At the same time ranchers were lobbying Congress to open Navajo and Ute lands to white livestock grazing.[51] Tensions increased. The end result of the conflict was the 1933 addition to the Navajo Reservation of the lands encompassed by or adjacent to Montezuma Canyon. What is important at this point is that Redshaw became the advocate for Navajos, and in some cases Utes, as they battled to maintain or obtain lands. He accompanied the Navajo agent, the Ute agent, and special investigators sent from Washington and, in a few instances, retrieved livestock stolen from Navajos. He explained to one Navajo that he was an Englishman, that he did not hate Indians, and that he would not take their lands.[52] He was as good as his word.

In 1931 Redshaw retired. He stayed long enough to complete the census but left soon enough to avoid the trauma of Navajo livestock reduction in the 1930s. His hired hand, Harvey Oliver, left because of dissatisfaction with the tribal council's authoritarian rule and the elimination of Navajo self-sufficiency. Redshaw feared that marking off parts of the reservation for school sections would allow white men to reclaim for their own purposes the land removed from the public domain. Today, Oliver believes this is happening: "Táábííchʼįidii said it was going to happen. 'These people will not tell you the truth about why they are doing this,' he said. 'They are a bunch of liars.'"[53] It was time for this government farmer to get out of the Indian Service.

Redshaw moved to Ucolo, where he remained for the next fifteen years. His accomplishments in his new home included acquisition of more than a thousand acres, which he parceled out to close family members; pioneered a telephone system that went from Ucolo to Eastland, Boulder, and then Monticello; served as a San Juan County commissioner between 1936 and 1940; donated five acres for a school and served on the school board; and developed a better road system for the outlying communities east of Monticello.[54]

But the reservation experience never seemed to get out of his blood. No matter where he went, Redshaw had in his vehicle a jug of water, a blanket, a shovel, and a tow rope. He still stopped and filled in potholes and helped to supervise road crews. Navajos came to his home, brought him mutton, and talked about the hard times caused by the slaughter of livestock.[55] And in 1938, as a county commissioner, he organized a meeting in Monticello, requested by the Navajos, to increase public awareness concerning the effects of livestock reduction.[56] In 1946, after two successive strokes, Herbert Redshaw died and was buried in the Burns, Colorado, cemetery.

Almost as if the San Juan River knew that Redshaw had left and livestock reduction had started, its waters gathered strength to undo what had been accomplished. In 1933 the river once again overflowed its banks, tore out the irrigation ditches, snatched away the headgates, wiped out Navajo farms, swallowed the government station, and forced abandonment of life on the floodplain. It also shifted from the south to the north side of the streambed and cut away every vestige of productive land there. The Shiprock Agency withdrew its program of maintaining a resident farmer in Aneth and requested that anybody desiring help come to their headquarters. The battle with the San Juan was over.

Was the government farming program a failure? Not really. It fit an era and a need that could not have been filled as successfully by other existing programs. The Navajos adapted to it easily because agriculture was already an important part of their economy. The government provided farm tools and equipment to a people who did not have the money to purchase them; it offered incentive to work as a community, yet rewarded individual efforts. Navajos were motivated to improve agricultural techniques and develop products comparable to those in the white economy. The program served as a vehicle to send children to school, produced a voice for law and order both on and off the reservation, and supplied men sympathetic to the Navajos' changing circumstances at the turn of the century. This last contribution was not measurable like the vanished headgates and ditches along the San Juan, but it was just as vital. The river may have won the contest for agricultural lands, but settlement and progress continued in spite of this setback.

For approximately forty years, the planting of crops remained on an individual, small scale. Then, in about 1970, technology provided a new answer to the age-old problem of using river water to grow crops. That year the Bureau of Indian Affairs completed a survey of possible farmlands bordering the San Juan River. To qualify as suitable for farming, a plot of land had to be at least eighty acres and have a vertical water lift of less than five hundred feet; the soil had to be free of strong alkaline and saline content; and the land had to have a gentle slope, less than 10 percent. The BIA identified 52,984 acres that met these guidelines.[57]

Eventually ten groups, including tribal, federal, state, and private agencies, participated in the project to turn the valley of the lower San Juan into a lush agricultural zone managed by local Navajos as a private, cooperative enterprise. In 1971 only 65 acres were under cultivation; in 1974, 370 acres were planted; and when the project reached its height in 1976, about 1,000 acres were yielding crops from five sites on both sides of the river ranging from the Utah-Colorado border to Sand

Island below Bluff.[58] Winter wheat, alfalfa, and oats were the main crops harvested.

One site, the Tahotaile (A-Wide-Expanse-of-Land-That-Extends-into-the-River) Farm Co-op, near Montezuma Creek, serves as an example of how the program functioned. To move the water from the river, a 150-horsepower pump forced it through pipes for 550 feet to a 14-million-gallon reservoir, where the silt settled to the bottom. Next, a rolling sprinkler system of aluminum pipe traversed the graded farmland. Finally, the families provided the necessary labor for weeding, harvesting, and marketing the crops.

Four major problems were encountered in the operation. The first was the silt, which produced wear and tear on the equipment but was mostly removed once it reached the settling reservoir. The second was the meandering of the river, which had a wide streambed in which to roam. The third problem was the fluctuation in the level of the river, which could vary from day to day and, in some cases, from hour to hour. But the fourth problem, individuals working in a cooperative effort, proved to be the final blow. Once the managerial system was relinquished to cooperative group control, individual differences hastened the abandonment of the farms.[59] Again the San Juan was left to run its natural course.

Today, the best example of what it takes to utilize the San Juan on a large scale also illustrates the price that must be paid. On the lower San Juan there are some relatively small (100- to 200-acre) Anglo operations that use hand-moved sprinkling systems to water fields of alfalfa and other crops. The vast majority of Navajo lands, however, lay agriculturally dormant. It is not until near Farmington, New Mexico, that one finds reservation land under the plow on a large scale.

The Navajo Indian Irrigation Project (NIIP) began in 1970 under the tribal-sponsored Navajo Agricultural Products Industry (NAPI). Part of the NIIP infrastructure consists of the Navajo Dam Reservoir and a seventy-one-mile canal and pipeline water delivery system that puts 508,000 acre-feet of water on 110,630 acres of farmland. The project swallowed $370 million, with an estimated $260 million more needed to complete future development. Fiscal reports suggest that it is "profitable" and annually pumps $35 million into the tribal economy.[60] With rising costs and shrinking availability of water, its future profitability remains to be seen. What is important at this point is to understand that it took a huge investment in time, money, technology, and materials to harness the San Juan—something that government agents in the past could hardly have comprehended. For the lower San Juan, this dream has continued to remain out of reach.

CHAPTER FOUR

NAALYÉHÉ BÁ HOOGHAN, "HOUSE OF MERCHANDISE"

Navajo Trading Posts as an Institution of Cultural Change, 1900–1930

Today supermarkets with electric-eye doors, soothing Muzak, and produce in displays worthy of *Better Homes and Gardens* are commonplace to most Americans. We see oranges treated with chemicals to make them turn the desired color, apples coated with wax, and glistening fruits and vegetables sprayed with water placed beside brightly colored packaging that screams "one-third off," or "fewer calories," or "organically grown, natural food." As we speed through the express-lane checkout and glance at a clock, we select the shortest distance to sprint to the car, located near the handicap parking stall. Weaving between the stationary cars, we manage to hit the main flow of traffic, never giving a second thought to the series of choices we just made, many of which were influenced as much by the environment and the store manager as by the shopper. In short, many of those value-laden decisions derived, whether consciously or subconsciously, from the culture in which we operate.

This chapter examines similar transactions at another time, in another place, and in a different cultural setting. The Navajo trading post started as an institution in 1868, reached its height between 1900 and the 1930s, and then declined. Recognized by many as the premier focal point where two cultures came together on equal terms, the post served as a vehicle for both change and preservation.[1] Most historians, however, look only at the economic transactions—the exchange of rugs, wool, and silver across the counter—rather than the role of the post as a vehicle of acculturation. In the following brief analysis, I examine the posts of the northern part of the reservation as facilitators of change in a people noted for adaptability. The Navajos accepted alterations selectively, as a means of enriching their lives without sacrificing cultural integrity. Only later, after the disastrous livestock reduction of the mid- to late 1930s, did their culture take on a rate and direction of change totally foreign to previous traditional practices and patterns.

Between 1900 and 1930 there were two types of posts that serviced the Navajo. The first belonged to licensed traders, approved by the BIA. The store and inventory may have belonged to the trader, but the land surrounding it was the tribe's and the license was the government's.[2] Federal regulations dictated the screening of traders, limited locations of posts, and controlled certain sale items. According to the BIA, to be involved in the business a "proper person" had to be of good moral standing, honest in his dealings, fair in establishing prices, concerned about his customers, and opposed to the sale and use of alcohol by the Indians. Anyone caught trading on the reservation without a license forfeited all of his merchandise and paid a fine of up to $500. One trader estimated that his store cost him $5,000 with $2,000 down and a 6 percent mortgage, along with an inventory of $1,500. A trader had no guarantee that his license would be renewed at the end of his tenure, which could last from one to five years.[3] The adage "damned if you do and damned if you don't" applied to the men who ran the posts: they were at the mercy of everyone from the local agent to the Washington bureaucrat, on one side, and to the Navajo customer, on the other.

Although the real may be far from the ideal, the general impression is that the traders of this era were basically honest, moral people who worked hard. Those who were not did not last long; they were forced out of the market by competitors who were. Most of the traders were white men, although a handful were Navajo. An Indian had an advantage in that he could establish a post anyplace, whereas an Anglo had to operate at a specified location. For example, John Wetherill opened a store in Oljeto in 1906 after receiving approval to locate on an abandoned mining claim that was surrounded by, but not part of, reservation lands. By 1910 he, his wife, Louisa, and his partner, Clyde Colville, decided that Kayenta, twenty-six miles away, would be a better site because of the traffic that flowed through Marsh Pass. The Wetherills again submitted an application with accompanying character references, which was later approved.

The second type of post avoided many government regulations by locating off the reservation on its adjacent borders. In the north, these trading facilities were found on the San Juan River, extending from Farmington, New Mexico, to Aneth, Bluff, and Mexican Hat, Utah, and to the western boundary and settlements along the Colorado and Little Colorado Rivers. Before the 1890s these posts flourished and were a never-ending source of aggravation to the agents, who watched their charges being siphoned off the reservation only to be cheated and sent home impoverished.[4] The national depression of the 1890s generally wiped the slate clean so that with the establishment of the Northern and Western Navajo Agencies in the early 1900s, closer surveillance of border activities was possible.

Over a thirty-year period, the number of posts fluctuated. The military expedition led by Lieutenant Colonel George Hunter in 1908 provides an educated estimate.[5] Hunter identified posts at Oljeto, Round Rock, Bluff, Tuba City, Teec Nos Pos, and Red Lake as those visited by the Navajos from the northern region. There were also stores in the Farmington-Shiprock area, although he did not mention them. One of Hunter's captains visited the Bluff post and reported that 950 adult Navajos had traded there within the past year, but only half of them had homes within a sixty-mile radius. Basing his population figures on traders' statements, Hunter concluded that from Navajo Mountain to the Carrizo Mountains, there was a total population of 1,512 men, women, children, and slaves. Even as a rough estimate, these figures are a strong indicator of Navajo mobility for trade relations. By 1930 there were additional posts, located at Ismay, Aneth, Mexican Hat, Monument Valley, Kayenta, Chinle, Red Mesa, Shonto, Inscription House, and Navajo Mountain, just to name the most prominent.

In general, the Navajos welcomed more posts to their area for two reasons: the closer they were, the more convenient it was; and having more options provided an opportunity to play one store against another for better prices. In either instance, travel was involved. For the Navajo, unlike for the white man, setting out on a journey had serious implications. The Navajo world was populated by supernatural beings, who could be either benevolent or vengeful, depending on the ceremonial precautions taken by the traveler. Before setting out, many people wrapped themselves in a protective shield of good thoughts, prayers, and songs of the Mountain Way and Blessing Way.[6] Just as in the myths and legends from which these songs came, the traveler identified with a supernatural hero who had also journeyed far and been protected. The Navajo felt compelled to invoke supernatural aid, especially when traveling to posts located in distant areas or across mythological boundaries that separated safe refuge from the lands of the enemy.

The San Juan River was established by the gods as the northern boundary of safety. Known by various names, Old Age River, Male Water, One-With-a-Long-Body, this powerful force is also described as a snake wriggling through the desert, as a flash of lightning, and as a black club of protection to keep invaders from Navajo lands. These elements serve as protective symbols to separate realms of safety and danger. Even today, when older people cross the river, they sprinkle corn pollen to the holy being within to ask for help. When questioned about going to a post on the other side, Navajos expressed how frightened they were as they loaded their sacks of wool and goat skins into a wooden boat, then watched a young man row them through the sand waves and across the San Juan to the Bluff Co-op.[7]

Fear was not only associated with crossing water. Navajo Oshley, a longtime resident of southeastern Utah, told of when he traveled to the unfamiliar Chilchinbeto post. As darkness fell, he heard soft singing as he approached an abandoned corral and what he thought was a ceremony. His horse became skittish, and a feeling of foreboding overwhelmed him. He hurried on and finally arrived at his destination, where he spent the night, but the next day curiosity got the best of him and he returned to the spot. There was no hogan and no ceremony, only a set of human tracks that changed into a pair of coyote prints and then headed for the trading post. Oshley was convinced that he had had a close encounter with a skinwalker, an evil personification created through witchcraft.[8]

In addition to danger, however, travel to a post also brought the opportunity for riches. Navajos sang songs to beguile the trader into giving a good deal. To the Navajo, thought is as important as action, so good thoughts and wishes needed to precede what occurred at the store. Prayers and songs could work wonders on the trader, one of them wishing "the white man will be generous with his money as well as with his food."[9] One trading song says,

Hard goods of all sorts are attached to it as it becomes mine.
Soft goods of all sorts are attached to it as it becomes mine.
It shall be beautiful behind it as it becomes mine.
It shall be beautiful in front of it as it becomes mine.
Good and everlasting one am I, as it becomes mine.[10]

Once the people arrived at the post, a new set of concerns arose. The stores, constructed of rock, adobe, or wood, followed a basic pattern. A front room called the bullpen, which held a wood-burning stove, had plenty of space for customers to gather and visit. On the outskirts of the room in an "L" or "U" configuration were wide wooden counters worn smooth by the blankets, wool, and merchandise that passed back and forth. Some posts had a floor elevated six inches behind the counters, allowing the trader to look out into the bullpen over the heads of his customers while also appearing larger in size, a slight psychological advantage. One trader put a wire mesh eighteen inches above the counter to prevent being lassoed and dragged over the top, although this fencing does not appear to have been a common practice. All goods were stored well out of reach of the customers, who identified articles by pictures and colors instead of labels. A disadvantage to this physical layout was that in the winter heat radiated from the stove into the bullpen but rarely made it over the counter to the feet and legs of the trader. Locks on the doors, a pistol or rifle nearby, and the trader's wits were the main means of safeguarding his establishment in times of trouble. Service for the customer and security for the owner divided the two worlds.[11]

The trader usually lived in a backroom that doubled as a kitchen and bedroom. Outside the typical post was a well, a corral for livestock, a guest hogan stocked with wood and some cooking utensils for long-distance visitors, and perhaps a storage shed for the ten- to twelve-foot-long sacks of wool. Most of the valuable items taken in trade or pawn remained in the post.

When people entered the bullpen, they saw brightly colored shirts and hats, bolts of cloth, cans of peaches, tomatoes, and milk, candy, and hardware. The staples of the trade, though, were sacks of flour, Arbuckle coffee—either whole or ground—sugar, and baking powder. Because Navajos resented higher prices in coffee but not in sugar, traders often sold coffee at cost and marked up the sugar to cover the expense and

The floor plan of the Coyote Canyon Trading Post illustrates the established pattern for most posts. The "bullpen" heated by a pot-bellied stove, the wide counters, and shelves with goods out of the patrons' reach communicated expectations of both customer and trader. Photo from the Milton Snow Collection, NE 18-46, Navajo Nation Museum.

profit on both items. Packing crates transformed into shelves, seats, and storage bins but were also sold to the Navajos for similar uses in their hogan.[12] Anything that enhanced life on the reservation and could be freighted in a wagon, or later by motor vehicle, was sold at the trading post.

The entire experience of buying and selling was laced with cultural meaning. When Navajos entered the store, a lengthy process was set in motion. The first thing they did was nothing. They entered, looked around, sat down, and greeted other Navajos in the bullpen. Personal relations and trade were not rushed. Eventually the customer approached the counter and started a light conversation with the owner, telling where dances and ceremonies were going to be held, where he had come from, and what he had been doing.

Most traders and their wives spoke Navajo; only a few depended on interpreters. Evolving from this commerce came a linguistic variation called "trader Navajo," a communication that emphasized the economic side of post life but missed the subtleties of more sophisticated speech. Some traders, such as Louisa Wetherill, Ray Hunt, and Stokes Carson, became so expert that Navajos detected little difference in speech. Regardless of linguistic ability, the universal sign of recognition was the handshake, a warm slight touch rather than a vigorous, tooth-jarring pump. The Navajo held the hand briefly and did not grip it tightly, since to do so boasted of one's physical strength and belittled that of the recipient.[13]

Navajos expected the traders to show some type of special kindness to each of the customers. For instance, there might be a box for tobacco and cigarette papers nailed down to the counter or a plug of tobacco from which the trader cut a 5-, 10-, or 25-cent slice. A little hard candy, a can of tomatoes, some coffee and bread, or popcorn induced the customer to feel relaxed and welcome. A coffee pot, matches, and blankets might be borrowed for the night, and occasionally a child might be given a shirt or some other article of clothing. A 103-year-old lady claimed that she never feared the trader because he gave her food and her brother clothing and called them his children.[14]

This last point is important. The Navajo language has titles that indicate kinship relations such as "sister," "mother," "father," "grandmother," "grandfather," and "son." These same terms can be used to indicate respect and social status for a person who is not related by blood but is only an acquaintance. Owners and customers used these terms freely as they bartered over the counters, but underneath the chatter were implied responsibilities and relationships. Navajos naturally placed the trader in the position of a parent who was obligated to provide for his or her children. Hilda Wetherill Faunce, as a new trader, illustrated her frustration with a monologue she heard many times. The customer started by saying,

My dear grandmother, come into this corner with me. We will speak slowly and not get mad. The children at my house who call you mother are hungry. They cry and call for candy and bread. One has a [bad] stomach. He said his mother would send medicine and apples and candy to him by me. Your children need shoes. In six months I shall sell my wool. Allow me, my mother, my sister, my pretty younger sister, to owe you twenty dollars until I shear my sheep. This will make all your children who live at my house warm. . . . See, my coat is worn out and no good. Let me have a new coat. Let me owe you four dollars for a new coat. Is this four dollars? It is very thin and ugly for four dollars. But I am poor, so I will take it. I tell all Navajos how nice you are, how you feed anyone who asks, and give apples and candy to all the children who come to your store. The Indians all say you are good. . . . It's a long way to my house, and my horse is tired. While he rests I have time to eat. Give me a can of pears and a box of crackers, because I live a long way off and come all this distance in the cold to trade . . . with you because I know you are good and we are friends. That's right, that's good. This is for friendship. Thanks my mother. Good, good. Now I go.[15]

Although to a present-day Anglo accustomed to a system of impersonal economic transactions this speech borders on wheedling and begging, in reality it shows the sense of responsibility and obligation emphasized in kin relations. Inherent in Navajo culture is the desire for cooperation and sharing fostered in a land that could be harsh and pitiless. The trading post was one more resource for survival, although to many white men, who had their own ethnocentric biases, at times this fact was hard to accept.

The Navajos also gave the trader a name that described a prominent physical or social characteristic. This practice fit in with a previously existing pattern, which taught that a person is not called by this name face to face because it could embarrass him or her by publicly calling attention to a noticeable characteristic.[16] Examples of names emphasizing physical qualities are Curly Head, Big White Man, Slender Woman, Red Beard, Swinging Arm, Skinny Hand, Hairy, Little Man With Big Ears, Looks Like A Mouth, and Rough Hands. Those centering on personality traits include Big Boss, One That Jokes Around, One Who Is Hungry, Lady Who Lies Around, and The Poor One. The latter name was given to O. J. Carson because he often said, "I can't lend you any money; I haven't any."[17]

The wide acceptance of women as traders also tied in with Navajo values. In a culture that was strongly matrilineal, Navajo women not only held the most important role in descent lines but also controlled substantial property and prestige. Both sexes accepted white women as competent traders, and in some cases they seem to have been preferred.

Louisa Wetherill is a fine example. She spoke Navajo better than her husband, John, did the trading while he was off exploring, was adopted by the most prominent leader in the Oljeto-Kayenta region, acted as lawyer and judge in local disputes, was given access to ceremonial knowledge, and received all of the property of her adopted father when he died. One Navajo described her by saying, "Asdzáán Tsosie is like a Navajo herself. Even when she speaks English, she speaks with the tone of a Navajo."[18] Hilda Faunce at Covered Water, Mary Jones at Bluff, Elizabeth Hegemann at Shonto, Mildred Heflin at Oljeto, and "Mike" Goulding at Monument Valley all had positive relationships with Navajo clients and earned respect as knowledgeable and sharp bargainers.

The daily life of the trader is so well documented that only a brief sketch is provided here.[19] The theme that runs through all the accounts is how important it is for traders to understand Navajo culture. For example, many have written about the Navajos' fear of the dead and how traders were often called in to bury the body as a service to the family. However, one trader earned the hostility of the community when he buried an important medicine man facing the wrong direction.[20] Jot Stiles, in a Tuba City trading post, watched a Navajo consumed with epileptic seizures. Realizing that his store and its inventory would be supernaturally defiled if the man died inside, Stiles vaulted over the counter and dragged him outside before it was too late. This action would hardly be expected in an establishment serving Anglo customers but met with strong Navajo approval. Stiles also walked the streets of Tuba City during a parade or gathering to identify those who owed him money. Other traders watched to see who came into their posts wearing new clothes purchased elsewhere. If that person already had a lot of pawn hanging on the wall or under the counter, the new clothes alerted the trader to how much additional credit would be allowed.[21]

For those not wise in the ways of the world, there were opportunities to become the butt of Navajo humor. Catherine and Frank Moore were living near the Oljeto trading post and doing some surveying when the store owner died. His wife and daughter put the corpse in a box and asked the Moores to manage the business while they went to Cortez to make funeral arrangements. The temporary traders opened the store doors the next day, hoping their slim Navajo vocabulary would get them through. A number of children who had been to school and spoke fairly good English were in the neighborhood, but the Moores did not know this. Some of them marched into the store and asked for everything in Navajo. After the traders had removed many items from the shelves, they finally brought down a box of shells, only to receive the reply, "Yes. Twenty-two shells. That is what we want." The silent Navajo adults and the pranksters broke into grins and laughter at the Anglos' consternation.[22]

Between 1900 and the 1930s the trading post fostered a variety of changes. As the Navajo people grew increasingly desirous of and dependent on the products of the posts, they increased the economic activity that allowed them to trade there. This is not to suggest that this was the only force moving them toward acculturation but just one of many. Anthropologists and historians generally agree that societies are constantly changing. The main questions, therefore, are in what direction, at what rate, and to what extent the change occurs. For the Navajos, the posts provided an introduction to white culture ranging from ruins to roads, from dollars to dyes, and from country fairs to current events.

Take Anasazi ruins as an example. In traditional society Navajos generally avoided these sites because of their association with the dead. The trader sometimes served as an effective force to decrease the amount of fear associated with the Anasazi. There are numerous accounts that indicate that both men and women operating trading posts encouraged the Navajos to set aside their anxiety and guide people to the ruins, assist in the digging of artifacts, and locate objects on their own. Indeed, the traffic became so intense that, in the 1905 *Report of the Commissioner of Indian Affairs*, traders were warned that the artifacts from Anasazi sites were "not private property to be disposed of at will." The report continued:

> It is well known that for some years past, Indian traders have greatly encouraged the despoliation of ruins by purchasing from the Indians the relics secured by them from the ruined villages, cliff houses, and cemeteries. . . . Much of the sale of such articles is made through licensed Indian traders, to whom the Indians bring their "finds." It seems necessary, therefore, to curtail such traffic

upon the reservation [Navajo, Southern Ute, and Zuni] and you will please inform all the traders under your jurisdiction that thirty days after your notice to them, traffic in such articles will be considered contraband. . . . A failure to comply with these instructions will be considered sufficient ground for revocation of license.[23]

However, this decree apparently had little effect on most traders as the traffic continued unabated.

Trade in artifacts varied in scope, some traders being less zealous than others. A man in Shonto reported that after extended windstorms in the spring or intense cloudbursts in the summer, Navajo shepherds brought in pots, ladles, and bowls that had been exposed by the storms. In exchange, they received five cents worth of hard candy in a brown paper sack. Two Navajos took this same trader to a site where they had been digging, only to find that the huge pot located at the corner of the ruin had burst into three pieces, the sand inside shattering the jar outward.[24]

Louisa Wetherill received a basket that had been discovered twenty-five years previously by a person who up until that time did not want to touch a thing that belonged to the Anasazi. The presence of the trader changed his attitude.[25] Another man sold a circular piece of sandstone, one foot in diameter, that was etched with an Anasazi petroglyph. He had used the rock for its healing power by rubbing sand off its edges and giving it to his patients. The cure was said to be effective against almost any disease.[26]

Wives were as active as their husbands in collecting artifacts. A Navajo woman led Hilda Faunce from her post at Covered Water to a mound filled with shards. Seizing a piece of broken bone, Faunce unearthed a skull and some vertebrae. Her Navajo guide herded her children away, fearing a "devil" may be present, while an old man warned Faunce to get the skull out of sight. She later found a bowl in the grave and proudly displayed it on her mantel.[27]

Navajos also entered the excavating business, some with excessive zeal. In 1906 one man took a plow and scraper and leveled a mound for a few pieces of pottery to sell at a post. He apparently destroyed much more than he saved.[28]

Traders also encouraged Navajos to enter the ruins by enlisting them to work for archaeologists as laborers. The degree of willingness varied with each individual, but many sought employment simply because of economic pressures. How daring they became once hired was another story. Moving from the more timid to the more adventurous, one encounters a wide array of responses. For instance, Bill Lippincott, a trader at Wide Ruin, employed Navajos to help dig a ditch for a pipeline to his store. As the men labored with their shovels, they uncovered pottery, mortars, and beads. The Indians refused to dig until the entire pipe system was rerouted, ensuring not only their immediate help but also future business at the post.[29]

The trader Richard Wetherill hired Navajos to dig in the Chaco ruins, which they did, until they found an Anasazi corpse and then promptly quit. Eventually others came looking for work, reaching a high of twenty Navajos employed in 1897. One of the problems Wetherill faced was that his Navajo workers took objects like arrowheads, figurines, and turquoise that were found during the excavation. He put more than one workman in a room, hoping that the rivalry would cause one person to report the other's actions. This was not successful. One jet frog figurine with jeweled eyes appeared at a trading post in Farmington, and the trader had to pay $50 to get it back. Wetherill also sent his wife among the Navajos to purchase any arrowheads they happened to have.[30]

Trading posts provided other forms of employment, including herding the trader's livestock, hauling supplies to railhead towns, doing odd jobs, and serving as guides. The net effect of many of these activities was to encourage the men to leave home. Navajo Oshley tells of how a trader hired him for $50 a month to herd sheep. His wife remained at Dennehotso, thirty-five miles away. Much of the money he earned went for a saddle and food that he bought at the post.[31] This in-house sale and trade was a common practice among traders to keep the cash flowing back over the same counter.

Old Mexican from Aneth hauled hay for the trader and traveled to Cortez, Mancos, and Durango to obtain supplies and drop off goods. He became so proficient that he decided to not only deliver the products from the trader but also sell and buy his own wares at a better price.[32] For a six-day round trip to Mancos, he received $12, and when he returned, he was warmly welcomed. Old Mexican said, "When I got back to Aneth a crowd was there waiting for me to pull in. They were expecting quilts and blankets on this wagon. They bought up nearly all I brought."[33]

Although he was a trusted worker, the trader sent him home, admonishing him that he needed to go back and care for his wife and children.

Home industries were the heart of the economy, the most famous being rugs and saddle blankets. There are a number of very good studies about the rise of the weaving industry, the role of the trader in encouraging a better product, the movement from utilitarian to artistic creations, the struggle to introduce better qualities of wool, and the attempt to keep vegetable-dyed designs a part of the Navajo heritage.[34]

Starting in the late 1890s, real commercialization of the craft began, as Navajo weavers grew desirous of entering the Anglo-American marketplace. This shift occurred in part because of a recent economic depression, in part because of the Navajos' abandonment of older, heavier blankets for lighter, machine-woven Pendleton blankets for personal use, and in part because of a craze for Indian decorations in Anglo homes. Traders met the demand head-on, encouraging Navajos to weave for the tourist industry and for export to outlets as far away as New York and Los Angeles. Their impact was obvious. In 1899 the weaving trade amounted to only $50,000 reservation-wide; fifteen years later it had skyrocketed to $700,000; and by 1923 a person could order a variety of blankets from the Sears and Roebuck catalog.

The trade had its ups and downs as demand fluctuated. For instance, a decline in weaving occurred as World War I markets gobbled up wool for military purposes. The general pattern existing up through the early 1930s, however, was that when wool was available and cheap, the rug industry prospered, but when it became scarce, weaving slowed appreciably. Before and after World War I, when wool was plentiful and the price low, the rug industry reached its height.[35]

Weaving varied from region to region, from family to family, and from person to person, some individuals commanding better prices at the post than others. Blankets called "quickies" or "bread and coffee rugs" were loosely woven, poorly designed, and bought according to weight, varying from fifty cents to a dollar a pound. A well-woven 3-by-5-foot rug might command up to $8 and a 9-by-12-foot not more than $20.[36]

As with most things in Navajo culture, weaving was not solely a matter of economics. The knowledge associated with it originated in the times of the myths, when Spiderwoman taught the first Navajos this trade. Songs and prayers accompany the creative process, but there is also danger involved. Improper use or a mistake in the songs can offend the holy beings and, instead of helping the weaver, cause harm or spoil the product. When asked if she used songs when weaving, one woman replied that it was too dangerous and that though her weaving would probably be much improved, she preferred not to get involved but just to take her chances in the market. Another suggested that she never let children touch any of her blankets before trading because they would handle them playfully and so the trader might not want them. She then associated playing with poverty.[37]

The traders helped to nurture the industry. While they shipped large amounts of raw wool to the railheads, they also kept enough at the posts to sell back to the Indians in the winter. This maintained steady employment and a steady flow of cash. By 1914 the traders in the Northern and Western Navajo Agencies were placing linen tags and lead seals on rugs to guarantee Navajo genuineness to the buyer.[38]

This protection and improvement process included the purchase of raw wool. Agents and traders realized that the Navajos sheared their sheep under primitive conditions. They used the same old corrals because there were only a limited number of places for watering. Vermin and disease infected the animals at these sites. Herders sheared the animals in the spring and early fall and often got sticks, sand, manure, burrs, and briars mixed in with the clippings. Agents sent out directives urging the traders to protect both themselves and their clients by purchasing only clean wool. Post owners realized that if the wool was found dirty when the product reached the markets in Kansas City or farther east, the purchaser would either refuse it or subtract a substantial amount that more than covered the cost of cleaning it.

In 1922 raw Navajo wool, characterized as "coarse in quality and light in quantity," sold for forty cents per pound with a three- to six-cent margin on market prices. By the time it was transported to the buyer's bin and cleaned, some clippings were reduced to 50 percent of their original weight. Two traders reported that between dirty wool and fluctuations in market prices, they suffered disastrous financial losses. They had purchased the wool in 1920 at thirty-five cents a pound, stored it for a year and a half because of poor market conditions, freighted it at one and a half cents per pound then sold it at nine cents per pound, with an estimated loss of $38,000.[39] The accuracy of these figures is difficult to determine, but they dramatize a very real problem.

A final set of figures summarizes the importance of raw wool and rugs. In 1922 in the Western Agency, 23,080 pounds of rugs sold for roughly $41,000, raw wool for $22,000, comprising 78 percent of all the commerce for that year, which included the sale of sheep, cattle, pelts, silver, and miscellaneous items.[40] It is not surprising that the traders and agents did all they could to improve the breeding stock, shearing practices, and disease control of the sheep.

In 1909 a new incentive for improving crafts and production helped the trader to instill the Anglo-American value of competition. The Shiprock Agency, founded in 1903 by William T. Shelton, sponsored its first regional fair. Trading posts from different areas had booths that competed in all types of industries. The traders and their clients took the cue, starting preparations months in advance. Specialty rugs declaring the name of the post, and products from that area, fostered regional pride and competition. Shelton invited tourists to attend, encouraged Navajos to sell traditional artifacts such as bow and arrows and silver work, and even allowed some Indian dances. By 1914 seven hundred blankets graced the traders' booths, five of which were purchased and sent to the Panama-Pacific International Exposition.[41]

Although silversmithing did not become an important commercial industry in the northern part of the reservation until the early 1930s, silver bracelets, necklaces, broaches, and bridles still served as pawn. One problem confronting the trader was the Navajos' love for silver coins, used as buttons and decorations on clothing. The Federal Criminal Code clearly stated that anyone who "fraudulently defaced, mutilated, . . . or lightened" U.S. currency could be fined $2,000 and imprisoned for up to five years. Agents contacted traders, requesting they discourage Navajos from drilling holes or attaching loops to coins for fastening them to their shirts. The traders did not like the practice any more than the government, since banks would not accept mutilated currency because it decreased its value and because it did not stack well.

Yet the traders had little choice but to accept the currency when Navajos in need cut dimes, quarters, half dollars, and dollars off their clothing. The only solution was to circulate this money among their clients, since few people accepted it off the reservation. Some posts even created their own money stamped with a unique design and used these tokens in place of regular U. S. currency, another practice frowned on by the government.[42]

As the outside world became increasingly aware of Navajo crafts and as trading posts became more numerous, roads were needed to transport goods and people. A key to any economic system is transportation; the isolated posts dotting reservation lands were no exception. The development of roads will be discussed in the next chapter, but their importance as promoters of commerce often was directly tied to trade. Dirt preceded macadam, as the net stretching across reservation lands spread from the posts, located where water and traffic flowed.

In the early part of this century, traders willingly worked to build roads into their isolated locales, improving routes to encourage customers. John Wetherill and Clyde Colville smoothed and widened the road through Marsh Pass that tied in with Flagstaff 160 miles away. Elizabeth Hegemann tells of working with her husband to blast away dirt and sandstone for a safe passage to Shonto, and Hubert Richardson headed a survey party over an old Ute war trail to the site of Rainbow Lodge.[43] Roads were the key to commerce.

Rain, drifting sand, and snow could present huge problems to the wagons and, later, automobiles that traversed mile after mile of sand, rock, and canyon. Navajos served as pathbreakers when the track was obliterated or built temporary bridges to span washouts. By 1916 the Denver and Rio Grande Railroad served as a magnet to the northern end of the reservation, drawing traffic to Thompson, Utah; Dolores, Mancos, and Durango, Colorado; and Farmington, New Mexico. The *Cortez Herald* applauded efforts to extend paved roads, especially the one from Gallup in the south to Shiprock in the north. One article claimed, "This road would be of material advantage to the Navajo Indians who do practically all of the freighting for different traders on the reservation. . . . With a good road, the Indians can haul [more], save much wear and tear on their wagons, and keep their teams in better condition."[44]

While some road advocates argued vociferously for their benefit to the trader and the Navajo, this was often a veneer for improvements that encouraged tourist traffic. BIA money supported many of the paving projects on the reservation, but for many whites, it was more important that the Gallup-Shiprock road, completed in the early 1930s, terminated near Mesa Verde National Park. One Indian agent, H. E. Williams, boldly declared "that the tourists, the Indians, and the government have the same common interest and purpose," suggesting that roads would "facilitate the necessary mingling with a reasonably good class of whites, to the end that the Indians will be better prepared for citizenship . . . [and] a new life different to that of the reservation and the trading post."[45]

By 1930 good oil-and-dirt roads extended from Flagstaff to Tuba City, opening up the Grand Canyon to an increasing tourist trade, with a lateral east-west artery extending from Tuba to Kayenta, then on to the north-south Shiprock-Gallup thoroughfare. Spur roads opened Natural Bridges, Rainbow Bridge, Inscription House Ruins, Keetseel Ruins, and Monument Valley to the sight-seer.[46] Little wonder that when a second car passed through Kayenta on the same day, John Wetherill quipped, à la Daniel Boone one hundred fifty years earlier, "[T]he country's getting crowded."[47]

Bridges were an integral part of this burgeoning network. Starting in 1909 the government made preparations for bridges to span the San Juan River at Shiprock and Mexican Hat and a year later at Tanner's Crossing on the Little Colorado.[48] One justification for the Tanner's Crossing bridge was that traders and the Western Navajo Agency were shipping across the river over a million pounds of merchandise per year, most of which was hauled by Indians at $1.25 per hundred pounds. "Goods damaged or washed away and the value of time lost at this crossing" required that a structure be built.[49]

As with the roads, however, this cry was at times only a camouflage for other motives. The Lee's Ferry Bridge, for instance, had an initial estimated cost of $200,000, half of which was to be paid by the Navajo tribe. Proclaimed as an "outlet for the Indians . . . [to assist] them toward a more advanced situation," the bridge spanned a section of the Colorado River that was sparsely inhabited by either traders and Navajos.[50] The $100,000 debt placed around the neck of the tribe became a topic of congressional investigation that eventually led to its revocation. The testimony in the reports of this incident is acrid, some people claiming that no Navajo lived within fifty miles of the bridge, that the tribe had opposed its construction from the beginning, and that the Navajos believed this to be an attempt to obtain oil royalty money. Other critics called the political maneuvering "highway robbery" in its purest form. Even the name was unsatisfactory. President Heber J. Grant of the Church of Jesus Christ of Latter-day Saints made a special trip to the Arizona legislature in Phoenix to request a name change. His aversion to honoring John D. Lee of Mountain Meadow Massacre fame encouraged dignitaries to christen it the Grand Canyon Bridge, although the name Lee's Ferry has remained to this day.[51]

◆ ◆ ◆

It is clear that between 1900 and 1930 the trading posts on the Navajo Reservation held an influential position between the two cultures. Each post had its own personality, its own economic emphasis, yet all shared the common goal of commercial exchange in a foreign cultural setting. As agents of change, the traders provided desirable goods, but the Navajos purchased only what they wanted. In a free market economy in which competition exists, the buyer has as much influence as the seller in determining the rate and flow of exchange. Whether the trader cheated the Navajos is not the issue here, but rather did the trader encourage change? The answer, obviously, is yes. The location and organization of the post, the traffic in prehistoric artifacts, the marketing of wool and rugs, the establishment of the Shiprock Fair, the construction of roads, and the employment of Navajos in a mixed barter and wage economy— all emphasized white values in the Indians' world. They encouraged the Navajos toward the "civilizing" process so important to their agents.

However, to look at the post solely as a tool of white imperialism is to suggest that the Navajo was a helpless pawn. This is far from the truth. The Navajo was a sharp bargainer who knew what he or she wanted and worked toward the means to obtain it. Traders stocked only those goods that would sell and charged prices that were competitive with other posts. While long-distance travel might be an inconvenience, much evidence indicates that Navajos were not averse to traveling to posts that offered the best prices. As soon as a customer entered the store, the trader was obliged to operate substantially on Navajo terms. The giving of initial presents, the use of kinship terms, the bestowal of trader names, the speaking of a "foreign" language, the dependence on pawn, and the social obligations placed on the trader indicate anything but passive acceptance of white imperialism.

The Navajos accepted and rejected according to their own cultural dictates, but they were also moving inexorably toward greater acculturation. In general, they were in the driver's seat but did not, could not, realize where the future would take them. Until the 1930s they selectively chose those things that fit into traditional, cultural patterns. With enforced livestock reduction and John Collier's BIA programs, the government catapulted the Navajos into the wage economy of twentieth-century Anglo-America. A growing dependence on roads, railroads, and consumer goods was already rooted in the Navajos' lifestyle. When the government removed the basis of their economy—livestock—the Navajos' increased mobility and desire pushed them into the depression of the 1930s and the New Deal programs of Franklin Delano Roosevelt.

The trading post, crippled but surviving, watched many of its customers turn first to it for help, then look elsewhere for employment and products. Other factors such as service in World War II, attendance at boarding and day schools, access to the media, purchase of trucks and cars, and participation in the Federal Trade Commission hearings of the early 1970s affected both the Navajo and the trading post as economic partners. The golden days of the trading post were over; the days of plastic, tin, and Saran Wrap had arrived.

CHAPTER FIVE

THE CHIDÍ AND FLYING METAL COME TO THE NAVAJOS

Thoughts on Technology and Initial Cultural Contact

As the five hundredth anniversary of Columbus's discovery of America came and went, Americans looked back to the time when the Western Hemisphere was abruptly opened to a European way of life. As the Arawaks stood on the shore of San Salvador Island, they were the first of many Indian groups to behold the mysterious boats filled with strange creatures, awesome technology, and men with a different understanding of how the world worked.

Shortly after this initial entry, the Spanish explorers started to record the natives' impressions, mostly for amusement, but today these give rare insight into the Indians' thinking. When Hernán Cortés arrived off the coast of Mexico in 1519, Indian runners quickly reported in the Aztec capital of Tenochtitlán the "towers or small mountains floating on the waves of the sea," containing men with "long beards and hair that comes only to their ears."[1] As the Spanish fleet landed at Vera Cruz, Moctezuma prepared a fitting welcome for the return of a god prophesied to arrive at this time. His messengers took gifts to the Spaniards and kissed the ground before their feet, but when the ships' cannons fired, the Aztecs panicked and fainted with fright. Later they related to Moctezuma their strange experience on board the "floating mountain."

A thing like a ball of stone comes out of its entrails: it comes out shooting sparks and raining fire. The smoke that comes out of it has a pestilent odor like that of rotten mud. . . . If the cannon is aimed against a mountain, the mountain splits and cracks open. . . . [They ride a] deer [without horns that] carries them on their backs wherever they wish to go. Their deer, our lord, are as tall as the roof of a house. . . . As for their food, it is like human food. It is large and white, and not heavy. It is something like straw, but with the taste of the pith of a cornstalk. . . . Their dogs are enormous, with flat ears and long dangling tongues. The color of their eyes is a burning yellow; their eyes flash fire and shoot off sparks.[2]

Depressed and fearful, Moctezuma waited for what his priests had prophesied as his demise and the fall of the Aztec Empire.

This early scene of wonder and awe has been reenacted numerous times as technologically advanced societies encountered less advanced societies. The process has continued even into recent years. As the Navajos of the Four Corners region shed the isolation of their reservation during the first half of the twentieth century, Anglo-American society introduced dozens of innovations that both helped and hindered, sometimes changed, traditional lifestyles and ideas. Wagons, windmills, pumps, sheep dips, radios, canned goods, and money combined with ideas on health care, livestock practices, the off-reservation job market, and marriage to bring about shifts in an increasingly fast-paced world. Soon the question became not whether change would happen but at what rate and in which direction.

Anthropologists have often noted the adaptability and flexibility of the Navajos amid these changing circumstances. Historically, the Diné have selectively adopted new ideas and technologies that fit their beliefs and physical needs. As change became mandatory because of the livestock reduction of the 1930s, the dependence on off-reservation employment in the 1940s and 1950s, and the burgeoning tribal population in the 1970s and 1980s, Navajos have become engaged in the general economy and life of twentieth-century Anglo America.

Two technologies created a significant shift in understanding and capability for the Diné: the automobile and the airplane. Each is explored here through the eyes of the older people who witnessed the change from horse to mechanized transportation, from self-sufficiency to dependence on a market system, and from traditional religious teachings to a more mechanistic worldview.

Much of what follows is based on what Navajo people have said. It is important to understand that those speaking looked back on this period of change with a smile and a twinkle in their eyes. The Navajos have a

wonderful sense of humor, and as they described what they encountered, they did not hesitate to chuckle at their first impressions of these
strange mechanical devices. What happened, from a twenty-first-century
perspective, provides an understanding of the experience any culture
may encounter when introduced to something new.

Like the Aztecs when they encountered the white man, the Navajos
faced some strange and mystifying events. Nothing could have been
stranger than a horseless wagon. Older Navajos today tell of medicine
men who foresaw the future and warned of the consequences of the new
technology. They told of paved highways, jet airplanes, and long vehicles, buses, that would carry people great distances. One man said, "Girls
will cut their hair and wear pants; they will hitch rides, wandering here
and there. When this comes to pass, everything will go wrong."[3] And for
many older Navajos, it did.

Starting around the turn of the twentieth century, the northern part of
the Navajo Reservation was increasingly exposed to the auto. In Kayenta
John and Louisa Wetherill attracted a group of daredevil tourists from Los
Angeles who wanted to see if they could conquer sand dunes, washes,
and canyons to reach the Wetherill trading post. Cars setting out from
Shiprock around this same time went to Aneth; others traveled from
Monticello and Blanding to Bluff, a place that would eventually become a
mere stopping point for tourists on their way to Mexican Hat and Monument Valley beyond.

On July 9, 1908, the first automobile pulled into Bluff. A newspaper
account recorded the Anglo community's initial reaction.

> Our quiet little burg has at last been invaded by a car of progress,
> the automobile of Mr. Bozman of Cortez. We heard a strange noise
> at the head of town the other evening and looking up saw it coming.
> Us kids then took to the high fences and shouted ourselves hoarse,
> "Hurrah for the automobile," Hurrah for the autu-mow-horse,"
> "Hooray for the ought-to-mow-hay," and the thing flew past and
> down the street to Frank Hyde's store.[4]

The Navajos were just as surprised but far more reserved in their
approach to this novelty. Early glimpses of this machine were disturbing. One man went with a friend to the Aneth trading post to chop
wood. When he got there, a crowd had surrounded something unusual,

so he decided to investigate. "Everyone was excited and talking. This `something' had small wheels similar to a wagon. One person stared in amazement and kept circling it. He was asked to turn the crank in front so he did. Then, with a loud noise it started up," much to everyone's amazement.[5]

Fred Yazzie remembers that when he was a boy, he was wrestling around during the second night of an Enemy Way ceremony when he looked off in the distance and saw two glowing eyes approaching the group. He was convinced it was Big Snake, a mythological creature of impressive supernatural power. He and his friends scattered and would not return until they were convinced of its safety. Once they got used to it, the boys enjoyed seeing its lights go on, hearing the engine chug, and watching it roll along over the desert floor.[6]

The Navajos, masters at picking out physical traits and assigning appropriate names, immediately christened the contraption *chidí* or *chogí* because of the chi-chi-chi sound of the engine. Some scholars suggest that another possible origin of the name could be the Navajo verb *nishjiid*, which means "it sits or squats"; others believe the word comes from *dilchiid*, which means "to point at something quickly."[7] Regardless of where the name came from, the vehicle itself became an increasingly important fact of life for the Navajo.

Other physical traits stood out as well. Some people thought the vehicle looked like a stinkbug because it held its rear end high, with its head tucked down. Others felt it must be a spider because of its skinny wheels and rocking motion as it traveled down the rutted wagon tracks.[8] The crank in front, narrow wooden-spoked wheels, rag top, rear spare tire, and "smoking tail" created more things to wonder about. John Bluesalt captured this curiosity when he described the first time he saw an automobile.

> As I observed the car, I realized it had a skinny pipe underneath it. This pipe was covered but rotated around whenever it moved. I wondered what made it run. Some people were scared of it. As for me, I was curious. I wanted to take a closer look and find out what it was made from, what made it run. I wanted to study it and learn more about it; could I possibly build one like it? I saw that the pipe underneath was connected to the engine. I saw the driver had a

To the Navajo the car was a new invention in the first quarter of the twentieth century. Some compared it to a stinkbug with its high rear end and rocking motion. Others said it stole children. Photo from Special Collections, Northern Arizona University Library, Photo #NAU.PH.658.674.

key with which he operated the engine; as he did so, the engine turned the pipe, which caused the car to move. If this pipe wasn't visible, I probably would not have wondered what made it move.[9]

New understanding about how cars functioned arose through trial and error. Navajos were familiar with wagons and transferred their knowledge of what powered horses to what made cars run. Hay was a logical place to start, especially since one person found scattered fodder dropped in a vehicle's tracks. Soon this understanding shifted to liquid fuel as a possible "food" for the car. In about 1924 Jack Lameman bought a Ford in Farmington and drove it in low gear to Aneth, approximately one hundred miles away. The next day he started for the trading post but went only a short distance before the vehicle died. Next he sought out the government farmer, Herbert Redshaw, who looked in the gas tank and found it empty. Lameman was chagrined. He swore that it could not be, because he had looked in it the day before and it was full. When he learned that a person had to put gas in on a regular basis, he vowed to go back to Farmington and return the vehicle, but Redshaw pointed out the problem of depreciation, so Lameman decided to "make the most of a very bad bargain."[10] He eventually became known to other Navajos by his auto, Mr. Red Car.

As the car became more user-friendly, the Navajos likened it in function and characteristics to their old ally the horse. Soon the headlights became its eyes, the tires its shoes, the battery its heart, the gasoline its water, and the exhaust its gas. Just as humans and animals are powered by water, air, and electricity, so is the car. Where the analogy broke down between the horse and the auto, other familiar items filled the gap. For example, the English translation of "brakes" reflects the old mechanical system used on wagons, literally interpreted as "it is pulled against it by means of a cord."[11]

This system of comparison extended further. Cars, like horses, came in many colors—black, blue, white, red, and yellow. Prayers and blessings were given to horses and autos in a similar fashion. Starting with the tip of the tail, moving along its back to the horse's forelegs, then ending with its mouth, the owner blessed his animal through prayer and corn pollen. On a car, one started with the tires, moved forward to the hood, then returned to the tires on the other side. One prayer of assurance is as follows:

> In beauty this horse will have a good trail.
> In beauty will it have protection from anything that will harm it.
> In beauty the owner will have a good journey in it.
> In beauty I will travel.
> Where the rainbow travels its trail.
> Where the sun ray travels its trail.
> Where the sun ray crosses over.
> With all of these you will be my horse.
> When the wind travels its trail.
> In beauty I will travel in it.
> We will travel a good journey together.
> In beauty I say this on this earth in the midst of heaven.[12]

After praying with pollen, the *hadahoneestiin* (mirage or heat wave) is applied with song and prayer to give endurance and protection for as

long as the car is in use. Some people hang feathers to prevent accidents. For example, if an eagle feather is hung in the interior and a tire
blows out, the car will come to a safe stop. The feather can also think
and serve as a guide and protector, just as do the life feathers in myths
and in ceremonies.[13] There may also be a miniature sacred bundle
placed inside to give speed and endurance. The bundle contains "shake-
offs" from various sacred birds and animals such as a horse's dust and
saliva, a hummingbird's feathers, dust from a horned toad, and material associated with a rainbow. In the past, bundles and feathers were
tied to the tail of the horse; now a mirror or another projection in the
vehicle's cab will do.[14]

Infant car seats have also taken on a traditional value of protection,
once associated with travel and the cradle board. Either carried, hung on
the pommel of a saddle, or placed on the seat of a buckboard, the cradle
board protected the child physically while surrounding it with religious
powers associated with the first cradle board used for Changing Woman.
Now the car seat has replaced the cradle board and is blessed by medicine men to ensure safety. A medicine man in Shiprock blessed 260 car
seats with white corn pollen before they were given to parents.[15]

Automobiles today continue to be imbued with traditional values.
George Tom from Monument Valley explained:

> An automobile is more than a horse; it can hear, make noises, and it
> runs. If it weren't alive, then why does it move? It is alive. It is per-
> fect to look at. But it is similar to a horse as far as its usefulness, and
> it is blessed just the same. We pray for either our automobiles or
> horses. We pray for the horse, "In beauty we will travel; without
> trouble and hunger. Be my good horse always. May our journeys
> begin with a rainbow. May the holy beings be with us wherever we
> go." This same prayer is spoken to the automobile.
>
> I have become familiar with some mechanical functions of an
> automobile. Everything inside it, including the smallest objects,
> has a part in making it run. When it comes time to fix a trouble
> spot, I lie awake at night trying to figure out the problem. Sure
> enough, I see the "flickering blue flame" on the spot. It certainly
> has life alright.[16]

Others explain that a car is made from things of the earth, just like
humans are. Iron holds part of the earth's spirit; rubber comes from liv-

ing trees, lightning from the storm clouds, oil and gasoline from the earth; water is in the cooling system, and air comes from above; all of these are natural things comprised by the car that make it work. One can bless these elements, and they will respond just as people do to prayers. The difference between the two is that the car cannot think or do for itself; it will not hesitate to go over a cliff, whereas a horse will go around and safely take itself home. Both of them, however, can be made sacred and protected by the holy beings.[17]

Many people were mystified about traveling so fast without the use of horses. Imagine the confusion when a Navajo's first view of a car was of it being pulled by two yoke of oxen or a team of horses. Mechanical failures were common, and so one group of veterans cautioned a novice about to embark on his first ride, "If it breaks down, it will not run again."[18] Sometimes this was only too true.

And like the horse, the car had many uses. When one man saw his first vehicle, he thought it offered an easy solution to herding sheep, but he soon learned differently. Another used it for long-distance travel to Enemy Way, Yé'ii bicheii, or Mountain Way ceremonies. Many Navajos received their metal census tags distributed from the running board of a Model T. The federal agent told them they were like brands used on livestock, but in this instance, they would help them get money from the government and the oil companies.[19]

Navajos' reactions to the automobile were often incredulous. One woman compared the sensation of riding to spinning herself around, then falling to the ground and watching the earth and plants move backward. Another explained that traveling in a car was like moving in a dream. Still others felt sheer terror. Long before some people ever saw the first vehicle hove into sight, they had heard stories about how these creatures picked up children and carried them far away. Mabel Begay remembers that when she was school age, people warned her, "Someone is out hunting and gathering small children like you to haul away." Whenever a car passed, she let her flock stray and crawled under a rock ledge to hide. She never went to school, and in fact, even at the time she was interviewed (1991), in her eightieth year, she had never talked on a telephone. Many of those children who did go to school were left crying and scared by their first ride and their fear of the unknown.[20]

Most of the people we interviewed stressed that in one way or another, their initial encounter with an automobile was associated with education. This in itself could be a terrifying experience for both parent and student. Many Navajos initially had strong feelings against children leaving because of the work to be done around the home. Herding sheep, carding wool, planting gardens, hauling water, and myriad other chores made parents reluctant to let their sons and daughters go to an alien world. Adults cautioned the youth to stay away from roads because this was where bums traveled to kidnap the little ones. Some parents hid their children, others sought assurance from traders and government officials, while others had little choice. During the livestock reduction program of the 1930s, Navajo policemen told one father that if he sent his children to school, he could keep the sheep and goats he had hidden in the canyons. The man sent his son and daughter to the Tuba City Boarding School, where they witnessed their first truck bringing in students from outlying areas.[21]

Roads were a constant challenge to travelers. Old trails were deeply rutted according to the dimensions of the wagons that traveled them. The automobile, with its narrow frame and thin tires, cut into the sides of the center strip and pushed loose sand into the ruts. Cars going too slowly bogged down and, wheels rotating too fast, dug a shallow grave.[22]

Ray Hunt, a veteran trader, remembers getting stuck in a wash between Shiprock and Teec Nos Pos and asking some Indians nearby to help break his vehicle free. One of the men took hold of the wheel, started to push, and was stunned when the tire turned but the car did not move. He reasoned that on a wagon, a turning wheel meant a moving vehicle. Not so with this white man's invention.[23]

Foul weather presented its own problems. Steep, rugged roads proved to be particularly vulnerable to snow and rain. Tracks either were washed out or became so slippery they were difficult to drive on. One group of schoolchildren on their way to Kayenta encountered a rainstorm. Slick roads and a wrong turn tossed the vehicle upside down in a ditch. Fortunately, the children were able to crawl out of the windows, uninjured.[24]

Another time, at another place, a snowstorm caught some passengers far from shelter. They walked all the way home but then faced the problem of getting the wood in their stranded vehicle back to their hogan. The next morning they herded their sheep to the abandoned truck, directed the animals in the path of the vehicle, and thus packed the snow enough for the car to be driven home safely.[25]

Road construction and travel started early and served for many as an introduction to the car. Imagine their surprise when in fall 1915 some Navajos encountered five white men blazing a trail between Los Angeles and Kayenta in an automobile. The Zahn family group, composed of brothers and uncles, wanted to be the first to attempt this feat, which entailed 250 miles of new road. They packed 4,600 pounds of gear, including dynamite, winches, cables, and shovels for "road" work; hard tack and jerked beef for food; and a compass for navigation. The Franklin Camel, which got its name because it did not require as much water as other vehicles, sagged under its load, especially after the men deflated the tires to minimum pressure to traverse the sand. Rarely clipping along at its maximum twenty-eight miles per hour, the four-cylinder auto traveled in low gear and carried its own spare drum of gasoline for use until it could reach prepositioned supplies.

According to the diary of one of the men, the travelers saw many Navajos along the way: "One Indian perched atop a mountain and shouted until we thought his lungs would burst. . . . Some Indians sat stoically by the road and refused to look up until we had gone past, as though to ignore the phenomenon."[26] Whenever the vehicle stopped, the Navajos disappeared, causing the white men to hike several miles before they could purchase meat and water. The Indians were friendly and willing to sell the food, but they feared getting too close to the car.

On October 26, 1915, the "pioneers" reached their farthest point of travel and camped on the San Juan River, twenty miles from its confluence with the Colorado at the base of Navajo Mountain. The return trip held more drudgery, when first and second gear in the transmission broke. John Wetherill sent a Hopi to rescue them by towing the car with a team of four horses. As the Camel picked up speed, the Indian released the animals and the driver shifted into third gear and was off to the races, which lasted until he drove up a dead-end canyon and had to stop. Four hours later the Hopi pulled into sight and the whites resigned themselves to the ignoble fate of being led by horses. Two days after this the Camel was in Kayenta. Repair parts arrived, and two weeks later the travelers arrived in Los Angeles, completing their 2,089-mile odyssey.[27]

Obviously, one of the main problems with owning an automobile was that gas was not readily available. Many Navajos and whites who drove the reservation roads carried their own spare drums of fuel. The vehicles often reeked with fumes from the gasoline that sloshed out of the container. Trading posts, the only stores serving the population in isolated corners of Navajo lands, eventually started to sell gasoline, although many posts had no permit and operated under primitive conditions.[28]

Often it was the traders who helped to provide cash for the purchase of a car. They bought cattle, sheep, wool, rugs, and silver from the Navajo, who in turn went to Farmington, Cortez, or other larger cities to make their purchases. The traders also advised their customers about the cars' care and repair. One man remembers seeing Navajos pulling their automobiles apart to determine what was wrong when all they needed was gasoline. Speaking of these early Navajo mechanics, he recalled, "They used to have some awful times with cars. They had no idea of how to get them going and some white people charged them $20 to $30—a whole day's wage—to work on their vehicles. There were just so many times you would see Navajos by the side of the road, working on their cars kind of backwards, because they very seldom knew what was wrong."[29]

Navajos were not the only ones who struggled to discover the reason for mechanical failure. Burt Dustin, a trader in Aneth, had problems with his first Ford. He took his car to the trading post in Shiprock, where there was a small mechanic's shop, and asked his trader friend to fix it. The trader put spark plugs in the car but then jacked the wheels slightly off the ground and waited for Dustin to return. The customer got into his car, well pleased at the purr of the engine, but was astonished that it would not move. The trader told Dustin that he might be able to hitch a ride to Fruitland, New Mexico, his destination, but on second thought, there was a boy in the back room who knew a lot about cars and might be able to fix it. While Dustin went to get the young man, the trader jacked the car down. The child prodigy found the "loose wire" and sent Dustin on his way, never the wiser for being the butt of a joke.[30]

Even the newspapers got in on the act. One article in the *Grand Valley Times* was titled "Navajos Demonstrate New Way of Starting a Ford" and told of when Herbert Hyde from Bluff took four Navajos to the state fair. Somewhere between Bluff and Moab the driver lost the crank used to start the Tin Lizzie. Hyde had the Navajos—"all huskies"—get out and push when the car stalled in the sandy ruts. According to the article, Hyde decided that "he did not need a crank, and he made it into Thompson without delay."[31]

Many years have passed, many changes have occurred on the reservation, since the first auto appeared. The trauma of livestock reduction in the 1930s and the introduction of the wage economy through the Civilian Conservation Corps, migrant labor, and government-sponsored job training programs have encouraged the Navajos to become increasingly dependent on the automobile. Unfortunately, there are few statistics and quantitative studies to indicate where and how rapidly the Navajo people adapted to this technology. The general pattern deduced by scholars from anecdotal evidence indicates that a few wealthy Navajos owned some cars beginning in the mid-1920s. Even in those days cars had become "quite an obsession among these Indians," according to one of the agents.[32]

Clyde Kluckhohn estimated that in 1930 only one family in fifty owned a car.[33] A study done in the Fruitland area indicated that in 1949 Navajo families owned only 10 vehicles but that by 1952 there were 150 in the same locale, and by the mid-1960s almost all Navajo camps had at least one vehicle.[34] The shift from wagon to car was complete.

Father H. Baxter Liebler, an Episcopalian priest who established the St. Christopher's Mission for the Navajos in the Bluff area, noted the difference. He arrived in 1942 and twenty years later wrote an article on the cultural change he encountered during that time.[35] Introduction of the motor vehicle into Navajo culture increased mobility, distances traveled, stores visited, and tonnage transported while decreasing the time, effort, and money spent shopping. Many aspects of a cultural revolution began to take place, from the introduction of new building materials that replaced the hogan with Anglo-type housing to greater exposure to disease and increased opportunity for health care. Even styles of clothing changed: the long skirts worn by women for riding horses were replaced with short skirts, for now women only had to slide in and out of a pickup truck. Thus motorized transportation reached into every aspect of Navajo life, whether hauling water longer distances, bringing livestock to market, having access to schools, or traveling farther to ceremonies. Most families became just as dependent on the car and truck as did members of the dominant society.

The 1990 census shows quantitatively just how great this dependence is today. Reservation-wide, 63 percent of the people sixteen years of age or older drive to work alone, with another 21 percent riding in carpools—

a total of 84 percent.[36] The next largest category was those who either walk to work or stay at home, at 12 percent. The mean travel time to work was twenty-three minutes.

Now that almost all families have at least one vehicle—often a pickup truck—to do all the chores, they are dependent on the mainstream economy to keep their transportation operational. A study completed in 1975 indicated that the largest expenditure of funds for Navajos went for transportation, followed closely by food. More than half of their incomes went to these two commodities.[37]

The growing emphasis on vehicles in Navajo life is disturbing to older people who depended on wagons and livestock for transportation and survival. One older woman said:

> Now people only live to have a vehicle. They are addicted to them. This is the only thing we see now. It seems every single person has one. Because of this, what was once called life—sheep, cattle, and the things that can preserve life—have been forgotten. People only think of automobiles. Money does not stretch enough to cover expenses of a car. The question is always, Where are we going to get the money? This is not good for us, but we are doing it anyway.[38]

Another woman blamed the younger generation's lack of interest in sheep, horses, and cattle on the automobile, because the youth just drive around all day and do not do things that are important. She compared the car to its driver, saying that both go places quickly, do not take time to pause and rest, and consequently wear down and break from fast-paced use.[39]

Others see the advantages of the car. Trips that once took a week now can be accomplished in a day. The variety, convenience, and ease of transportation is dazzling, although the cost of purchase, maintenance, and fuel is considered exorbitant. Loans, credit ratings, and full-time employment have become the measure whereby a person may purchase this necessity of life.[40]

Some Navajos use crystal gazing or hand trembling, two forms of divination, to know where to go to buy a car and to make the salesman kinder. Prayer is another tool used to obtain an automobile. An eighty-year-old man in Aneth shared his experience with prayer in getting divine help to purchase a vehicle:

I have bought many cars—at least twenty times. The vehicle I have outside was repossessed after I missed two payments. My grandchild said I could purchase another one using his credit. I prayed to God for help. My grandchild came back saying it was alright to buy a car after he had talked to the salesman. Then me and another grandchild went with the others so we could drive the vehicle back. I prayed again for the car. This salesperson has said no to me before, that I would not be able to purchase another car for six years. Instead, he told us to take it home. If you pray earnestly, you will touch their hearts and turn their thoughts around. That is why prayer is important. It is not to be forgotten; it is the law.[41]

Even the roads hold teachings for those who travel. The name for a hitchhiker is "prairie dog," because he stands upright and waits by the side of the road. Other beliefs are more complex. For instance, the Navajos have traditionally followed the practice of arising at dawn, facing the east, and praying to the holy beings with white (ground) corn or pollen. In the evening, they face the west and pray using yellow pollen. A man once explained that paved highways were something never dreamed of by the Navajos but that the holy beings had a hand in guiding the white man in road construction. As one travels on the pavement, the white lines on the right, or the breakdown lane, represent white pollen; the center markings on the left, yellow pollen. People travel the good road between these markings that serve as a reminder that all will be well.[42]

A parallel to the automobile on the ground was the airplane. Known to the Navajos as "the car that flies about" or "the metal that flies about," this creature was initially just as strange as the auto, although it had little application to reservation life. It was thought of as the thing that moved through the heavens. The tail was said by some to be a person standing up, directing the rest of the plane. One woman believed that its noise came from dragging over the rocks and mesas, while another was told that the shining specks in the sky were two supernatural beings returning to the earth.[43]

Many of these early sightings evoked fear. As with the automobile, parents cautioned youngsters that planes were looking for children to kidnap.[44] Even adults were afraid. One man remembers that as a child, when he and his family were living at their winter camp, they heard a strange engine early one morning. He looked up and beheld a biplane so close he could see the pilot inside. The boy's mother, terrified of the machine, fled to a rock ledge and crawled underneath, waiting until the danger passed. "She thought the plane would drop something down on top of [them]. She said that white men do such things."[45] The plane then flew on to Bluff and landed on an improvised runway located where the Utah Navajo Fairgrounds are today.

Another person spoke of this same event as a time of great celebration. Word filtered through the Navajo community that on a certain day a plane was going to land in Bluff for the first time. A lot of people went to see this new phenomenon and to help clear sagebrush for a place to taxi. The gathering became a social event, with roasted goat for the main course of the feast. At noon a reddish object appeared overhead. Everyone raced on horseback to the landing strip and spent a long time inspecting the strange contraption of the white man.[46]

During World War II, the Navajos became aware of their adversary, Smelling His Mustache (Adolf Hitler), across the ocean. Aircraft seemed the most logical means for being attacked, and so the Navajos kept a watchful eye on the skies. One group believed that a skirmish was imminent and went to Mexican Water trading post where the trader received "wire messages" (telephone calls) to warn of the enemy's advance.

On the "morning of the war," these Navajos brought in their livestock, left the sheep by a spring of water, and moved through a narrow canyon where they tied their donkeys. The people then carried their belongings up on a ridge and sent scouts out to keep an eye out for the approaching enemy. One of the women later reported, "We saw many planes. They were flying low, which made the war seem real. We came down in the evening and continued to do this for two weeks. I believe the other Navajos did likewise. Later we heard the war was over. It was our victory."[47]

As we look at these early views of planes and cars, we are confronted with a choice. We can be amused by the naïveté of a people who did not comprehend a new form of technology, or we can understand how something strange and mystifying was adapted into an existing worldview. Indeed, culture in its broadest terms is a "sense-making system" that forms people's perceptions and thus their reactions to a new experience. Soon after the car became familiar, a clear understanding of how it oper-

Even stranger than the car was the airplane. One wonders what this traditional Navajo woman and her children think of this machine. Photo from Milton Snow Collection, NF5-1164, Navajo Nation Museum.

ated started to evolve, and its desirability became abundantly evident. As Bruce Trigger points out in his study of early European and Indian contact, "Native people were not constrained by their traditional beliefs to the extent that a rational assessment of the dangers and opportunities of the novel situations in which they found themselves was precluded."[48]

There are interesting similarities and differences in the Aztec and the Navajo experience. Perhaps the most obvious similarity is that both peoples attached religious significance to what occurred. Technology and its impact were prophesied. Whether some of these beliefs were "recalled" after the fact is not important, because prophecy places events in a meaningful context for the living. Prophetic utterances bolster faith in the existing religion while showing humankind that God or the gods know what is happening and have a hand in its outcome.

Because the Navajos live in a universe filled with spiritual creations, they gave technology animate qualities that were comparable to what already existed. Attributing eyes, feet, a heart, and the like to a car or believing it a sentient being was rational, when one believed that everything on this earth was imbued with a spirit from the holy beings. And because the car served in a capacity similar to the horse, the transfer of understanding was logical. Prayers and blessings to protect either the vehicle, the horse, or the traveler were an important part of the Navajo belief in strengthening one's resolve to live a holy life.

Joseph Campbell explained that in order for a system of beliefs to be a viable force in a person's life, it must meet four criteria.[49] First, the beliefs must have a mystical function in which a person lives with awe and gratitude toward the supernatural forces of the universe. Second, they must be in tune with the knowledge and science of the times, giving an adequate explanation of how things occur that does not conflict with the understanding of the physical world. Third, the beliefs must "validate" the teachings and practices of what is morally acceptable in a certain culture. Fourth, they should be a guide to spiritual harmony and strength in a useful life.

For the older people raised with traditional Navajo values, these beliefs still provide a vital explanation of how the world, in all of its variety, was created and empowered with supernatural forces. For the younger generation, these teachings are not as available as the white man's schools that provide a nonreligious, secular explanation of the world and its operation. The car and the plane are just two of hundreds of different forms of technology that are physically desirable but also affect the Navajos' understanding of how the world behaves.

♦ ♦ ♦

So while the car has solved many problems associated with transportation, physical ease, and economy, it has also raised questions, not all of which are tangible. One might ask if the Navajo people will continue to accept the teachings about the car as a spiritual creation? Or ask how much longer the markings on the roads will remind the people of their prayers blessed with corn pollen? And if these teachings do change, what will replace them? If the past is any indication, the Diné's adaptability and resilience in a changing world will not fail to provide a newer view sufficiently satisfying to the people, yet nonetheless Navajo. The form and direction this will take is left to future generations, but it most likely will be as it is chanted in the prayer for the car:

In beauty will it have protection from anything that will harm it.
In beauty as its owner will I have a good journey in it.
In beauty I will travel it.
In beauty I say this on this earth in the midst of heaven.

CHAPTER SIX

HISTORY REPEATS ITSELF

Navajo Livestock Reduction in Southeastern Utah, 1933–1946

Livestock was one of the most important foundations of traditional Navajo economy through the first quarter of the twentieth century. Horses provided transportation and occasional food for the winter months; goats and sheep served as a continuing source of sustenance, blankets, and clothing and as a means for entering the barter economy of the trading post. Livestock also became synonymous with social status and psychological security, as Navajos watched their herds multiply and prosper. Suddenly this all came to an end.

The U.S. government determined, as a result of the economic and environmental disasters of the Great Depression years, that there were too many animals on the Navajo Reservation, that they had to be eliminated to save the grass, the topsoil, and the surrounding area from the effects of erosion and overgrazing. With rifle and butcher knife in hand, the government agents set about to save the world from excessive Navajo herds. To the People, an entirely different process was under way.

The livestock reduction of the 1930s was one of two major tragedies in the Navajos' tribal memory. The trauma of the first tragedy, the roundup and incarceration of the people at Fort Sumner between 1864 and 1868, has been passed down by word of mouth for generations as a time of defeat, degradation, and removal at the hands of the white man. The destruction of their livestock was, to the Navajo, an economic form of the same thing—defeat, degradation, and removal from their traditional life.

This chapter examines the Navajos' social, psychological, and religious reactions to this crisis. Although there have been a number of studies that look at the role the government, Commissioner of Indian Affairs John Collier, and Navajo spokesmen played in this drama, surprisingly little has been written explaining what the Navajo herders thought about their circumstances.[1] The most prominent works—Donald L. Parman's *The Navajos and the New Deal* and Lawrence C. Kelly's *The Navajo Indians and Federal Indian Policy*—rely on government sources to evaluate the livestock reduction program, providing an eagle's-eye view of its effects.[2] Policy and procedure and their implementation can be subjects for perceptive clinical analysis, but they are divorced from the dust and blood of the slaughter corrals and canyons where the traditional Navajo way of life ended.

Here I take a different approach. Based on oral interviews that I conducted between 1988 and 1991 and those done by Fern Charley and Dean Sundberg between 1971 and 1974, a very clear picture emerges of stock reduction in southeastern Utah from the Navajos' perspective. Most of the people we interviewed lived through this period as adults, participated in the traditional livestock economy, and witnessed its destruction. All shared feelings of bitterness at what occurred.

Each of the interviews was translated by Navajos fluent in both English and Navajo. When dealing with translations of languages as dissimilar as Navajo and English, a certain cultural perspective is lost. Every effort has been made to provide translations that convey the meaning and the feeling of the original, but inevitably much of the power and emotion that characterizes Navajo thought is dissipated by English words that carry a different connotation.

It is important to note that when history is written from oral tradition, the view provided is based on the personal experience recalled. Some things are remembered, other things forgotten or changed. For example, the Collier administration's efforts to ease the Navajo people into voluntarily reducing their herds and its attempts to pay for the livestock are often forgotten. Anger and bitterness speak louder, and Collier is often viewed with hatred, although his efforts were motivated more by concern and a desire to help.

The ramifications of stock reduction (in this discussion primarily sheep and goats) extend far beyond the solely material realm of crippling the relatively self-sufficient Navajo economy. Indeed, long after the actual events, the emotional wounds still fester and occasionally erupt in unexpected forms and circumstances, which show that for older people it was only yesterday that their pastoral life ended.

Navajos in the past explained their relationship with livestock simply: "Sheep are life." In the time of myths, when the holy beings created the world, the landscape was foreordained to support the livestock industry. One of the four sacred mountains, Dibé Ntsaa, or Big Sheep Mountain, was "made of sheep—both rams and ewes."[3] The holy beings associated with this mountain pour forth their wealth in livestock and are appealed to by herders for supernatural help in prospering. The gods work through this and other mountains to provide livestock to support the Navajos. "The mountains were put here for our [Navajos'] continuing existence. . . . All of the living creatures, like sheep, horses, cows, etc., said we will help with furthering man's existence."[4]

Medicine men gather soil, *dziłleezh*, from these mountains and bring it home to protect Navajo land and livestock. One person explained that by blessing the animals with prayers and dziłleezh, rain comes to nurture the land:

> Livestock is what life is about, so people ask for this blessing through *dziłleezh*. From the sheep and cattle, life renews itself. Who would give birth in a dry place? This does not happen. You get many lambs and calves from the plants around here. On the tip of these plants are horses, cattle, and sheep. They are made of plants which are sheep.[5]

The holy beings provided special plants to maintain the sheep's health. Silky sophora, for instance, is so popular as feed that the Navajos call it "sheep-dig-it-up." In addition to eating the flowers and roots, the sheep are also given it if they come in contact with deer hair. Navajos believe that when sheep are around deer or their residue, they become contaminated with excitement and are uncontrollable. This herb quiets the sheep.[6] Conversely, some Navajos chase their sheep around waving a fawn skin so that they will learn to forage for themselves and not be lazy.[7]

Separating domestic and wild animals is also important in food preparation. Deer bones are cut differently than sheep bones, the former having only one joint and the latter having a second or false joint. The sheep is cut in the second joint, and if the butcher fails to do so, lambs will be born crippled or deformed.[8] Deer bones are not cracked for the marrow; sheep bones are. Indeed, the process of killing and preparing sheep as food is ritually circumscribed, reminding the participant of the sacred bonds connecting humans, animals, and the supernatural.

Another example of this reciprocal relationship is expressed just before a sheep is killed. Some people take wool from the chest, flank, and rear as they pray to the victim, then place the fleece first in its mouth, then in another sheep's mouth, explaining that this is not the end and that the herd will continue to grow and prosper.[9] The sheep or goat is killed by cutting its throat as the head faces to the north. The skull is not completely severed until the carcass is ready to hang up and be divided for cooking.

Compatibility between humans and livestock is an essential ingredient in this relationship. As a person tends the flock, the sheep watch their caretaker. The animals eat to become fat in order to better serve their master when they are killed. If a person takes care of the animals, they will provide him or her with what is needed. Some Navajos even suggest that one of the sheep in a herd will separate itself from the other livestock, signifying it is ready to give its life for food to its owner. Charlie Blueeyes, a Navajo who lived and worked with sheep all his life, explained, "The sheep are made of money, gold, necklaces, and many goods. They are carrying pop, flour, and everything we consider wealth and good."[10]

For the Navajos living in a world circumscribed by taboos, it is only natural that words and actions affect the stock. Prayers and songs constantly remind the petitioners of their dependence on the holy beings to help the herd prosper. Navajos sing over their flocks, their corrals, and the lands on which the animals graze. During the time of the myths, the gods placed sacred baskets filled with plants, flowers, pollen, and dew drops to attract the sheep, so now, when the animals come to their pen, they are fulfilling the measure of their creation in a holy way.[11]

Conversely, "Dying livestock is a message from the gods, 'You are doing something wrong.'"[12] One should not speak badly about the animals, or something bad will happen; count them too much, and the herd will get smaller; place a sheep's head on the ground in an upright position, and the herd will run away; waste part of a butchered animal, and the flock will decrease; kill too many sheep at the same time, and they will disappear; and burn wool, then the sheep will turn poor.[13]

From a purely practical standpoint, livestock stood between poverty, starvation, and death, on the one hand, and survival, wealth, and status, on the other. Navajo testimony is replete with parental teachings about the value of sheep. One woman explained how her mother took her aside and said,

> I will not live for you forever. Therefore, learn to take care of the sheep, for it will be your mother and father and support you. Its meat you will use as food; its wool you will use in many different ways. If you are willing to learn how to card, spin, and weave with your hands, you will have all that you need and want. If you are careless, you will be begging for handouts from other people. . . . Your wealth will not diminish and die, for this is the "life of life" and "strength of life." It is the "life of life" because these animals are alive.[14]

After a baby was born, the mother buried a child's (usually a boy's) umbilical cord in the sheep or horse corral so that these animals would think well of it, provide easily the products of the flock, and encourage its interests and heart to always return to home and the livestock. One person described this relationship by saying, "If there's livestock around, I call that home."[15] Even when a child was still wrapped securely in a cradle board, unable to walk, the mother would take it out and place it with the animals as they grazed so that it would become used to the sights, sounds, and smells of the livestock industry.

Susie L. Yazzie remembers being carried piggyback behind the sheep, then later walking with them while holding her aunt's hand. In snow knee-deep to adults, she herded them in her moccasin-wrapped feet, remembering the stern council, "If a child stays home with nothing to do, she will be irresponsible."[16] The sheep provided a perfect training ground to prevent idleness.

Navajos, skilled stockmen, became intimately aware of each of their sheep and goats. Rather than part of an impersonal herd on the hoof, each animal had its own personality and characteristics. A shepherd knew which ones were most likely to wander, which were weak, and which were docile or belligerent. The owner literally lived with the animals from birth to death and was usually present for both. During the lambing season, snow, cold, and fog often endangered the newborn lambs, so the herders built fires to warm themselves and the animals after birth. If the snow was too deep, the women and children wrapped the newborns in blankets or the folds of their clothing and carried them home to the corral.[17]

Processing and weaving wool was another activity closely connected to the vitality of the herds and the family income. At an early age girls watched their mothers clean, card, spin, dye, and weave imaginative patterns into rugs and blankets. When the youngster was ready to try her hand at the task, a family member built a loom, and regardless of what the end product looked like, she was congratulated and encouraged to weave again. Family members counseled that this was a good way to make a living because the girl "had all the goods, right in her hands."[18]

From this wealth came status. An evaluation of a family's position in society derived directly not only from the number and quality of sheep and goats but also from how well they were cared for. Sloppy work with livestock translated through Navajo eyes into laziness, ignorance, or a bad attitude toward property and the important things of life. Losing sheep because of poor herding practices or gambling was synonymous with intolerable profligate living.[19] When a person cared so little about his livestock, the Navajos believed, this outlook carried over to other areas of his life. He was not respected in his community and would not be elected to leadership positions. Conversely, the person with the biggest and best herds in an area was often called on to lead his neighbors.[20] As Richard Hobson points out in his classic study, *Navaho Acquisitive Values*, "The Navahos value their sheep perhaps more than any other material object. . . . An old Navaho woman reported that on pay day, her people 'don't want to take the money, but would rather take the sheep.'"[21]

The events that set livestock reduction in motion were rooted in the distant past. Although the Navajo Reservation expanded at a sporadic but significant rate during the late nineteenth and early twentieth century, land acquisition did not keep pace with the growing number of Navajos. In Utah the land additions of 1905 and 1933 only recognized what was already occurring on the public domain. The last addition appended 54,000 acres to the reservation, most of which were rangeland. Ironically, the year after this "Aneth Extension," the BIA reported, "These Indians will be willing to dispose of all of their range stock in exchange for a farm of adequate size to support their families."[22]

Little did the Northern Navajo agent, B. P. Six, understand the role of livestock in Navajo culture. He did, however, watch the herds expand.

During 1930 in the Montezuma Creek and Aneth area, 19,514 sheep and goats passed through dip vats filled with medicine to prevent scabies. The Oljeto and Shonto areas produced 43,623 more animals, while some Utah Navajos undoubtedly went to vats located at Kayenta, Shiprock, Dennehotso, and Teec Nos Pos. Still others probably skipped the process entirely, but if the totals from the Aneth and Oljeto areas are combined, at least 63,137 sheep and goats ranged over the reservation lands of southeastern Utah.[23]

By 1934 the entire Northern Navajo Agency reported that government officials had killed or sold 70,000 animals and that the Utah Navajos' herds were now down to an estimated 36,000.[24] Because the nation was experiencing the depths of the Great Depression, the agent could price a sheep at only $2 and a goat at $1. The annual report went on to say, "[A]n excessive number of goats and sheep were slaughtered for food. There is every reason to believe that the next dipping record will show even a greater reduction than indicated by the number sold."[25] Horses and cattle suffered a similar fate.

The cold, hard statistics of livestock slaughter matched the scientific logic of trying to save the range. Depleted vegetation, soil erosion, silt accumulation at Hoover Dam, expanding herds, restrictions on off-reservation grazing, poor animal quality, and the faltering national economy were all part of the motivation to reduce livestock and modernize the Navajos' livelihood and management of resources.[26] In Utah, as in other parts of the reservation, science proved to be an economic and emotional disaster for the Navajos, who depended on their herds for survival.

Starting in 1933, the goat herds were the first to be selected, gathered, then killed. A year later, the sheep came under the knife, followed by horses and cattle. The reduction that had started out as voluntary and just one more incomprehensible government program, soon became a major threat to the Navajos' subsistence economy. Richer Navajos were more powerful and harder to coerce, so often the poorer people, those who could least afford the losses and still maintain self-sufficiency, were the first to suffer. Impoverishment and dependency on the government became larger parts of reservation life.

What was the Navajos' reaction to all of this? Stunned disbelief and shock. What had at first seemed like one more government requirement turned into a symbolic and economic war of attrition and destruction, comparable in the tribal memory to events seventy years before—the roundup of Navajos and their transport to Fort Sumner.

Hite Chee, a Navajo man from Monument Valley, clearly linked live-stock reduction to the past.[27] He told of how during the 1860s Navajos had their sheep "gunned down," causing starvation among the people. Many of the Navajos who stayed behind and many of those who went on the Long Walk died after the soldiers killed the animals. "There got to be much hunger around here and it was even killing the children. . . . I guess they thought we would eventually be exterminated as a people," Chee said.

> There were no sheep left. Before that, there were quite a few sheep running around. The bones of the horses that were laying around were boiled; it was not enough for a stew. Hunger killed some of them [Navajos], but the people were strong. . . . [Finally, the lead-ers of the two opposing groups] spoke to each other. They [white men] said: "From here on we will not do any harm to each other again. . . . Here are your sheep, the ones we have done away with." . . . This was what the Navajo people were given. . . . There were many [sheep] later. After so many years there came people called "Horse Rangers." The talk of sheep and goats [by which the white men] came about. [They said,] "They were a nuisance and so much trouble around," and they [whites] started planning again. That is how it came about. . . . Then they shot all of them [the livestock].[28]

One might ask how representative Chee's point of view is. Sam Ahkeah, chairman of the Navajo Tribal Council from 1946 to 1954, said that livestock reduction was "the most devastating experience in [Navajo] history since imprisonment at Fort Sumner."[29] What parallels existed in the Navajo mind between livestock reduction and the horrors of the Long Walk, when soldiers and their Indian allies destroyed the Navajo econ-omy, forced more than eight thousand tribal members onto a faraway dis-ease-ridden reservation, surrounded them with enemy troops, starved them with meager rations, then sent them home to a land constricted by artificial square boundaries? Although the trauma of the 1860s ended seventy years before the livestock reduction, generations of Navajos had recounted tales of horror around their fires in winter hogans.

To the Navajos, the parallels between the two events were striking. Some people reasoned that they had angered the white men, "stirring them up like bees in a nest," and so the Anglos had become tired of the Diné. The sheep and goats were a nuisance and so "they [whites] started planning again."[30] When the enemy arrived, they caught the Navajos by surprise. One man said, "Had we been informed, perhaps we could have done something to prevent what was done to us. But it came suddenly, like a wind that rises with no warning."[31] Just as during the Fort Sumner period, when the enemy "sneaked right up to [their] feet," the People were unprepared for what happened.[32]

The Navajos quickly labeled the government's intent. One woman heard people encouraging others: "We are going to have to fight for our food, the livestock. That is good to do."[33] A man spat out, "If you take my sheep, you kill me. So kill me now. Let's fight right here and decide this thing."[34] A woman watched her goats disappear in a cloud of dust and thought to herself, "I guess it was just like that when we had enemies who stole our flocks to satisfy their own needs. . . . My grandmother used to tell of these kinds of things."[35] Others testified that when they were told to give up their livestock, they felt "like a rifle was pointed at us to obey those orders. The life which we led back then was full of misery. Some of us have scars on our bodies from fighting the police," but "what could people say when they were conditioned to follow orders after Fort Sumner? After the white man conquered us, we had to follow orders."[36] This time, instead of the U.S. Cavalry, Utes, Hopis, and other Indian allies, the "soldiers" were government agents, range riders (known in Navajo as the One-Who-Leads-His-Horse-Around), and tribal government officials sympathetic to Washington's plans. As during the 1860s, those who resisted were removed, handcuffed, and incarcerated. Some Navajos referred to the livestock agents and police as "troops": "The troops asked our councilmen to carry out the request. The troops waited for those that refused."[37]

When Navajos did refuse, the BIA from Shiprock sent policemen "dressed in uniforms with a five-pointed star badge, and they carried handguns. They came in their BIA patrol vehicles."[38] And fights broke out when the words were heated enough. John Chee and a man named Imitation scrapped with a government official and a Navajo policeman, the latter drawing a knife during the fight, thus securing the epithet

"Sharp Edged Policeman." They almost choked the agent to death before members of the crowd separated the fighters. Chee later regretted not having beaten his adversary more vigorously, but his subsequent jail sentence gave him plenty of time to think about it.[39]

Chee was not the only one who fought with a vengeance. Jane Silas and her husband had heard rumors that the "troops" were coming to catch Hastiin Bi'álátsoh (Mister Thumb) and cut his throat because he refused to relinquish his sheep. Jane feared the same treatment, because she owned too many horses. As she and her husband returned from a ceremony in which they were encouraged "not to run from anything," the troops arrived and blocked the trail. Jane recounts,

> Several of us took off again. A man named Billy's Beard told me to remove and wrap up my necklace and bracelet that I was wearing. He told the rest of the others to do the same because he said the jewelry would cut us when we started fighting. "Here come the police," someone said. We saw our Navajo Council woman named Baal among the police troops that came to us. We gathered at a nearby water tank and watched Hastiin Bi'álátsoh, whose throat was to be cut, take off on his horse. "The police are coming with their guns; do your best," we were told. We stayed to face them; we did not care what happened. When they arrived, an uncle of mine confronted our council woman, scolding, "Baal, I thought you taught us differently, to be good and all that, and here you are doing the opposite. You are doing the worst possible; you have become a leader of chaos. What happened to your wise teachings? Have you gone crazy? Which mouth did you speak those good words from?" The woman hung her head. My uncle continued, "We will now whip and batter you. I will knock that crazy head off your shoulders, Baal!" She broke down and started crying, begging us not to carry out the act, saying, "This is it. Let's quit this conflict; let's have peace." Then we all dispersed on our horses. They left us alone from then on.[40]

Those Navajos who helped the Soil Conservation Service and BIA officials became the most controversial of the "enemies." Seen as equivalent to the "traitor Navajos" who helped the army round up those hiding in the 1860s, government and tribal employees were abused by those who felt their influence during the reduction. White men who had married Navajo women were no better. For instance, Nedra Tó dích'íi'nii explained that Charley Ashcroft, a trader in Monument Valley, was a "white" man with a Ute father. Charley had enemy blood on two counts, and even though he married a Navajo, he was a traitor: "He was doing things against [them]. He was on the other side. . . . People used to say to us, 'Why were you all in darkness? Why didn't you know better? Why didn't you do something right away when you moved back? [Probably referring to the return from Fort Sumner.] You people came back and John Collier just took all your livestock.'"[41]

Ashcroft served as a range rider, and many Navajos believed that it was he, not the federal government, who directed the slaughter. They pictured him riding around, telling his four assistant Navajos to kill the animals regardless of what their owners wanted. Because he knew where the people lived and the number of sheep each had, he was effective in rooting out the flocks hidden in the canyons or grazing amid the monoliths. "Try very hard to take all the stock away," he said. Nedra said, "They did as bad a thing as our enemies did to us long ago. That is what I think they did when I think about it. . . . They also told us they would ship us off somewhere. They said some land was bought somewhere for people called the Navajo."[42]

As with most things in the Diné's world, the holy beings knew what was happening, had prior warning of events to come, and were petitioned for aid during the struggle. For example, Navajo Mountain, according to local beliefs, was the birthplace of Monster Slayer, a supernatural hero who made the world safe for the Diné. During the Fort Sumner period, many Navajos fled to this isolated region, believing the powers of the mountain and Monster Slayer served as a protective shield against the forays of the Utes, the Hopis, and the army. Navajos climbed the mountain and offered prayers to "talk back the people who were captured."[43]

During the livestock reduction, the canyons and passes again provided protection, but this time for the flocks of sheep and goats. Many of these animals were dispersed in small groups over a wide geographic area or given to friends and relatives as presents or for safekeeping. Some family members stayed away from home with portions of their herds while the authorized number grazed around the camp.[44] Navajos offered prayers of protection at water seeps, in the San Juan River, to places where the wind lives, and to the holy beings in the mountains. The people believed the gods answered these prayers.[45]

Medicine men also performed ceremonies to protect the sheep. One sing called "Ntł'iz ni'nil" (Putting-Down-the-Sacred-Pebbles) was performed for all livestock and became increasingly important as the herds diminished. Ceremonies encouraged the Navajos to actively thwart attempts to destroy their animals. Some Diné believed that these ceremonies, "conducted by powerful medicine men," caused events to "calm down."[46]

Perhaps one of the clearest indicators of the "battlefield" trauma suffered during this time comes through the imagery used by Navajos to describe the destruction of the herds. People familiar with accounts of enemy attacks on the Navajos in the 1860s will quickly recognize how the same descriptions were used to depict the condition of the livestock.

As in war, events happened quickly, by surprise. Some children were bringing home the sheep in the evening when government agents approached them. The men told the youngsters to bring the sheep closer together so they could catch them, and once this was accomplished, the slaughter started. "We watched in horror as they slit the animal's throats. It was strange to stand among the blood-soaked dead sheep with the few that were left. . . . It was a violent crime."[47]

A relative of Nedra Tó dích'íi'nii, a four-year-old girl out herding sheep, approached and told her that her horse had "bad blood" and needed to be taken. He let her ride it home, then took the animal while she was in the hogan. He had "pulled the horse out from under her." Range riders came back the next year for more and were asked, "Who is going to pull the wagon? You are taking all our horses!" While they were there, a pregnant donkey ran away with the horses and hid behind a hill to give birth to a mule. Nedra's family shooed the newborn away for its own protection. The three men rode their horses about, "shouting after the livestock [and] if they didn't catch them, they just shot them. . . . They came constantly, trying to kill them. The goats would be crying as they were shot down by guns. They just fell . . . [and] were all bedraggled. Some of them were blind and were lost wherever they went. . . . I used to ~ii.ık that they [range riders] had almost wiped us out for good."[48]

The scene at the collecting corrals was equally gruesome. Ada Black remembers: "The goats' throats were just slashed and [the animals] put next to a woman. The goats were bleeding; they were churning inside the corral. . . . The remaining goats were hauled away and were shot with rifles. The bones were piled high, when placed on top of each other."[49]

Older people often described the disaster as "chaos" and "waste" as the "poor creatures," some of which were "pregnant," were "shot right there" or "killed just over the hill" in "cold blood" while "others were still alive and crawling around." "Women were crying," animals were "running around crying for their mothers," while others were "cornered against a canyon and shot to death." The Navajos "felt like [they] were all tied up and couldn't do anything," that "the stench of death was too much," as they witnessed this "cruel and sorry scene." The people's source of food was "brutally wiped out . . . without any good reason."[50]

The carnage after the slaughter was sickening. Mary Tsosie recalls, "Sheep heads and feet were strewn all the way down the wash. . . . [T]he heads were rotting everywhere. . . . I heard that even the dogs didn't care to bother them anymore . . . [because of] all the rotting stench."[51] Many mention how the bones remain in piles today, and the dried blood on the rocks can still be seen.[52]

The government had to accept the blame for this tragedy. Navajos still relate how U.S. officials talked to their forefathers when they left Fort Sumner and how little trust was placed in their words. The Navajos remember being told, "'Now you can all go home in pretty good shape. . . . Now everything will be better for you all and you must follow the road that leads back to your homes. . . .' Some people said to him, 'You sound like Coyote talking.' They were laughing at him about this. . . . After this we were put in poverty by the [confiscation of our sheep and horses]."[53] The federal government's credibility with the Navajos was sorely lacking long before the livestock reduction started.

Tribal policemen, Soil Conservation officers, range riders, and local BIA officials administered the program. Many of these public servants did not fare well and often faced the possibility of a physical confrontation. For instance, in Aneth, range rider Emmet D. Harrington, with his interpreter Benjamin Harvey, arrived at the hogan of White Man Hair on April 8, 1938.[54] The owner, along with Jim Hammond, Sakizzie, and seventeen other people, had gathered there for a protest meeting. Harrington told Harvey to give each Navajo a paper on which they could declare how many animals they owned. This was a poor time and place for such an action.

The men had already agreed that they would not accept these papers. Tall Man criticized Harvey as being a "schoolboy" who "lined up with the white people like Harrington, causing trouble for us." At this, Sakizzie jumped down off a nearby rock, approached the range rider, and told him, "Now I have given up my heart, my head, and my life, and I am going to take that paper away from you people. We can use sticks or stones or whatever weapon we might have to do this."

As Sakizzie spoke, he moved to the left side of Harrington's horse, while a man named Black Horse went to the right and White Hair Man held the bridle. Sakizzie rummaged around through Harrington's pouches after the Anglo's interpreter warned him to let them do what they wanted. The Navajo took the hated papers in a sack, harangued the interpreter again that he was working against the Navajos and that he had "never been taught by his mother and father." Sakizzie concluded by testifying, "I have given up myself to die. You can kill me now if you want to." Harrington and Harvey left, feeling lucky that the angry group had not gone further. The police arrested the five major antagonists but released them eight days later.

Other government employees were not as fortunate. In Teec Nos Pos, some Navajos spotted a range rider and an official. They captured, tied, and beat the two men with their fists and a board, giving the range rider the severest punishment.[55] Later, in this same area, five Navajos visited the district supervisor at his home. They clubbed him, tied him and his interpreter up, put them in the back of his pickup truck, drove a few miles north, and stopped. Six policemen quickly pursued and exchanged shots with the kidnappers, but no one was injured. Although the kidnappers released their two captives, they went into hiding, and the search resumed, culminating in seven arrests. The culprits spent three months in a Prescott, Arizona, jail.[56]

The BIA cultivated informants who reported names of people hiding sheep or not cooperating with the government's program. Arrests soon followed. Jealousy between those who lost livestock and those hiding them arose, feeding the cycle of spy and counterspy. It seemed like people were "crawling among themselves."[57]

As stock reduction became increasingly a matter of force, more violence and longer jail sentences resulted. A Navajo woman attacked a range rider, tied him up with his own bandanna, and sat on him until he urinated on himself. She and her husband spent a whole winter in jail. Some policemen arrested a chapter official late at night because he refused to cooperate with the government. They put him in jail and killed his herd. Jack Crate spent a year behind bars and was "almost killed there because of [his] horses" and protests. Chester Bitsue ended up in Alcatraz for a year because of his refusal to cooperate, and when he was released in California, he got lost. He found his way home by crystal gazing for directions.[58]

Not only were some of the people confined to jail, but in Navajo thought, officials implemented other restrictions, just as they had at the end of the Fort Sumner experience when the government controlled the people through reservation boundaries. One man said, "Even though they fenced us in, they're still not happy."[59] Some Navajos mentioned how they were going to be removed to the Salt River country in Arizona and not returned until the soil was restored. Medicine men believed that their medicine bundles were going to be centrally located in Window Rock and would have to be signed out for each ceremony, while others believed school programs were the government's attempt to control the young people.[60]

Even land surveys became part of the master plot to reduce the Navajos to poverty. Right after the horses were killed, men came to the Monument Valley and Navajo Mountain areas to survey reservation boundaries. They gave many of the Diné small metal tags and erected stakes that had "messages" inscribed on top. The Navajos saw this as one more effort to bring them under control, with the end result that the "white people from California want to move here."[61]

Out of all this turmoil emerged a lone figure, the lightning rod and focus of all the fear, hate, blame, and tension in the hearts of the Navajos— John Collier, head of the BIA and a driving force behind the livestock reduction program. Regardless of the fact that Collier wanted to foster Native American self-determination through his Indian Reorganization Act and other programs, to the Navajos, he stood for one thing: he was the man who destroyed their flocks.

Just as Kit Carson became the living symbol of the Long Walk, so did John "Collie" or "Collins" represent the evil of this period. Some Navajos believed he "hated" them and that he looked at them with "hungry eyes" because they were "getting rich by having too many sheep." To others, he was a "white cowboy" who brought in his friends to kill the goats. Still others thought he was "crazy" because he liked to "steal, cheat, and lie." As one white rancher explained, he never had a conversation with Navajos about livestock that did not end with "John Collier is a son-of-a-bitch."[62]

Stories abounded regarding the head of the BIA. One man said that Collier was the "number one enemy of the Navajo people" and that when some men working in a Civilian Conservation Corps (CCC) camp saw a mouse or rat scampering about their tents, they laughed and joked, "There goes John Collier."[63] Another person felt that Collier made himself a leader of the Navajos so that he could take advantage of them: "He did whatever he wanted with us and he ground our faces against the hard sand."[64] But to most Navajos, he was a faceless bureaucrat who reduced them to poverty.

One story in which the Navajos triumphed—an important thing for an oppressed people—tells of how Collier came to Kayenta and confronted an irate livestock owner. The two men started sparring verbally, the white man saying there was no room for more sheep and that they were making "narrow gullies." The Navajo replied, "It's none of your business. You're not the one who labors over them." Collier countered that there were no plants, which brought the reply, "What do you mean there's no plants? There's a lot of them on the mountains!" When the argument ended, the head of the BIA was "near to tears."[65]

By 1946 the reduction had run its course, leaving the Navajos' economy devastated. Tribal figures indicate that dependence on agriculture and livestock had decreased by 57 percent in a little more than a decade, although this figure varied by region, by outfit, and by individual, depending on the extent of the losses.[66] John Holiday, for example, drove thirty-seven horses into the stock corrals and came out with only thirteen. Of his 600-plus sheep, he kept 354.[67]

Just as discouraging as the physical poverty and deprivation was the psychological turmoil. One theme that threads through Navajo testimony is their understanding of why the livestock were killed. When the Diné moved back from Fort Sumner, they said, "We will go back to our own land. The people will multiply, the horses and the sheep too, the corn will reproduce itself, plants of all kinds will always grow . . . and it will rain."[68] This last point is important. The Navajos believe that the sheep pray to the gods, who send rain to help the plants grow. Consequently, the Diné believed there was plenty of vegetation before the sheep were killed. "During the mid-summer, vegetation, like sunflowers, colored the place. It grew in such abundance that the livestock walked in tunnel-like paths amidst it. . . . There is very little now for a sheep to take a bite of. All of this is due to the lack of precipitation. . . . Maybe they [Anglos] reduced that too."[69] When Collier killed the sheep, he also hindered the male rains and damaged the vegetation, one of the main things he sought to protect. But, according to the Navajos, he used this as an excuse to "cheat" them at a time when there was abundant forage. Without the livestock's prayers for rain, the whole weather cycle collapsed.[70]

Now everything is different to the Navajos. The grass is gone. Russian thistle has become sharper and tougher, able to puncture a tire. It is so tough it can kill horses and sheep that eat it and can make a person ill if scratched by it. Weeds infest the land and droughts are common.[71] The land is desolate and reflects the older people's feeling of what happened to their way of life because of the reduction.

There are several words that describe this state of being. The term *yíni 'biiłhé* means "to die from worrying." John Holiday felt that many of his people perished "before their time because the turmoil was too great to comprehend."[72] In the same sense, *ch'íínaíí* means literally "the life goes out," from depression, sadness, and melancholy.[73] Navajo testimony repeatedly makes reference to just such an effect: "Because their livelihood was destroyed, they let go their own lives"; "My husband died because of it"; "Just imagine taking the animals away from the children—animals which they loved—and killing them within their sight. Many of our people suffered mentally and some died from it"; "Those men took our meat off our tables and left us hungry and heartbroken"; "A lot of older men and women died because of this, because the livestock was their life and that was taken from them. I was involved in the project and I felt the anguish"; "They took so many away from us. That is why we do not sleep well sometimes. All we think about is that"; "Some of our ancestors died of grief. The Anglos destroyed our main reason for living."[74]

These emotions and beliefs are not new to the Navajos. They plagued the older people who were rounded up and sent to Fort Sumner. Diné returning from there told of how healthy relatives just seemed to give up and die. Victor Frankl saw a similar phenomenon in Nazi concentration camps during World War II. The difference between those who survived and those who perished often came down to who had the will, desire, or hope, rather than sheer physical strength and endurance.[75]

Is this pushing the effects of livestock reduction too far—to compare Nazi concentration camp inmates to the old people's feelings about losing sheep? From their perspective, sheep were life, and the psychological trauma was real, as were the social and cultural costs to their traditional way of life. In the Navajo universe, people die as much from unseen, intangible things as they do from physical, observable phenomena. When the old people say that after livestock reduction "all that represented life went sour," they are not just being poetic.[76] Anguish and death visited many Navajos—how many will never be known—because of the loss of the sheep and other animals.

Starting in 1934, the U.S. government, under the Taylor Grazing Act, began scientific range management using animal unit months (AUMs) to express the carrying capacity of the land. When the government introduced this system on the Navajo Reservation in 1936, the land was divided into grazing sections evaluated by how well they could support one cow, one horse, or five sheep as a unit of measure. The tribal government then allotted a family a permit to graze a certain number of livestock on a specific piece of land. While this was common sense to the scientific community, it limited Navajo herders to such an extent that very few could remain economically self-sufficient. Men left home to earn money; women herded the sheep and goats that were left, wove their rugs, and hoped their husbands would return to help keep the family intact. The end result—dependence on the wage economy and a new way of life.

Today old people tell their children about the two times the tribe was devastated. The teachings about the Long Walk period have been passed down from generation to generation and mythologized. Livestock reduction, in contrast, still aches, vivid in memory. The pattern in each instance is similar: surprise, betrayal, destruction, confinement, and the start of a new way of life.

Livestock remains important to the old ones, but the youth, raised in a world of American wants and desires, find new things, other than livestock, to pursue. As Betty Canyon said, "Today, people in our society live as if they were some small children, tending a household, while their parents are away."[77] Her view derives from traditional values of responsibility to the family and the herd, and in that context she is probably right. Many of the teachings, practices, and beliefs associated with caring for livestock are no longer important to the younger generation's survival. As far as the elders are concerned, the "parents" of these "children tending a new household" may never come home.

CHAPTER SEVEN

SEEING AS BELIEVING

Navajo and Anglo Perceptions of Tourism in Southeastern Utah, 1910–1990

Few things have drawn nonresidents to southeastern Utah like its scenery. Large red monoliths, pine-clad mountain slopes, the swirling brown water of the San Juan River, peaceful canyons snaking their way across pinyon and juniper mesas, and wide-open spaces that meet the sky beckon tourists to enjoy nature's spectacle. Add to this a worldwide interest in American Indians, and one has a winning combination that lures people to experience another way of life in a dramatic setting.

Travelers' accounts of their adventures with the land and its inhabitants go back to 1765, when Juan María Antonio Rivera entered southeastern Utah in the Montezuma Creek area, before returning to his base camp on the Dolores River and, eventually, to Santa Fe. His brief description of the Utes living along the San Juan and his comments about the landscape became the first of dozens, perhaps hundreds, of reports that explained what lay in this scenic corner of the earth. He, like those who followed, always found listeners—those who would later decide they wished to have similar experiences.

By the early 1900s the encouragement and support of tourism had itself become a lucrative profession. Images and experiences were packaged, bought and sold, and recycled for the next group of travelers to such an extent that roads, railroads, and towns arose for the express purpose of receiving and increasing the tourist dollar. The Fred Harvey Company, with its grand-scale marketing of the Southwest and "Indian Country," provides one of the best examples of the type of elaborate production that attracted people from all over the United States. Land,

Indians, and heritage formed the pillars of a mystique, supporting economic growth for the region.

However, there was also tourism on a smaller, local scale that appealed to the more adventurous, more mobile sector of society. The land and the people encountered were just that much more removed, seemed more "genuine," than some of the slicker packaged deals encountered on railroads and in easily accessible sites. The Model T and other automobiles provided unparalleled freedom to take to the roads, which were themselves more numerous and improved. Some of them were even paved.

Paralleling the increased mobility and abundance of tourist dollars was the camera to record what had been seen and done. By the turn of the twentieth century, George Eastman had founded the Kodak Company, which offered an inexpensive camera, one and a half inches thick and six and a half inches long. It produced a two-and-a-half-inch-long by three-and-a-half-inch-wide celluloid negative that was easily developed, durable (compared to glass plates and other earlier materials), and relatively inexpensive.[1] The stage was now set for tourism to infiltrate, as never before, the dramatic landscape of southeastern Utah.

To the Navajos, who had lived on this land in comparative isolation for generations, the onslaught of travelers was bewildering. The Navajo perception of their land was rooted in their belief that it was imbued with power and religious significance. The earth was a living, breathing entity that nourished, blessed, healed, and protected its people. Teachings from the chantways made that a certainty.

Still, the Navajos, like the Anglos, were a product of their own historical and religious experience. Although their beliefs did not share the technological, scientific orientation of the white man, they bore just as much fruit, of a different nature. A beneficial relationship arose between the two groups as each agreed to participate in the economic venture of tourism. Here I examine the exchange between the two differing worldviews as they merged in the landscape of canyon country. Economic development resulted. But perhaps more interesting than the dollars and cents is the understanding that grew up between the Indian and the white man. Tourism provided the vehicle for a cultural exchange that was less threatening and more balanced than any other commercial endeavor between Navajos and Anglos in southeastern Utah between 1900 and 1980.

The two most photogenic topographic features on the northern part of the reservation are Rainbow Bridge, near Navajo Mountain, and Monument Valley. According to Navajo mythology, the holy beings created Rainbow Bridge at the beginning of this world to help the earth surface people. While there are a number of different teachings about the rock arch, each speaks of a concern for those in need. And, interestingly, each deals with travel.

Floyd Laughter from Navajo Mountain tells a story about two Navajo "tourists" who wandered far from their homelands in the beginning of time. This man and woman did not want to listen to their people, who encouraged them to stay in one place. The couple kept wandering until they arrived, lost, on the east coast. There they met some holy beings, the Underwater People, who asked, "Where did you come from?" They were told, "From the West," to which came the reply that this was not the place they should be, that the food was not good for them, and that they must return to their land. The couple then asked how they could do this. The holy beings fashioned a rainbow from the sun's rays, placed the couple on it, then fired it like an arrow from a bow to the west. The husband and wife landed on the western shore but realized they had gone too far. They traveled back to the east, scanning below until they spotted Navajo Mountain and the San Juan River. There they decided to land. The rainbow-sunray slowly came to earth, its two ends permanently sealing themselves onto the rocks. "Let it be," the couple said. "Leave it like it is." Then a spring appeared below the rock formation and the weary couple stopped to drink. The flowing water remained there as a holy spring until Lake Powell covered it with its own waters.[2]

Another story linking Rainbow Bridge to travel tells of Big Snake, Wildcat, White Shell Woman, and other holy beings as they visited various geographic locations in the Four Corners country. When they approached Rainbow Bridge, a voice spoke, saying, "Do not go to the other side of Rock-arch, but instead, walk around this side of [it]."[3] They did, but from that time on, the formation was known to the Navajos as Standing Rock Obstacle.

Yet another story tells of when the Navajo Twins, Monster Slayer and Born for Water, returned from visiting their father, Sun Bearer. Their means of travel was the rainbow, now located on the north side of Navajo Mountain. Next they went to the top of the mountain, where, according to local teachings, they now reside, giving power to the prayers and offerings left there by the People.[4]

Because Rainbow Bridge and Monument Valley are holy places, reverential behavior, defined by Navajo custom, is expected.[5] The spring near Rainbow Bridge was a place where offerings were left for increased wealth. Prayers for sheep, horses, cattle, jewelry, and a safe crossing of the San Juan River were given at this spot.[6] The arch also provided protection from danger, especially on water. Ernest Nelson tells of prayers he offered there and on the San Francisco Peaks in behalf of a young relative going to Vietnam. One day the soldier found himself on a watercraft caught in heavy enemy fire. The boat overturned, drowning many of its crew, but the holy beings created "a miraculous water tunnel . . . in the depth of the water" that allowed the young man to escape.[7]

Buck Navajo, a medicine man from Navajo Mountain, explains that the first water basket was created near Rainbow Bridge and the first Navajo war dance, the Squaw Dance, also originated there. He says that when "a ceremony is held to request moisture and rain, water is collected from that ridge and brought back to where the [main portion of the] ceremony is being held. An offering is taken to that ridge and placed beneath Rock-arch. That is the way the story goes. It is said that it is a Rainbow. All the Rainbows in the world originate from there."[8] It is predicted that if the arch ever falls, it will produce harmful effects for the Navajo people.

Although the beliefs surrounding Rainbow Bridge extend back to the beginning of time, the Navajos recognize that their discovery and use of the powers located there are fairly recent. Oral tradition tells of how a man named Blind Salt Clansmen, who belonged to a band of Navajos escaping the terror of the Long Walk period (1860s), stumbled onto the formation while herding horses.[9] He remained silent about this discovery, and it was not until about the 1880s that word of its existence began to circulate.

Anglos began entering the area, first as miners and later as archaeologists and government officials. W. F. Williams claims to have first seen Rainbow Bridge with his father in 1884. He listed a half dozen other men who wrote or carved their names on the arch or canyon wall nearby.[10] As there had been sporadic mining activity during this time and a gold rush in 1892–93, Williams's claim is credible.

By 1909 rumor of the arch had spread to the point that Dr. Byron Cummings from the University of Utah, guided by John Wetherill and a Paiute named Nasja [Né'éshjaa-Owl] Begay, set out to be the first to officially record the location of the "bridge." A government surveyor, W. B. Douglass, also sought the honor at the same time. The race was on. Eventually the two parties joined forces, making their way over the tortuous terrain. On August 14 the competitive spirit that had characterized the outset of the two expeditions became outright rivalry. Cummings and Douglass vied for the honor of being the "first" to see the formation. Nasja later specified that Cummings should be accorded that recognition.[11] A year later the rock formation's fame was guaranteed when it became a national monument, whose boundaries eventually expanded to 160 acres, administered by the National Park Service. Still, the characteristic American desire to be the "first" to see the "biggest" (the arch is 275 feet wide and 290 feet high) and to recount the event in a dramatic "story" was in keeping with the best tradition of tourism.

As news of Rainbow Bridge spread, a desire by more and more people to see it forged new paths with growing opportunities. John and Louisa Wetherill, traders in Kayenta, were the first to capitalize on the interest. Their post was located at a crossroads of traffic on the northern end of the reservation. Because Wetherill had been outfitter and guide on the expedition of "discovery," it was natural that he hold the initial corner on the market, a corner that would last for about fifteen years.

As Wetherill's fame grew, so did the flow of traffic to his door. There were three broad categories of visitors at his home.[12] The first included writers such as Zane Grey, poet-artists such as Everett Ruess, and wealthy tourists such as Charles Bernheimer. The second group was composed of politicians, most notably Theodore Roosevelt. Archaeologists and anthropologists such as Earl Morris, Clyde Kluckhohn, T. Mitchell Prudden, and Alfred V. Kidder made up the third group. While many of these people were as interested in Louisa Wetherill's understanding of the Navajos and the exploration of the Anasazi ruins at Betatakin and Kiet Siel, Rainbow Bridge also served as a lure to an unfamiliar land.

It did not take long for a collective image and feeling to be attached to Rainbow Bridge. Each new visitor's response was colored by personal experience, but the elements were much the same. Scenery, the Indian, hardship, Wetherill's skills, and the aha! experience of seeing the arch coalesced into a formula that all writers followed. Although many confessed fatigue during the trip, no one ever seemed too tired to write just one more line of wonder and admiration. A few examples give a taste of the pervasive flavor of the early accounts.

Zane Grey visited Rainbow Bridge in spring 1913, a year after publication of his *Riders of the Purple Sage* and two years before *The Rainbow Trail* would reach a growing audience. His experience of going to the arch was as much a confirmation of what his characters had experienced in *Riders* as what Grey would write about in his future work. Although he claimed to have never been in the Monument Valley–Navajo Mountain region before, his visit left a near-mystical impression:

> My dream people of romance had really lived there once upon a time. . . . Something of awe and sadness abided with me. I could not enter into the merry pranks and investigations of my party. Surprise Valley seemed a part of my past, my dream, my very self. I left it, haunted by its loneliness and silence and beauty, by the story it had given me.[13]

With this reflective mood established, it is not surprising that his travel to Rainbow Bridge was colored by his penchant for drama. True to Grey's formula for writing, he spared no adjectives. Phrases such as "secret of the great bridge" were placed next to the description "colossal shafts and buttes of rock, magnificently sculptured, standing isolated and aloof, dark, weird, lonely."[14]

His treatment of his Paiute guide, Nas ta Bega (Nasja Begay), and Indians in general was just as dramatic. When Nasja, with a "dark, inscrutable face," pointed to a distant range, he "made a slow sweeping gesture. There is always something so significant and impressive about an Indian when he points anywhere." And when the party finally reached the bridge, Grey connects the rock formation to the Indian, the wilderness, and the American West. He describes his guide: "Dark, silent, statuesque, with inscrutable face uplifted, with all that was spiritual of the Indian suggested by a somber and tranquil knowledge of his place there, he represented to me that which a solitary figure of human life represents in a great painting. Nonnezoshe [Rainbow Bridge][15] needed life, wild life, life of its millions of years—and here stood the dark and silent Indian."[16] Thus Grey plays off the romantic image of the noble savage and wild landscape, so prevalent in popular literature at the turn of the twentieth century. Later tourists appear to have interpreted their experience through Grey's eyes, perpetuating an attitude, shaping their reality.

There were some travelers, however, who were more negative toward their Paiute and Navajo contacts. For instance, W. D. Sayle visited Rainbow Bridge in July 1920 and could hardly veil his contempt. Navajo men were "bucks" and the women "squaws." On a number of occasions Sayle had to establish "friendly relations" with the "chiefs" he encountered by giving them a big red bandanna. All the items that he and his party obtained from the Indians were "trinkets." When the travelers purchased a sheep for dinner and the Navajos prepared it, Sayles writes, "This was to a city man a weird and savage scene." But, he adds thoughtfully, his group was as "much a curiosity to them as they were to us."[17]

Kluckhohn, an anthropologist, took a far different approach. His interest in and sensitivity to the culture is evident in his description of the Navajo people he met along the way. He visited Rainbow Bridge in 1925 but seemed far more taken with the Wetherills, the Indians, and their artifacts than the rock formation. Navajo sand paintings hung above the fireplace, woven rugs covering the floor, blankets draped on the walls, and "Indian handicraft of every description" moved Kluckhohn to say that the interior of the Wetherill home was "one of the most attractive in America."[18]

But if material culture attracted Kluckhohn's attention, the linguistic skill of Louisa Wetherill, known as Slender Woman to the Navajo, held his fascination. She was a veteran of thirty years of reservation life, spoke the language without a white accent, and was often asked by the Navajos to preside as judge and jury in local disputes. With an anthropologist's eye, Kluckhohn studied with appreciation her role in the culture. And he often interjected in his narrative bits of information concerning Navajo linguistics.[19]

But the eye of the average tourist during those early days was fixed far more on entertainment than accuracy. Winifred H. Dixon reported her experience with Wetherill and a Navajo guide, Hastiin Chee, during the late 1920s. Her dramatic rendering of Chee and the Navajo people is an interesting mix of admiration and disdain that leaves one wondering how she truly felt. For example, she pictures Chee riding his horse like a "centaur," his smoking a cigarette as a "Buddha breathing incense," and his blowing his nose like "Adam and Eve must have."[20]

In the same breath, she pointed out that Chee wore "an old sack coat and a mangy fur cap with a band of quarters and dimes, his most cherished possession"; that he had a "childlike," "innocent" smile; and that one night he and a companion "began a savage chanting, with rhythmically placed falsetto yelps and guttural shouts."[21] Another Navajo who joined the expedition later fared no better. Dixon was convinced that he was there for the daily rations and that he made himself just useful enough to be allowed to follow camp. He was "fat and venerable" and "looked so like an old woman that [they] dubbed him Aunt Mary."[22]

This ambiguity—somewhere between disgust and the idealized noble savage—is encapsulated in a single event. Dixon recalls how she awoke one morning, as dawn banded the windy sky. As she peered out of her tent, she spied

> Hostein Chee, the Red Man, beside a campfire blazing shoulder high. His body slanting back, his face frozen to exalted calm, he gazed fixedly at the glory of the sky. His inscrutable nature seemed touched and wakened. I called softly to Toby.
>
> "Look—he is saying a prayer to the dawn!"
>
> We looked reverently. The white men were sleeping, but the Indian kept his vigil. He raised both arms above his head, removed his hat—and scratched vigorously. This done, he repeated the process wherever he felt the need. . . . Yet even engaged in so primitive a gesture as scratching, [Chee] invested it with the stately grace we noticed in his every move.[23]

For the more masculine traveler, less interested in how a Navajo blew his nose, scratched his backside, or donned his checkered underwear, there was also a rip-roaring Wild West saga of bravery and battles surrounding the development of travel to Rainbow Bridge. This story began in 1924, when a trading family consisting of Cecil, Hubert, and S. I. (Samuel Irby) Richardson explored, mapped, and built a road to within thirteen miles of Rainbow Bridge. Veteran Arizona traders who operated posts in Blue Canyon, Cameron, Kaibeto, Shonto, Leupp, Red Lake, and eventually Navajo Mountain, it was only natural that they would have a growing interest in the tourist trade that had been beneficial to John Wetherill.[24]

Hubert and S.I. received permission from the BIA and other government agencies to forge a trail into this isolated part of the reservation in order to expedite the delivery of services to Navajos in the interior. Their plan was to have tourists begin in Flagstaff, then travel to Cameron, Red Lake, and on to the western side of Navajo Mountain where a trading post would be established. To facilitate the construction of the undeveloped part of the trail between Red Lake and Navajo Mountain, they hired John Daw, a Navajo scout for the military in earlier times. He knew well the old Ute, Paiute, and Navajo trail system in the Navajo Mountain area.[25]

At this point, according to the Richardsons, pressure began to mount for them to stop their venture. They believed that John Wetherill was using his influence with the government and the Navajos to prevent competitors from threatening his lucrative business, since he and his partner, Clyde Colville, "were failures as Indian traders."[26] Navajo workers built the road—grubbing sagebrush, dynamiting obstacles, digging out embankments, and filling in road base—while John Daw mapped ahead.

Suddenly the work crew disappeared, leaving Daw and the Richardsons alone to continue the task. Kayenta Navajos, in the employ of the Wetherills, had driven off the local Navajos with threats. Next followed a period of tense waiting as the enemy stalked the camp, verbally threatened, and physically attacked the small party of workers. Fistfights, rock throwing, stick bashing, and even a little dynamite tossing resulted. Not until some of the local headmen appeared, angry that the Kayenta Navajos had moved into their territory to stop a project that they wanted completed, did the hostilities cease. The Richardsons now had a clear path to establish a trading post and guest lodge near Willow Spring on the western side of Navajo Mountain.[27]

Work continued. The Richardsons, with Navajo, Mexican, and Hopi labor, quarried local sandstone for building materials. From it they fashioned the store, a large living room, a dining room and kitchen, and a long porch facing west. The entire structure was roofed with peeled logs and packed clay. Above the main building they constructed guest cabins

This photo of Richardson's car was taken on the newly blazed road leading to Rainbow Lodge. Accessibility became the key for opening up the natural wonders of southeastern Utah to the tourist trade. Photo from Arizona Historical Society, Flagstaff, NAPHS 666-352.

for tourists and a guide shack for the trail bosses who would lead trips to Rainbow Bridge. Below the post was a log barn and large corrals for the horses that would be rented. And finally, there was a warehouse built from Arbuckle Brothers' Coffee packing boxes that stored supplies brought in during October to last the trader and his wife through the long winter.[28] During the winter, the area was as isolated as it had been before the road was built.

The twelve-mile trail leading from Rainbow Lodge followed a relatively direct route to the bridge. At one point, the Richardsons used $10,000 worth of dynamite to blast through obstacles and made a switchback that zigzagged down the two-thousand-foot wall of Cliff Canyon.[29] As the trail was on the west side of the mountain, much of the eastern trail developed by John Wetherill was of no use for this more direct route. Apparently pressure was exerted to have geographic features and part of the trail named after members of the earlier exploration party, but the responsibility for that lay in the hands of the BIA, not the Richardsons. Once the trail was completed, the main road, which started out from Red

Lake as a one hundred-mile trace but was eventually shortened to seventy-four miles, saw increasing automobile traffic. The last twelve miles to the bridge was always by horse and mule pack train.

The history of Rainbow Lodge is a story in itself, one that needs to be told at another time. Management of the lodge remained primarily in the family, with S.I. relinquishing his share to his brother, Hubert, in 1927, who later turned it over to his brother-in-law, W. W. (Bill) Wilson. Bill and his wife, Katherine, remained for twenty-five years. They retired in 1952, having spent their energies promoting the tourist trade and minimizing the trading post business.[30]

As these owners and operators came and went, they received Navajo nicknames. Bill Wilson was known at various times as The One with a Bad Hand, Man with Blue Eyes, and Man from the Pine Trees.[31] The first name was given to him because one of his hands had become permanently disfigured from rope burns when he lassoed a wild horse; the latter name was probably because he originally hailed from Detroit, Michigan.

Over the roughly thirty-year period that Rainbow Lodge existed, it and the bridge became a destination for approximately 8,700 tourists.[32] Touring companies became a major part of a system that moved people to this remote area for their encounter with the Wild West. Based on the rates of a 1934 brochure, an individual could spend a fairly significant amount in a single trip to Rainbow Bridge, considering that this was during the Great Depression. Automobile transportation from Flagstaff to the lodge (332 miles round trip) for one to four passengers cost $100. The Fred Harvey Tours Company offered a line from the Grand Canyon, while Clarkson Tours did the same from Santa Fe, New Mexico, and Winslow, Arizona. Once at the lodge, it was $2 a day for accommodations, $3 a day for food, and $30 for the two-day pack trip with everything included. A five-day trip encircling Navajo Mountain was $100.[33]

Gradually, more and more inroads were made into the once-isolated domain of the Navajos. A trading post on the east side of the mountain soon added other amenities, as roads improved and a network of branches threaded through the pinyon- and juniper-clad mesas and hills to Navajo homes. Civilization marched boldly into the interior, bringing with it improved wells and eventually telephone lines, a boarding school, a clinic, and various types of commerce.

But this was in the distant future. At this point, in the late 1920s, it was the tourist who came as the ambassador of the dominant culture. What the Navajos thought of all this is recorded in the memories of many of the gray-haired elders living at Navajo Mountain today. Some of them worked at the post, wrangled horses, guided pack trains, and catered to sight-seers. Their experience provides an interesting view of this strange phenomenon, tourism, so prevalent in Anglo culture.

Joe Manygoats recalls the earliest days of the post, when Old White Man (S. I. Richardson) arrived with two wagons filled with merchandise. Richardson sent a message through John Daw (Big Policeman) to the local people, even before he had arrived, that he wanted to meet with them. He set up a tent and traded food and goods, then asked permission to relocate to the place where the lodge would later be built. Many of the local leaders, such as Yellow Salt, Long Salt, Standing Oak Tree, and Small Canyon, spoke for the people and agreed that the long trip to Kaibeto, Shonto, and Kayenta was too inconvenient and that a post closer to home was desirable. The Navajos helped Richardson get his supply wagons in and assisted in the construction of the post and lodge.

Joe was just a young man when he started working at Rainbow Lodge, probably in the early 1930s.[34] He was on the payroll for four years; his pay was $2.40 a day and was received weekly. He remembers working there with several other Navajo men under a white foreman who supervised the day-to-day operation of the business. It was strictly summertime employment. The men did a variety of odd jobs such as digging a ditch for a pipe to bring water to the post. They also dragged in by horse large amounts of firewood, then attacked it with a two-man saw, creating a pile of wood as high as a hogan.

Navajo women worked at the lodge too. When she was sixteen, Velta Luther cleaned the cabins and washed the clothes of the tourists. She remembers when the travelers arrived: "They usually took off their clothes and just left them lying around all over the place and under the bed. I would gather them up and wash them in one of those washing machines made out of metal; the ones that made the wosh, wosh sound."[35] She also swept and mopped the rooms, cleaned the windows, and aired the bedding. Later she worked in the store, dusting shelves and stacking goods. Her employment lasted for two years.

But the main task for most Navajos was working with the horses and mules that were rented by the tourists. Joe recalls "wrestling" with the large stubborn mules and holding their ears as the men tightened the packs down on their backs. There were usually eight or nine mules, plus all the horses ridden by the tourists. Many of the dudes did not have an inkling of what to do once mounted: "All they did was sit in the saddle and hold the reins. We even had to help them on and off the horses. . . . They were such a burden." The guide led the tour and did most of the talking, while the Navajo helpers checked for safety, unpacked and fed the mules, set up camp, and at night placed lighted wax candles on rock ledges for picture taking.

Occasionally, a group would travel the long way around the mountain and back to the lodge. One time Joe remembers taking this trail, which had an extremely steep section covered with black volcanic gravel and many sharp traversing turns. The Navajos had named it "Long-Upward Hill" and took particular care for the inexperienced riders' safety. Without warning, Joe's mule started bucking uncontrollably, then plunged down, pell-mell, over the switchbacks and through the knots of bewildered, shouting, and screaming tourists. By the time he reached the bottom, he gained control, then sheepishly joined the group. Nothing else was said.

One diversion that was difficult for the Navajo guides to get used to was swimming. Robert Chief remembers his older brother, Tom, telling how the white bathers turned the crystal-clear pools into swimming holes: "The tourists went swimming stark naked and he was at first embarrassed about it, but he slowly got used to it. It didn't seem to bother anybody that everybody was naked. He sat around in the shade of the cedar trees listening to the birds sing or watching the puffy white clouds play tag while the tour group all went swimming."[36]

Floyd Laughter, another young Navajo, began an employment relationship with the people at the lodge in the late 1930s that lasted fifteen years.[37] He became very good friends with the tour boss, a white man named Miles Hatchett, who eventually turned all of the responsibility over to Floyd to run groups on his own. Miles even helped Floyd to correspond with customers, which increased business. This venture was extremely lucrative for Floyd, who otherwise would not have had access to the eight separate sleeping quarters, a huge horse corral and camp-grounds, and all of the horse tack, camping gear, and equipment necessary for the trips.

He and other Navajos earned substantial sums of money renting horses. Floyd recalls the rates were $10 for a riding horse and $5 for a packhorse, and since a person would typically rent from two to five horses on each tour and the trip was usually three days, he might earn $100 to $200 for one tour. With large groups that required thirty horses or more, the cost of a tour shot up to $4,000.

Still, Floyd earned his money. He and ten other men had responsibility for maintaining the trails by removing rocks and other obstructions. After a group of tourists arrived, the real work began. Following the initial packing and saddling, he would stop and tighten saddle cinches before ascending or descending steep sections of trail. The tourists varied in age from children to elderly, and so his ability to anticipate hazardous situations and help people through the rigors of trail rides was appreciated—so much that he received tips in thanks. Then there were all of the cooking and camping details, the packing and repacking, and the return trip with stops along the way. One elderly couple appreciated his efforts so much, particularly because their arrival was spur of the moment, that they paid $600 for the two-day trip.

Some trips were very difficult. Floyd remembers the time 225 members of the Colorado Club arrived. One guide was provided for each group of fifteen people, and thirty-five packhorses were needed to carry the supplies. There were no major mishaps, but Floyd was relieved to say good-bye to the crowd of travelers.

In summarizing his fifteen years in the tourist trade, Floyd remarked that he generally enjoyed the people. Some of them taught him English, which he was anxious to learn because he had no formal education. He said, "I may never learn to speak their language fluently, but I was more than determined to learn their work and to hold a high position in their type of work. The white men are not the only ones to get educated and earn a retirement; I will do the same and work until I retire too." He went on to employment with the National Park Service at Navajo National Monument (Betatakin), retired, and reached his goal, but he was quick to point out that the money working for the government was not nearly as plentiful as it had been when riding trail for Rainbow Lodge.

The land that the tourists passed through was breathtaking, but they had no knowledge of the history and spiritual meaning it held for the Navajos. Every bit of the trail, from the lodge to Rainbow Bridge, had a name and special significance. For instance, Willow Spring, which supplied water to the post and was supposedly discovered by the Richardsons, was actually a well-known site, one of many where Navajos made sacred offerings to water. Thus the Navajos called the lodge "Watercoming-out." As the travelers wended their way toward the bridge they passed through such Navajo landmarks as Grey Hill with Thorns, into Water Flowing, and across the valley into The Owl's Flowing Water, which was considered Paiute country. They then went out to Where the Eagle Sits, sometimes called The Home of the Eagles, and on to Amidst the Thorns, then Solid Rock Wall, and finally into the valley called Water Flowing in Sumac Berry Bushes, where they camped and ate supper.[38]

Karl Luckert, in *Navajo Mountain and Rainbow Bridge Religion*, has documented rock formations, springs, alcoves, and other topographic features near the bridge that are important to the Navajos. There is a cave where the Holy People dwelled, a rock person who stands as a sentinel, with other holy beings frozen in stone closer to the Rainbow. Talking Rock Girl, Talking Rock Boy, and a spring related to those on top of Navajo Mountain are other sacred sites. Below Rainbow Bridge, where the male San Juan River joined the female Colorado River, was a place where two spiritual bodies created water children of the cloud and rain people. Before Lake Powell covered their bed, the San Juan actually mounted his mate, the Colorado, giving rise to a place for moisture-producing ceremonies.[39]

The intensity of belief associated with these sites is illustrated by an experience of Joe Manygoats. He tells of a large hole beside the trail to Rainbow Bridge on the south side of Navajo Mountain. This rock cleft goes far down into the earth. There is a corresponding hole on the north side of the mountain, and if a person goes near either one, a whirlwind will attack them, since these are the wind's homes. Joe recounts:

> One day while I was working for Rainbow Bridge, me and my coworker were asked to go down to the Rainbow Bridge campsite to fix the boxes of bedding, food, and horse feed storage areas. On our way, we stopped to investigate the hole located just off the

trail. My coworker threw a rock into the hole to see how far down it would go. It took a long time before we heard it hit bottom. We felt a funnel of strong air coming from this hole; it scared us off. This was also the wind's home. It is dangerous and forbidden to go near these kinds of places, but you can do so by talking to it and "naming" it by its sacred name. It is much calmer then.[40]

As time passed, the lodge changed ownership. In 1946 future Arizona senator Barry Goldwater bought Hubert Richardson's half interest in the business and went into partnership with Bill Wilson. Goldwater claimed that as a moneymaking proposition the lodge "never made a cent" and that profits at the trading post were marginal at best.[41] His interest lay in the love of the country and in providing a retreat for himself and people like him who wanted to get away from the busy life of mainstream America. He and Wilson got along well as co-owners, but the actual operation remained in Wilson's hands.

Goldwater built a rough dirt airstrip south of Navajo Mountain, approximately three miles from the lodge. He would fly in from Phoenix, buzz the lodge, then land at the strip. Some of the Navajos did not like the noise, complaining that it bothered the War God (Monster Slayer) at the top of the mountain. Their beliefs seemed justified when Goldwater's aircraft tipped over on a landing as he was teaching his sister-in-law how to fly.

A general impression among the Navajo people who remember Goldwater's involvement is that he was a tough businessman. They believe that he was making a good profit that did not trickle down in their direction, while at the same time there were issues within the growing Navajo community concerning the use of water from Willow Spring.

There were some other rumblings of discontent, and although most Navajos agreed that Rainbow Lodge had been a good thing for the community and was generally welcomed, there were a few who did not feel that way. On August 11, 1951, Rainbow Lodge burned to the ground. Goldwater believes the fire was caused when one of the white guides went in to the bathroom to take a shower, left a lighted cigarette on the windowsill, and allowed a breeze to fan it into a conflagration that could not be stopped. The guest houses and a newly built garage, now converted into a dining room, were untouched by the fire and remained operational for another year.[42] Then the business was abandoned and most of the materials salvaged by neighboring Navajo families.

At least some Navajos perceived the fire in different terms. One man told of how his grandfather believed he had been cheated by the trader there. The grandfather "knew the ways of darkness" and performed a ceremony to have the post destroyed. In the grandson's words, "He prayed to have bad things happen to the traders and it wasn't long after that lightning struck the trading post and burned everything. The owners did not rebuild but moved away to California. The curse has never been removed from the place."

The burning of the lodge signaled the end of an era but not the end of interest in Rainbow Bridge. Plans to rebuild the business never reached fruition, but in ten years' time there would be no need for it anyway. The completion of the Glen Canyon Dam in Page in 1963 created ease of access to the bridge that was undreamed of twenty years before. By 1965 the waters of the Colorado and San Juan Rivers had backwashed to the point that they were lapping up Bridge Canyon and fast approaching the foot of the monument. The establishment of marinas at Hite, Bullfrog, Wahweap, and Halls Crossing provided jumping-off points for the most casual of tourists who appeared on the shores of Lake Powell.

Before long the National Park Service, which until this time was not terribly concerned about managing such an isolated site, became intimately involved in its control. Docking facilities less than a mile from the bridge allowed continuous access and pushed the number of visitations to astronomical proportions. For example, in 1964 there were 5,670 tourists who visited the site; six years later there were 40,000; by 1997 an estimated 1,000 visitors a day went to the monument; and more than 235,000 people visited Rainbow Bridge in 1999.[43]

What has been the Navajo reaction to all of this? Unlike their feelings about Rainbow Lodge, where there was direct benefit and involvement and tourists came and went on a manageable scale, the Navajos feel that tourism now offers them little and is destructive. A sampling of these attitudes shows that far more than dollars and cents and tourism are at stake. Now that the lake waters cover one of the sacred springs, medicine men have to guess where to leave their offerings, and another spring above the arch is too exposed to public use. The National Park Service docking facilities bring more people, encourage swimming, and allow "many unholy things to be done and planned [there]. For example, a lot of beer cans are being thrown around and they eventually end up at Rock-arch."[44]

In addition, Navajo ceremonies must be performed during the day, which is impossible because of the presence of tourists. People who travel from all over the reservation to be healed for bad dreams can no longer avail themselves of the powerful forces within the bridge. Problems in general beset the Navajo people because the powers there have been abused and medicine men can no longer appeal to them. The dry years in the 1970s were offered as proof of this desecration.[45] Keith Holiday, from Navajo Mountain, put it this way: "Medicine men no longer go over there. When they did the world was in harmony because they made offerings in this place. There was abundance of rain during that time. . . . Now it is gone. It [the traffic] probably crushed it all to pieces."[46] The word that is heard most often in interviews with Navajo people who are concerned about Rainbow Bridge is "trampled." One person said, "It looks like the sheep slept there," and went on to comment that there is no vegetation, just rocks, sand, and fence.[47]

There have been stirrings from the Navajo community to try to bring about a change. On August 11, 1995, a small group of Navajos called Protectors of the Rainbow closed the monument to any outside interference, then held a cleansing ceremony for four days. The National Park Service enforced the group's wishes, rerouting scheduled boat tours and closing down any activity beyond the dock facility. It has also implemented policies to remove graffiti and to prevent climbing on the bridge.[48]

This peaceful resolution was only temporary. An underlying issue is the question of how much and what type of protection can be afforded this site. And the problem is not limited to Rainbow Bridge. Rangers at Devils Tower National Monument in Wyoming have discouraged rock climbers from ascending its face; Chaco Canyon National Park in New Mexico closed its Great Kiva after Pueblos and Navajos complained it was being defiled; and park rangers now prevent tourists from going to the Lion's Shrine at Bandelier National Monument in New Mexico for the same reason.[49] Indian people do not want to see their sacred sites profaned.

Part of the problem is reconciling American Indian practices with Anglo-American law. While the National Park Service is able to grant temporary closure of these sites, it cannot completely prevent public use. One court ruling said, "We do not believe [the Navajos] have a constitutional right to prevent tourists visiting the Bridge 'in a respectful and appreciative manner.' Were it otherwise, the monument would become a government-managed shrine," an obvious infringement of First Amendment rights.[50]

One might ask if the Navajo people might have better results if the tribe controlled these tourist sites. To answer that, one must turn to the Navajo Tribal Park in Monument Valley, then listen to what the local people say. The park is located in one of the most scenic parts of the reservation, made famous by the movie industry and local entrepreneurs like Harry and Mike Goulding. In May 1960 the Navajo Nation dedicated the park and its facilities. Development of the 94,000-acre park cost an initial $275,000, which included a visitor center, campgrounds, and a network of roads that wind between and around some of the most heavily photographed monoliths and mesas in the world—the Mittens, Totem Pole Rock, Three Sisters, and Merrick Butte. The growing number of visitors attests to the park's popularity: in 1960, there were approximately 22,000 fee-paying tourists; in 1983, 100,000; in 1993, 292,721; in 1999, 380,575.[51]

The older people living in the area have mixed emotions about what is happening today. Some of them appreciate that their children and grandchildren are employed as tour guides, as workers in local restaurants, and by selling arts and crafts near the visitor center. For some, it has become the main source of income. One person noted, "Many receive lots of money. When a bus stops, many of the tourists come and buy many of the items the people are selling. . . . This is what they do, the ones who put their things in the sun."[52] Others feel the money is going to the tribal government in Window Rock and hope that it is returning to them through chapter (local government) funds. However, there are others who have the same complaints as the people at Navajo Mountain. The most notable problem is the sheer volume of people. As one man put it, "The Anglos just flock and stream into the area. I do not know how to slow this down. Now they are crawling all over behind our back. There is no hope."[53]

A common Navajo perception is that movie studios are making huge amounts of money from the land and the people while they receive little in return. Some of the film companies are doing this "secretly" and are guarded by police to keep the "complainers" away, while no one locally gets paid for the use of the land. All of the money being paid for filming remains in Window Rock. "These white people take hordes of pictures only to make huge profits by showing them [movies] in foreign countries. Millions gather in huge theaters to watch movies for large fees."[54]

Even more fundamental to the elders is the effect that "trampling" the land has on rain and moisture-producing sites. Rooted in the livestock economy of the old days, they are concerned when sacred rock formations, springs, and mesas are opened for public use. Guy Cly recalls how offerings of sacred stones would bring the rains, first gently, then in a downpour. "Puddles would form and rain would splash down into the puddles and create a haze. It would rain hard."[55] John Holiday, a medicine man in Monument Valley, said,

> These places are very sacred. When we lack rain, we always place our offerings in these sacred areas. About five years ago, a man from the valley came to visit me. He said, "We never have rain and are experiencing drought." So we took some sacred pebbles as offerings to Totem Pole Rock. We asked for rain in all four directions. Then it started pouring as we were halfway home and the wash filled with water. It has rained more often since then. It was truly a sacred and holy blessing. If these holy places are destroyed, then I do not know what will happen.[56]

He went on to say that before the tourists came there was a lot more rainfall. "Now, there is nothing—it is hopeless."

Control of natural resources and decisions about how they will be used rests in the hands of the younger generation. Tourism has been trumpeted as the salvation for the Navajo Nation as the extractive industries of coal and oil play out to their inevitable end. In July 1997 former Secretary of the Interior Stewart Udall published an article titled "More Tourists, Please," in which he prescribed the need for the construction and operation of "world class" facilities on the reservation.[57] He believes that the problems of poverty will be solved by attracting wealthy tourists who will drop large bundles of money in restaurants, lodges, and entertainment meccas spread throughout Navajo land. In a word, big money means big profits and the end of Navajo poverty.

Monument Valley would be one of the key areas of development.

Albert Hale, president of the Navajo Nation at the time, responded. Calling on history as his judge, he pointed out that from the time of the Harvey Houses and the Santa Fe Railroad, the writings of Zane Grey, through to the movies of John Ford, the Four Corners area has been publicized and visited by the wealthy. The Navajos have remained in the same economic state throughout their experience with tourism. While Hale was not suggesting that the tourist be pushed away, he insisted that when visitors come to the reservation they stay in Navajo motels and use Navajo owned and operated facilities. In his words, "For a century we have had tourism that says, 'Take nothing but pictures, leave nothing but footprints.' That is precisely what the last era of grand hotels left us—nothing but footprints."[58]

From the era of the Wetherills to the Richardsons to the Wilsons and the Goldwaters, Rainbow Bridge and Monument Valley have proven to be only marginally profitable for the Navajo people. Now the People's voice is getting stronger, as the Navajo government becomes more responsive to local needs and as a more sensitive public moves beyond the stereotypes and assumptions of yesteryear. The twenty-first century brings a new dawn in man's relationship to the land—one from which the Navajos can benefit as they examine their past.

CHAPTER EIGHT

INDIANS PLAYING INDIANS

Navajos and the Film Industry in Monument Valley, 1938–1964

Paint-bedecked Plains Indians sit astride prancing steeds, waiting to descend upon the encircled wagons; blue-coated soldiers charge over the red earth in pursuit of a retreating enemy; men grapple in a death struggle to overpower their tenacious foe. All of these clichés played across the nation in movie houses packed with thrill-seeking audiences hungry to watch stereotypical Indians in the Wild West. Viewers, perching on the edge of their seats, silently cheered the heroes, booed the villains, and left contented that good had conquered evil and right prevailed. Very few questioned the authenticity of the portrayal or entertained the possibility that Indians had legitimate grievances.

Many westerns were the creation of John Ford, the director whose masterful eye for setting and keen sense of contrast catapulted images of the West onto the screen and into the minds of a receptive audience. Ironically, these images, so much a part of Ford's West, were the antithesis of how he felt about his Native American actors. His warmth and generosity toward them far surpassed "duty" and kindled a friendship that lasted until his death in 1973.

Ford left on record how he and others felt when working with Indians, but few people have taken the time to ask how Indians perceived their involvement in westerns. The Navajos—who largely represented Indians on screen—looked through very different cultural eyes at their experience and how it affected their lives. This chapter explores these views of events and attitudes toward the films directed by Ford.

Starting in 1938 and continuing for the next twenty-six years, John Ford appeared in Monument Valley on a fairly regular basis to create such film classics as *Stagecoach, Fort Apache, The Searchers, She Wore a Yellow Ribbon, My Darling Clementine,* and *Cheyenne Autumn.* The story of how Harry Goulding left his trading post for Hollywood, armed only with some photographs; how the landscape's beauty sold itself; how cast, crews, and director were enamored with its charm; and how Harry and his wife became major promoters for these various ventures has itself become a well-known story, as the trader, on a number of occasions, recounted the film industry's genesis in the valley.[1]

There had been other earlier traders, such as John and Louisa Wetherill of Kayenta, who had similar ideas but lacked vision on such a grand scale. In 1917 they tried to promote an "elaborate moving picture advertising scheme of the Monument Valley and Rainbow Natural Bridge country" in cooperation with the Santa Fe Railroad Company.[2] Because of this and other promotional schemes, the trickle of tourists swelled each summer to an increasingly larger flow.

Travelers made their way with camera in hand through the deserts to the hogans, much to the surprise of the Navajos. Fred Yazzie, a lifelong resident of Monument Valley, tells of living near the base of Eagle Mesa when some Anglos approached him with a strange object. One man pointed his box at Fred and his father as they butchered a sheep and, amazingly, produced a paper with a black-and-white image of what had happened just a few minutes before. This was in 1919. Two years later other white men came with a different type of object that had "strings" (film) going into it and that made a "chii, chii, chii" sound as one of its parts rotated.[3] Moving pictures had arrived.

Professional photographers followed on the heels of the amateurs. When Fred was nineteen years old, he began to understand moviemaking. Surprisingly, one of the earliest films focused on the Long Walk period, when Anglos came to Monument Valley to capture and send Navajos to Fort Sumner. The soldiers burned replicas of hogans, Navajos once again wore the old-style clothing and carried bows and arrows, and Indians and whites chased each other around the red rocks of this scenic region. Fred remembers, "We did not really know what was going on; we were just told to do something in a certain way and we did."[4] By the time Ford became a familiar visitor, some of the Navajos were well aware of what acting was all about.

The Great Depression took its toll on the reservation. Livestock reduction had decimated the herds of sheep, goats, horses, and cattle, so the Navajos welcomed any kind of employment. The CCC and other government programs helped to alleviate the suffering, but the movies provided substantial sums of money without the red tape and with a number of side benefits. The twenty-six years of the Ford era saw many changes, but Navajo informants seemed generally satisfied with their employment and pay.

Recruiting took two forms. The first was through Harry Goulding and, later, Navajos such as John, Johnny, and Jack Stanley or Frank and Leon Bradley, all from the Kayenta—Monument Valley area, who were consistently used in the movies. The success of this recruitment program is apparent in the film credits; the names of the extras added authenticity and color to the production. For instance, in *The Searchers* Indians who played the part of Comanche braves included Away Luna, Billy Yellow, Bob Many Mules, Percy Shooting Star, Pete Grey Eyes, and Smile White Sheep.[5]

In later years, Rusty Musselman, a trader from Bluff, became extensively involved in outfitting equipment for the sets and also traveled from hogan to hogan offering employment. A primary criterion for "visible" actors was the "great face" that Ford insisted on. Selection was based on what an Indian "should look like," harkening back to the romantic stereotypes of the noble and ignoble savage. Musselman started looking for the personality features he thought Ford wanted. If someone looked "more like a wild Indian" than another person, he would get the job.[6] Other criteria for selection were being tall, having long hair, and owning one or more horses, for which an actor was paid extra.

A second means of recruiting was by word of mouth. Job seekers appeared on some sets by the droves. Men and young people, sometimes entire families, rode from all over Monument Valley as well as Kayenta, Shonto, Navajo Mountain, Rough Rock, Chinle, Tuba City, the Gap, and fifty miles in any direction just for an acting part. If for no other reason than excitement and curiosity, people came to watch the strange occurrences. Food and material goods attracted others who hoped that there would be something for everybody.[7]

Movie companies were always looking for extras to participate in crowd scenes. This movie, filmed outside Kayenta, Arizona, used many local Navajos to play non-Indian roles. Photo from Milton Snow Collection, NF11-39, Navajo Nation Museum.

The pay varied over the years, of course, but for the typical extra, the rate was between $5 and $20 for a day's work, the money being handed out either in the evenings or once a week. Navajos did not pay for their meals and considered the food part of their compensation.[8]

Navajos insisted that they be paid in coins, ranging from dollars and half dollars to nickels, because of their distrust of paper money. Coins were "real" money that makes a sound when you pick it up. Not only were they used to pay for goods, but they were also turned into decorations for belts, bracelets, bow guards, and buttons, or melted down to be fashioned by the silversmith's hammer.

During the early phases of the film industry, this money went a long way to meeting the basic needs of an impoverished people. The staples of flour, coffee, sugar, and salt were inexpensive, but a pair of boots cost $2, a pair of pants or shirt $1.50. Goulding and other traders loved to see hard cash instead of pawn flowing across the counters; it also provided a new firsthand experience for the Navajos. Fred Yazzie claims, "It was through making the movies that we got to know what money was."[9]

Film crews provided for other types of peripheral income. Navajos sold blankets, jewelry, and other articles to souvenir-seeking filmmakers. Some Indians purchased items from fellow tribal members and sold them at higher prices; for example, they might buy a bracelet for a $1.50 and sell it for $5.00. Others entered the bootlegging business and sold corn liquor, prohibited on the reservation, for after-hours refreshments. Covert stills in Oljeto or a couple of suitcases filled from the bars of Cortez provided enough liquor for thirsty throats and a profit for the entrepreneurs. They did, however, have to dodge the Navajo police who were brought in from Tuba City or Gallup to prevent disturbances. In later years movie companies paid for the protection and preferred Navajos from outside the area to avoid peer pressure and crossing family ties when it came time for an arrest.[10]

Legal concerns and economics came together in other forms. More than 260 miles of road were either constructed or improved, a great deal done by Navajo labor. The tribal headquarters in Window Rock, Arizona, took responsibility for issuing permits to movie companies for filming on the reservation; the Bureau of Land Management handled the off-reservation permits. Eventually the tribe also sent Navajo inspectors to ensure that the countryside was not damaged.[11]

Yet the land, more than any other feature, was the thing that Ford loved and was willing to pay for. In 1946 he said,

> I think you can say that the real star of my Westerns has always been the land. . . . My favorite location is Monument Valley; it has rivers, mountains, plains, desert. . . . I feel at peace there. I have been all over the world, but I consider this the most complete, beautiful and peaceful place on Earth.[12]

Indeed, Ford made the land synonymous with the Indian in a thematic statement that pitted savagery and wilderness against the white man and civilization. The former qualities mesh with the timeless, pure landscape filled with a natural beauty that is also an ever-present threat. The land and the Indian were inseparable.[13]

Another important aspect of Ford's movies was heavy dependence on horses. Although Hollywood brought in well-trained trick horses or animals noted for their beauty, the majority of the stock was either

Navajo or belonged to or rented by traders. Sometimes more than two hundred horses were needed for a day's filming or as backups, and not all of them were manageable. Guy Cly tells of Navajos riding unsaddled horses that ran and then bucked their riders onto the hard, red sand. Kee Stanley got one that chose to buck while passing under a tree. Kee went up and came down but left his wig hanging in the branches, much to the enjoyment of those watching him try to salvage his dignity.[14]

Navajos worked as wranglers and brought in livestock for the films. The job of head wrangler usually went to an Anglo, who could make up to $100 in a workday that was fourteen to sixteen hours long. Musselman had to keep saddle horses, wagon and stagecoach teams, and work-horses as ready replacements in prepositioned corrals or drive them out to where the day's filming was being done and then back again at dusk. He tells of one white man, working as an extra, who trooped along a line of horses looking in their ears. When asked what he was doing, he admitted to a cardinal sin for any person used to working with livestock. He said he could not remember what his horse looked like; he only remembered that it had a wart in its ear. Musselman left disgusted.[15]

The movie companies also brought in "dead" horses for battle scenes. These props simulated so closely the real thing that more than one Navajo struggled to tell the difference. Harry Goulding tells of having Chee, an older man serving as "chief" this particular day, lead a charging horde of Indians over a hill to attack a beleaguered wagon train. Chee received some hurried instructions, then was off to the attack not really knowing what to expect. When he crested the hill and saw all of the "dead" horses and men, along with all of the living whites armed with rifles, it was too much. He veered away from the set, charged through the camera crew, and led his mounted warriors in a pell-mell retreat that took him as far away as possible until Goulding caught him. The trader asked why he had fled. Chee replied that he did not want to fight all those well-armed white men with only rubber-tipped arrows.[16]

Other props included stagecoaches, wagons, pushcarts, blacksmith shops, and anything else found in a frontier setting. Musselman stocked and rented from his trading post between $20,000 and $30,000 worth of equipment for various movie sets. Some were antiques bought locally or in Colorado, other items were built for a specific movie, and others were brought from Hollywood and sold after the production.[17]

Temporary buildings were constructed all over Monument Valley. Constructing the fort near the Mittens for *She Wore a Yellow Ribbon* and the town of Tombstone near Eagle Mesa for *My Darling Clementine* put Navajo workers into the building trades. Many of these laborers received instructions from white bosses, then quickly and skillfully applied their knowledge to the tasks with favorable results. Carpentry, concrete work, wiring, and painting were a few of the skills Navajos learned.[18]

For six years after the filming ended, these two sites remained as silent witnesses and fooled many a tourist. Twentieth Century Fox and the tribe agreed to protect the sets and hired two caretakers—Leon (Lee) Bradley (the "mayor") and Fred Yazzie—to prevent vandalism. Yazzie agreed to watch Tombstone, or Ghost Town as the Navajos called it, for $100 a month. On one occasion, when Ford flew in to check the condition of the premises, Fred asked if he could use some of the buildings as a base of operations for a guided tour business and as a stable for some of his horses. Ford approved and even said he would provide $1,000 to help get the enterprise started. The plan never became a reality; the tribe felt the old sets were an eyesore, and some Navajos felt that Fred would reap a large income at their expense. Individuals bought the dwellings with the understanding that they had to remove them within an allotted time. As the deadline approached and the owners ran out of time, whites and Navajos living in the valley helped with the demolition and took the materials.

Sometimes Navajos were given the remains directly after a filming sequence or claimed the right to them because the structures were on or near their property. Today, parts of movie sets still remain, but instead of housing Billy the Kid or General Custer, they protect sheep and serve in summer as shade houses.[19]

Just as important as the material benefits of the films were the feelings they generated. Harry Goulding recounts how the Navajos arrived, in the best tradition of a John Ford spectacular, for the filming of *My Darling Clementine*.

> They brought about 1,500 head of cattle, bawling all the way. Forty-five prairie schooners came from somewhere and a couple of old stagecoaches, not to mention the hundreds of Indian wagons and ponies and dogs and cats that go along with Indian camps. . . .

Old-timers said that the noise and smell was like old times, the days before the army forced peace on the tribe.[20]

In the evenings people gathered around the workers' tents strung out in two straight lines below Goulding's trading post. They sang songs in English and Navajo, played cards, watched stuntmen's tricks, and ate together. Many slept in four- or eight-man tents, while others preferred living out of an automobile or resting beneath the stars. The mess hall and laundry facilities drew on the limited water resources, much of it hauled in from Kayenta, as did the hundreds of cattle, sheep, and horses. Still, for the Navajos there were never plusher times.[21]

Gambling was a prominent pastime shared by both cultures. The men's prowess in feats of strength and skill were always a welcome addition to stir excitement as each group chose its champion. John Holiday volunteered to Navajo wrestle one of the white men, with bets amounting to $200 for the winner. In this type of contest, the winner was the one left standing. Holiday sized up his burly opponent and noticed that he had a thin waist. As the men started to grapple, the Navajo grabbed the narrow waist bobbing before him and gave a terrific bear hug. The man went limp and did not revive until water was splashed on his face.[22]

Another bet was made over hauling firewood. One day Navajos and whites were scouring the desert floor for wood when they came upon a log so large that none of them could encircle it with their arms. Many men tried to lift the ponderous load but to no avail. Billy Katso rose to the occasion. He put a horse harness strap around the log, set it on end, padded his shoulder, hoisted the beam, and staggered to the truck several yards away. He won the bet and collected a sizable sum.[23]

Perhaps one of the most amusing wagers focused on a small sweat lodge when Mr. Ocean Water's Son led a group of movie employees on a guided tour of the monuments. The eighteen white men seated on the sight-seeing bus gaped in awe as their guide explained there were eleven men crammed into the small conical-shaped hogan dug in the side of the hill. Although the various sets of clothes arranged outside testified to the number, no one believed it. Each man offered $25 if there were that many inside. As the disgruntled participants interrupted their sweat and crawled into the blinding sunlight, those outside started the count. All eleven emerged, much to the chagrin of the losers, and even after the whites inspected the interior of the lodge, they could not comprehend how so many could fit into such a small space.[24]

If any single person symbolized the fun and positive relations between Indians and whites, it was John Ford, known to the Navajos as "Tall Leader" or "One Eye" because of a patch he wore. Ford truly respected Navajo customs. In 1956, during the filming of *The Searchers*, the Monument Valley community decided to make him an honorary member of the tribe. He selected the day, had three cattle barbecued, shipped in a truckload of watermelons, provided prizes for the horse races and footraces, and came in on the heels of the winner of the older men's competition. Around noon, the Navajos presented an unblemished deerskin as they chanted and performed the adoption ceremony. Shine Smith, a trader fluent in both languages and probably at least partly responsible for the non-Navajo "adoption" spectacle, inscribed the gift as follows:

> We present this deer hide to our fellow tribesman Natani Nez [Tall Leader] as a token of appreciation for the courtesy and friendship he has extended to us in his many activities in our Valley. In your travels may there be beauty on both sides of you, and beauty ahead of you.[25]

A witness remarked that Ford and John Wayne "felt a lot of atmosphere . . . and they reacted a little to it.[26] Goulding reported the effects of this rapport when he quipped, "You could see 'em [Navajos] when they looked at him, just spelled all over 'em that he was like them. That damn man, sometimes I wonder if he didn't come from a Navajo squaw."[27]

One time, when heavy snows buried the valley, Ford heard of the Navajos' plight and ordered food and supplies parachuted in to his people. This was in addition to the $200,000 spent there the previous summer during the shooting of *She Wore a Yellow Ribbon*.

It was fortunate for everyone that Ford had a sense of humor and was sympathetic to the Navajos. Murphy's law—if anything can go wrong, it will—often came into play as men from different cultures and animals with minds of their own worked together on a film. Stories of humorous incidents abound. Imagine what Ford must have said when One-Who-Winks-His-Eyes, dressed in a breechcloth and mounted on a fiery steed, galloped down a sand dune, fell off his horse, and crashed through a Hollywood hogan. Or when one of the "dead" extras tossed a pebble at another extra, noted for teasing, and the two dead men ended by slugging it out in the middle of a scene. Or when Rusty Musselman hid behind some boulders out of the camera's view but provided such an irresistible target to the Navajos perched on the cliffs above that they pelted him unceasingly with rubber-tipped arrows.[28]

Sometimes the Navajos singled out an individual for special treatment. For example, one white man was noted for being afraid of bugs and lizards. One of his friends urged some of his Navajo helpers to slip him a present. The next day a dead rat appeared in his tool box. This person also believed that Indians still killed whites, so two Navajos followed him around, brandished their knives, and gave him threatening looks, much to the amusement of everyone but the butt of this humor. Some informants mentioned how funny it was for spectators to sit on the sidelines and watch the actors pretend to die over and over again until they got it right.[29]

Still others enjoyed watching the finished product to see "Comanches" speaking Navajo and saying ludicrous things that at times had nothing to do with the action. Dolly Stanley-Roberson, Jack Stanley's niece, remembers going to the local chapter house for a viewing of *The Searchers*. The audience remained quiet during this serious movie until the Navajos appeared in Technicolor. "Then it was like watching home movies. Everyone would laugh and call out names of who they saw on the screen. The whole movie became more like the funniest comedy ever filmed."[30]

There was no joking when it came to Hastiin Tso (Mister Big or Big Man), however. Goulding's stories about this medicine man have become legendary.[31] The very first movie filmed by Ford in Monument Valley depended on Hastiin Tso's ability to control the weather; the director's skepticism changed to belief, causing him to place Tso at the top of the payroll list, with a daily wage of $15. According to eyewitnesses, Tso received his weather requests at four o'clock in the afternoon so that by the next day the clouds were positioned in the right place for the cameras, the snow lay on the ground, the dust storm arrived on schedule, or the winds that threatened the crews and their equipment subsided. He received $100 to make low-lying clouds dissipate and ordered snow in October when it rarely appeared before December.[32]

Many of the stories about Hastiin Tso's control of weather are confirmed by Navajos who knew him. There were, however, other medicine men who held similar powers in the same region. The people believe that the northern end of Black Mesa south of Monument Valley serves as a funnel to prevent harmful winds from battering other parts of the reservation. Powerful medicine men like Hastiin Tso ceremonially encourage the winds to pass by as part of these protection rites. Hilda Wetherill, who lived at the Covered Water Trading Post in Arizona, explained how such a man saw a twister headed directly for the store. Making gestures as if throwing kisses with both hands and pushing away with outstretched arms, he caused the wind to veer off a mile and a half away from the post.[33]

Hastiin Tso obtained his power from the knowledge taught by his father. He performed the Enemy Way, Blessing Way, Male Shooting Way, Evil Way, and Wind Way ceremonies as well as a variety of prayers and accompanying lesser rites. According to Navajo informants, Tso used these powers in a coercive way to gain employment with the movie company. He went to them for a job but was turned away. He tried to rent his horse to them and failed. So he spoke to one of the managers and told him that it would be overcast for one or two months so that they could not film. A sandstorm blew in that lasted two weeks, the sand so thick in the cloudless sky that it temporarily blinded people who moved about in it. This was followed by almost two months of overcast. The movie people, losing money all of the time, relented and hired him. The next day the sun shone and the cameras rolled.[34]

This story contradicts Goulding's version of Tso's relationship to the movie industry. According to Goulding, Tso was a willing accomplice, always on call to deliver to the director whatever weather was needed. Although the accounts vary, both sides agree: "He really had sacred powers in the prayers that he had . . . and those things happened according to what he asked."[35]

Cecil Parrish and some other men went hunting one time with Hastiin Tso. The medicine man asked the men in the group if they would like snow, presumably for better tracking conditions; the party agreed, and by sunset the ground was covered. Some Navajos suggest, however, that this power is what killed him. His control of the weather for the movie industry became so well known that when drought persisted year after year, some people blamed it on his tampering with the holy beings. He failed to use the other part of the ceremony to bring the clouds back. When others used prayers to bring the rain back, the power killed him. Close relatives say he died from injuries incurred while riding a horse.[36]

When he was not working for the movies, tending his garden, herding livestock, or performing ceremonies, Tso hauled flour, sugar, coffee, and other merchandise in his wagon to trading posts. His shipping routes extended to Gallup and Flagstaff. One time when he was in need of money, he pawned his wagon for goods from Goulding's, then took the vehicle out of hock a few days later to haul firewood. He did this three successive times at different posts until Goulding caught on that Tso was reaping the benefits of having a wagon to use while procuring the necessary supplies.[37]

Some of the most important Navajos in the filming industry were not medicine men but mixed-bloods who looked the part and spoke English fluently. Frank and Lee Bradley were the children of an Irish trader father and a Navajo mother. Frank's facial features bespoke this ancestry—piercing eyes, prominent nose, and ears that earned him the Navajo sobriquet "Bat." His twelve years in the military, including a stint at the front lines in France during World War I, and his election to the tribal council in 1935, provided him with an excellent command of English that served him well as a translator for movie crews and Navajos.[38]

Frank, who lived in Kayenta, and Lee, who lived in Monument Valley, selected many of the Navajo actors for various parts. They screened the hopefuls for their hair, height, and face, gave directions as to what the cameramen wanted, and ordered the amount and type of livestock for the Navajos to bring in to the set. One time Ford needed seven men for a certain part and was about to send to Hollywood for some actors. Instead, the Bradleys supplied the men, who met the director's highest expectations.[39]

The most successful of the Bradley recruits were Frank's in-laws— John, Johnnie, and Jack Stanley. All three had what Ford desired in appearance, and each had specific talents to bring to the screen. John spoke English because of his schooling in Riverside, California; hence his Navajo name, School Boy with the Curly Hair. Jack (Black Hat), his brother, spoke only Navajo, was raised as a medicine man knowledgeable in the Lightning Way, and did not trust white men but understood that his people needed employment and therefore helped to recruit.

Johnny (Big Man), like his brothers, seemed to have natural acting ability. All of the Stanleys became members of the Screen Actors Guild. In addition to their work in Monument Valley, they were called to work on films in Hollywood.

They became so popular with John Wayne that when he was filming *McClintock* near Tucson, he insisted on using them and "fifty other good men" from Monument Valley.[40] And when they died, Wayne and others from the movie industry helped with burial costs by buying caskets for their funerals.[41]

Musselman insists that the Stanleys, like many Indians, were natural-born actors. He tells of the time Rock Hudson and another white man were acting as Indian chiefs. Hudson was to present a token to the other man, but no matter how hard he tried, he could not do it with sufficient grace to satisfy the director. After shooting the scene seven times, the exasperated director was losing patience when one of the Stanleys emerged from the crowd, took the item, and went through the motions perfectly the first time. Everyone roared with delight to see an unlettered Indian best the high-paid actor. Hudson was embarrassed.[42]

Although the movie industry proved an economic boon to the Navajos, there was also a dark aspect that few outsiders knew about. The older people especially felt there were certain practices that were harmful to the land and its people. Their protests often fell on the deaf ears of money seekers, unless they took physical action. Little Mister Gambler once rode into the midst of the moviemakers, both whites and Indians, flailing about with his leather whip and saying that they should get away from his land. The crews packed their equipment and left because in those days the "elderly men were very much in command and the white men used to abide by their rules."[43]

To the Navajos, the land is sacred and holds many powers that can bless if respected or curse if ignored.[44] The movie industry unwittingly used many of these places in their filming without understanding that holy beings resided there and that the graves of Anasazi and Navajo alike were scattered from the mesas to the rocks to the deserts of Monument Valley. Where a person lies buried becomes holy and should be left alone. As Fred Yazzie explained, "We were doing things in sacred places. The Anglos would tell us to get up in those sacred sites and roll imitation rocks down on the horses and wagons traveling beneath us. . . .

They told us to do bizarre things, but the money pulled us in to the business."[45]

Older Navajos insisted that these strange ways, especially pretending to kill or be killed, should not be done within the lands bordered by the four sacred mountains of Colorado, New Mexico, and Arizona. Because the Navajos making movies broke this teaching, the reservation no longer receives sufficient rain from the holy beings but only drought and unmanageable snows.[46]

Moreover, the Navajos, while playing the role of Plains Indians, wore their hair down instead of in the traditional bun. Ordinarily, the hair was only taken down for washing, as a religious expression in a ceremony, or at death. The long strands were said to represent the rain that streams from the clouds as they float across the desert. To wear the hair otherwise is disrespectful to the holy beings. On the other hand, dressing up as a Sioux or a Cheyenne did not seem to bother the Navajos. Most informants commented that they had to wear old ragged clothes and that some of the elders would not allow their faces to be painted, but generally they approached the role-playing like any other job.[47]

The single most serious complaint echoed by most people was having to pretend to kill or be killed. John Adair and Sol Worth encountered a similar problem when they gave cameras to Navajos to make their own film. There were culturally defined topics and ways to film them that were unacceptable. Adair explains, "Apparently the use of a symbolic representation of a person or an object was closely tied to their feelings about the use of the actual person or the thing the image referred to."[48]

Navajo actors feared that what they did on the screen was a foreshadowing of what they could expect in the future. The Stanley brothers are a good example. People tell of how the white men constantly shot them as they rode horses or ambushed from the tops of cliffs. "Bullets" fired from slingshots splattered the rocks nearby before a rubber dummy replaced the human and toppled below. Or one of the men, astride a galloping horse, tumbled from his mount in a battlefield littered with the dead. These scenes "invited death to stalk the People." According to the Navajos, all of these men died because they had acted out these scenes so often that death became a reality.[49] This was true of others, such as Lee and Frank Bradley, Keith Smith, and sisters and relatives of these actors. "[All of them portrayed] 'death scenes' and all died at a young age. It's probably because they have done what our people are forbidden to do."[50] Some elders saw this fate as justified, reporting an underlying tension between the Navajos in Monument Valley and the "big names" from Kayenta. Supposedly most of the money stopped in Arizona and never made it across the state line to the Utah people, whose land was being used most frequently. A few Navajos indicate that this jealousy led to witchcraft, with dire effects.[51]

Some elders refused to participate in distasteful movie scenes. Older men insisted they would not be shot, although the younger ones laughed and joked about killing white men. When filming *Billy the Kid*, someone commented that when Billy died and was buried among the buttes, "[i]t felt like it was very real, . . . it was ugly and they [the actors] were in the midst of foretelling a tragedy."[52] Another man told of riding a horse through burning tentage for one movie, then expressed his feelings about the work: "If you get scared easily, it is not good. It is like you are going in there to die when you are part of moviemaking."[53]

Medicine men performed ceremonies to protect and cleanse those people who requested them. A "return to normalcy" prayer (Blessing Way); the Enemy Way; offerings of sacred white shell, turquoise, abalone, and jet; or a ceremony designed to remove a specific ill could be used to ward off harmful effects. It is believed that those people who are living today were the ones wise enough to take these measures. Others that are now suffering from the ill effects are having ceremonies performed to undo the curse they placed on themselves.[54]

Even Ford felt bad about the Navajos constantly being killed, but for a different reason. The script so often called for the Indians to lose that one author suggested the director filmed *Cheyenne Autumn* as an "apology" to Native Americans. Speaking of this film, Ford said,

> There are two sides to every story, but I wanted to show [the Indians'] point of view for a change. Let's face it—we've treated them very badly. It's a blot on our shield. We've cheated and robbed, killed, murdered and massacred, and everything else. But they kill one white man and God! out come the troops.[55]

Cheyenne Autumn (1964) was the last of the Ford films shot in Monument Valley. The end of an era had arrived. By 1973, the same year Ford died, the Navajo tribe opened a department of film to handle requests by moviemakers who wished to use this lovely backdrop of red rocks and sand. Charging $1,000 a day or more for professionals, the department keeps much of the money that used to trickle down to the people.[56] Movies like *Back to the Future III* and advertisements for everything from cars to batteries and cigarettes take advantage of the wide-open spaces to sell an image. In some respects, the image is not so different from the one that Ford created—wilderness, freedom, and the American Indians. But there is still that magical feeling when a person first enters the valley, the same feeling that fostered its early film history, when Indian played Indian.

CHAPTER NINE

DIGGING THE
BONES OF YÉ'IITSOH

Navajos in the Uranium Industry of Southeastern Utah

Navajos believe that during the time of creation, the earth was the home of many different types of evil creatures who derived from impure sexual practices. One of the most fearsome of these beings was Big God (Yé'iitsoh), whose father, Sun Bearer (Johonaa'éí), wrapped him in zigzag lightning and sent him to earth. The monster lived in a cave on Mount Taylor, dressed in flint armor, carried a large club, and sallied forth from his home in search of human prey. This tall, fierce being became a scourge to the Navajos.

One day Big God visited the home of Changing Woman and asked where her boys were. She denied they existed, explaining that the tracks he saw around her home were really made by her fist as she fashioned designs with her hand. After he left her twin sons emerged from hiding, vowed to get help from their father, Sun Bearer, then started on a journey filled with trials. After passing all of the tests along the way, as well as those given by their father, they returned to earth. From their father they procured hats, shirts, leggings, and moccasins, all of which were covered with flint, arrows of chain lightning, sheet lightning, sunbeam, and rainbow, as well as large stone knives. Before the Twins set forth to destroy the monsters, they tried their projectiles. After seeing their effectiveness, one remarked, "We cannot suffer in combat while we have such weapons as these."

They found Big God near Grants, New Mexico. He threw his four clubs at the Twins, but their supernatural power protected them. Sun Bearer helped the Twins by stunning the giant with lightning while they set to work with their own weapons. Flint flew from the monster's body, scattering over the land as he tottered and fell in the four directions, never to rise again. The boys killed and scalped their enemy, his blood flowing forth to become the lava beds outside of Grants. The victors tossed his head away, and it became Cabezon Peak, while his bones covered the ground, forming fields of petrified wood.

The Twins reported to Changing Woman what they had accomplished, but amid her rejoicing they felt faint and dizzy. She had Kingbird and Chickadee shoot spruce and pine arrows over them and treated the boys with lightning-struck herbs to get rid of Big God's ghost. This was the first Enemy Way ceremony held to cure a Navajo from the effects of war. The Twins also received names—Monster Slayer (Slayer of Alien Gods) and Born for Water—to honor their wonderful deed.[1]

Another story about Big God tells of how he had strong arms, clawlike hands, bones of stone, and long dark hair. He hated the Sun, could reach it at anyplace in the sky, and grappled with it at every opportunity. Big God lost fingers, hands, and limbs but had the power to regenerate them. The lost appendages were scattered over the land in the form of petrified wood (*Yé'iitsoh bits'in,* "Big God's bones"). Finally, the Sun killed the monster with "millions and millions of its rays," and today "the country north and south of the Colorado River over which the battles were fought is still covered with these bones."[2] Starting in the 1940s, Big God's bones meant big business.

The Colorado Plateau is dotted with rich deposits of petrified wood, found primarily in the Morrison and Chinle geologic layers of the earth's crust. Water eroded away the once-living matter of a tree, a bone, or other organic matter and replaced it with mineral deposits. Uranium, an element that easily dissolves and actively replaces organic materials, is often associated with these petrified objects. It floated in the waters that covered the land millions of years ago, finding its way along streambeds and in lakes, only to be incorporated into the once-living tissue of prehistoric life. And there it remained until men sought its power. Two of the largest deposits of uranium were found on the Navajo Reservation—one at Grants, New Mexico, the other in Monument Valley, Utah.

Uranium is found in the Morrison and Chinle strata of sandstone. Vanadium is also found in the Morrison formation but unlike uranium, is not radioactive. Long before there was interest in uranium, miners were searching out deposits of vanadium to be used in strengthening steel and fortifying paint.

The earliest attempt at vanadium mining in this region was by John Wetherill.[3] During World War I, promoters told him that if he could get a shipment of this ore to Flagstaff, they would pay him for it. He worked hard to fulfill this agreement but failed to obtain the price he felt he should have received. He lost interest until some other white men approached him in the 1940s for information about the location of the ore. Wetherill took the men to the two mines (later known as Monument One and Two), promised to help them work through the tribal bureaucracy, and went with them to Window Rock to present his claims. The men gave tribal officials the maps of the mines' locations and were promised that they would be given first consideration but, according to one account, lost both leases to Vanadium Corporation of America (VCA) through shady dealings.[4]

In 1944 the Office of Indian Affairs leased its first uranium claim in Monument Valley. The mine, located on the eastern tip of Oljeto Mesa, yielded fifty-two tons of vanadium the first year. The tribe was anxious to receive its 10 percent royalty, so when a group of miners led by Wayne Carroll and Lee Shumway bid $505 for the forty-acre claim, called Utah One, the government at Window Rock agreed.[5] The men set to work with relatively crude equipment and Navajo labor to gouge out the minerals located on the cliffs above. Monument One, owned and operated by VCA, opened soon after on the valley floor south of Oljeto.

The miners transported the ore in a cable-and-bucket system down to the loading platform and onto trucks for shipment to Moab and the scrutiny of Howard Balsley, purchaser for the Vitro Manufacturing Company of Pittsburgh, Pennsylvania. From there, equipment loaded the minerals on a train at Thompson, then shipped it back East. After a few years, Shumway and Carroll canceled their lease, closing the first mine to yield payments for vanadium on the Navajo Reservation.[6]

As atomic bombs exploded over Hiroshima and Nagasaki, the world suddenly awoke to the fruits of the Manhattan Project and the possibilities of nuclear fission. What had transpired in secret now became public, and Americans learned that the government had been advertising for vanadium but really wanted its companion, uranium, to work its magic. VCA notified the tribe that it was seeking rich deposits of uranium to mine and that a government-established royalty was available for those who provided the resources.[7] Although prospectors found many of the major uranium mines farther north on the Colorado Plateau in the vicinity of Moab, the news was enough to generate tremors in Monument Valley. The race for Big God's bones was on.

In 1949 Riley and Barbara Baker, living in Cameron, Arizona, stumbled onto four large petrified trees, some two hundred feet long, with lengthy yellow streaks of carnotite assaying at 60 percent uranium and 20 percent vanadium. The Atomic Energy Commission bought all uranium for national defense, at $4 a pound. Just this small amount was capable of releasing energy comparable to burning 150 million pounds of coal.[8] Not too much later mining opened in the Lukachukai Mountains and still later in the rich fields of the Grants Uranium Belt, one hundred miles long and twenty miles wide.

Harry Goulding, at his Monument Valley trading post, took a growing interest in the possibility of having mines in his own backyard. By June 1950 he, with the help of Navajos who brought in samples, had located seven deposits of uranium.[9] But it was nineteen-year-old Luke Yazzie who discovered the largest concentration. Yazzie had studied the ore samples that Goulding left on his countertop. When he found some heavy rocks with a yellow stripe through them, he hid them away, thinking that they might be gold. Eventually he showed the trader a sample and received a free soda pop, lunch, and the impression that he could become rich.

Goulding invited Denny Viles, field manager of VCA, to visit the site. The trader realized that he could not receive the royalties from this discovery, but he was anxious to improve the Navajos' standard of living, which in turn would benefit his own operation. He showed Viles the grinding poverty that was part of reservation life and exacted a promise that wages paid to Indians would be comparable to those paid to white men.[10]

Viles noted the clicks on his Geiger counter and took samples from the site; two years later Monument Two was in operation. All that Luke Yazzie got was a pick, a shovel, and a promise of continuous employment until the mine closed. He worked for fifteen years at a monthly salary of $130. During one part of a later exploration phase, miners drilled a hole not far from Luke's house and struck artesian water, an equally precious commodity for the Navajos living in a desert environment. One foreman suggested that even though no uranium was found, the hole should be cased to provide water for Luke and others in the area. Viles agreed to do so, but the sides collapsed and the project never reached fruition.[11]

According to Yazzie, "What they [Goulding and Viles] promised me at the beginning was a big lie. . . . They took advantage of me. It seems like they profited the most from the mine. . . . I feel like I helped everyone else, including Window Rock and the United States Army."[12] Goulding, on the other hand, believed that the mine would be bid on, no matter who found it. Later the policy changed so that a Navajo who located a deposit could stake his own claim and receive some of the benefits.

Soon others started the search that continued throughout the 1950s. Geiger counters issued to Navajos served as one of the primary tools of discovery. One person said she believed the instrument located gold by making a buzzing sound when it got close. Some prospectors tried to find ore by putting uranium on the end of a stick, then "witching" for it just as they would water. Others simply used their eyes to locate yellow streaks of rock where erosion had removed the sandstone face.[13] Eventually thirty-one mines of varying sizes were established on the reservation in southeastern Utah and northeastern Arizona.[14]

One unique method of locating uranium was through supernatural means—crystal gazing. Only a few Navajos mentioned using or hearing about these techniques; others claimed this practice is not harmonious with traditional beliefs. This form of divination depends on supernatural power, prayers, and songs. The knowledge and ability to use it is a gift given to men and women who faithfully live the principles of Navajo religion.

In crystal gazing, the medicine man communicates with Big Star (part of Scorpius), which reflects its light into the crystal to reveal an answer. One medicine man is said to have located a deposit by performing the ceremony from the summit of a hill. Through the crystal, he saw a "fire on top of the mesa," told the miners where to drill, and, sure enough, they found uranium. The ceremony cost $200.[15]

By means of various techniques, both Navajos and Anglos located uranium. Small deposits throughout the Monument Valley region gave rise to mines such as Daylight, Sunlight, Starlight, and Moonlight. But the biggest one, Monument Two in Cane Valley south of Mexican Hat, was by far the most important. John Meadows, foreman of the Navajo crews that worked there, described the mine as having excellent grade ore close to the surface. Originally this site had been an old riverbed that had become dammed by wood that eventually became petrified. The uranium within extended for a mile, was 500 to 600 feet wide, and approximately 40 feet deep. Black pitchblende and yellow carnotite were the two most prevalent forms of ore extracted from the mine and sent to the VCA mills.[16]

Workers flocked to the mines for the new employment opportunities. At any given time, approximately 140 Navajos drilled, blasted, dug, and shoveled their way to a steady paycheck of $1.25 an hour at Monument Two. Only 10 percent were white workers, involved primarily in the technical or managerial aspects of the operation. Experienced laborers teamed up with new men and taught them how to operate a loader, set a fuse, or run a mucking machine. Those who had not gotten experience working in the mines of southwestern Colorado were not as easily employable and so in some instances had to plead, saying they did not have anything to eat and needed a job. Traders like Goulding or Ray Hunt at the Mexican Hat post spread the word when vacancies arose. Once employed and trained, however, a skilled miner could stay at work by moving from one mine to the next, as the old ones petered out. Those who did not stay in the Monument Valley area could move to other sites in the Four Corners region.[17]

On October 14, 1949, tribal policies changed so that Navajos could obtain a prospecting permit, lay claim to a mine in conjunction with the tribe (who received not less than 10 percent of the profit), and receive part of a personal royalty.[18] Seth Bigman, for instance, went into partnership with an Anglo named Leonard Young but had to split the profit three ways—the tribe, the mining company, and himself. Theoretically, he was to receive 10 percent of the proceeds, amounting to between $15,000 and $17,000 a year for three years.[19] For political reasons, Young did not receive any of this royalty, but he did operate a trading post just outside of the Starlight mine until it closed.

Cecil Parrish and Koli Black had to split their 10 percent royalty after they received a permit from Window Rock. They also employed Navajos while working in partnership with an Anglo company. Harvey and Ada

Black signed a contract with a white man to help work their claim but felt they did not receive in payments what was rightfully theirs. The mine remained open for less than a year. The Blacks believed that one reason this and other mines closed was because of the accidents that started to plague many of the small, poorly supervised operations.[20]

The construction at mining sites varied according to the size and sophistication of the company working it. Out of the desert sprang the headquarters, air compressors, and loading areas for the ore. Next came housing for the whites living at Monument Two, while the Navajos, some coming from across the reservation, lived in makeshift homes, with relatives or, in some cases, in their cars. An estimated 75 percent of them took up residence within a mile of the Monument Two operation.[21] Miners bought their own food out of their two-week paycheck which usually amounted to about $100 in the early days.[22]

Water in the desert was at a premium. The first mines depended on water hauled from Kayenta or Goulding's post in a 450-gallon truck. VCA drilled wells and either pumped the water into tanks or left them capped for future use. For many of the Navajo workers, the only satisfactory way to get clean after a hard day's work was with a sweat bath built near their camp. Some mines later installed showers and facilities for washing clothes, but many Navajos complained that the grease and grime never left the fabric.[23]

The average day for a miner followed a routine that seldom varied. At one point, Monument Two operated three eight-hour shifts, while the smaller mines had only one day crew. Shone Holiday, who worked in many of the mines in Monument Valley, tells of his experiences, which are representative of those of many others. He arose at dawn, sprinkled his white corn meal to the east, and said his morning prayers. After breakfast he packed his lunch, walked to the mine, and (in later years) donned rubber work clothes. He next entered the shaft to prepare his equipment: turn on the compressor, lubricate the jackhammer, and move it to the site of the day's work. A carbide headlamp, later replaced with a battery-powered light, provided sufficient illumination to guide him along the passageways. In some mines water that had seeped in during the night had to be pumped out before the work started. One of the men would take readings to find where the most uranium was located; then Shone drilled that area by sections, for about three hours. When it was

Underground miners faced backbreaking labor and danger. Navajo prayers and
ceremonies gave protection and perspective to what the workers faced. Photo
from Milton Snow Collection, Navajo Nation Museum.

time for lunch, some of the men ate in the mines, in the midst of radioactive dust and grime. Others, like Shone, chose to go outside to eat,
inadvertently prolonging their lives by not ingesting uranium particles.

Following lunch, the men placed wires, caps, and dynamite into the
holes they drilled; then all but two men left before lighting the fuses. In
larger mines, the night crew did the blasting so that the dust and debris
could settle. Although later mines had blowers to clear out the fumes
that smelled like butane, the bothersome odors of dust, gas, and powder
permeated the passageways. In mines where no blowers were used, the
men complained of dizziness and severe headaches. The final job of separating the ore and removing the debris preceded sending the two products to the surface in carts or buckets, where the men loaded the ore for
shipment.[24]

Mining has always been a dangerous livelihood. Accidents from
cave-ins, with the equipment, or with explosives were just a few of the
common hazards that plagued especially the smaller, more impromptu
mines. A few harrowing experiences illustrate what many Navajo miners

faced each day. Shone Holiday lost a cousin in the mine they were working together when at the end of the day a section of ceiling the size of an
acre collapsed. The workers retrieved the body, but it was too late to
save the life. Another time, he had a heated argument with his supervisor over whether the columns supporting the roof should be removed
for their rich ore. The boss got his way and "chased us all down into the
shaft." They were barely finished when the roof collapsed and buried
the machinery. One man tells of workers remaining down in the mine
when explosives were detonated. Others mention mud slides, falling off
platforms that were used to stand on when drilling the ceiling, and the
small daily injuries from not wearing steel-toed boots, breathing without nose and mouth filters, working without proper ventilation, and
failing to check levels of radiation exposure. Contaminated clothing,
equipment, and materials found their way to the homes of workers,
where wives and children unwittingly came in contact with radiation.[25]

Many white miners in other parts of the Four Corners region encountered similar dangers, resulting in maiming and death; it was not just a
Navajo "problem."[26] The results for both groups were the same—quick
death or injury or slow death from cancer or respiratory ailments.

Tragedy also struck outside the mines. All of the ore had to be shipped
by truck to various mills—at Monticello, Utah; Naturita, Colorado; and
later Durango, Colorado. Monument Two had as many as thirty trucks
operating at any given time. One route took the ore through Teec Nos
Pos, Shiprock, then Durango, while a second route moved its cargo north
over the cable bridge at Mexican Hat. The cable bridge's weight capacity
was limited to eight tons, so the large trucks unloaded their uranium into
smaller shuttle vehicles that ferried the ore across the bridge to a pile at
the top of the hill, where it was again loaded back into the fleet of large
trucks to begin the long haul through Bluff and Blanding to the mills.

One man learned of the wisdom of the shuttle system too late. His
truck and trailer, burdened with heavy equipment, exceeded the eight-
ton limit. By the time he reached the bridge and read the sign, he had
maneuvered the vehicle into a position where he could not turn around.
He shifted into low gear, opened the door of the cab, and prayed that the
load capacity sign was wrong. It was not. When the truck and trailer
reached the bottom sag in the bridge, the whole section gave way. Truck,
machinery, and driver plummeted to the water thirty feet below and

sank into the brown silt flow of the San Juan River. Luckily, the man jumped free of the mess, swam two hundred feet downstream, dragged himself ashore, and roared out with a thunderous "I quit" that echoed along the canyon walls.[27]

Another driver was not as fortunate. After a new steel bridge replaced the cable structure, a man piloting a truck and trailer lost his brakes and could not find a turnout. He leaned on his horn as he careened down the hill, across the bridge, and into the cliff running perpendicular to the road. The truck killed not only the driver but also three Navajo men sitting in their GMC pickup nearby and splashed uranium ore from the base to the top of the forty-foot sandstone wall. The men of the cleanup crew did not realize that people besides the driver were involved in the accident until they discovered the twisted wreckage and bodies at the bottom of the ore.[28]

With such a potentially dangerous environment both in and out of the mines, it was only natural for people to seek protection. To the Navajos, this often translated into using supernatural means to ward off harm. This approach tied directly to their perception of the earth as an animate, sentient being infused with the power of holy beings. For at least some Navajos, the spiritual, supernatural aspects of digging into a living creature required prayers, offerings, and ceremonial understanding.

Different myths, the basis of ceremonies, provided explanations of how the supernatural forces of the earth operated.[29] Often the earth was associated with Changing Woman, a beneficent deity who provides sustenance and shelter for her offspring. According to the Navajos, "Digging hurts our mother. What she was living on, her veins, we are digging up." So prayers and ceremonies were offered in propitiation.[30]

Talking God and Growling God could be petitioned through prayer for forgiveness or for help in mining operations. George Tom, in reflecting on his mining experience, felt that the earth should not have been disturbed, but because it had been, lives were lost. He said, "Because we did the forbidden to our earth, . . . the earth's waters intervened from within and refused to let mining proceed." He also believed that "certain rocks were capable of moving around or relocating to different areas. They were hard to find; only 'lucky' people could find them [ore deposits], whereas if another person were to drill in that same spot, he would find nothing."[31]

Another man believed that people who did not show proper respect to the rocks were the ones who got hurt. Because these miners had no "sacredness in their manner" and joked about their activities, the mines held danger. On the other hand, the rocks would "feel kindly to the people who were using them to pay for food for their families," as long as they showed proper respect. According to this informant, the only person he knew who was hurt in the mines was a man who kidded about his job; a vehicle flipped over on him, serving as a reminder that his attitude should change.[32] Shone Holiday summarized humankind's relationship to the earth: "We [Navajos] believe that the holy beings are everywhere. They protect us from harmful things if we ask them. If the individual fails on his part, then he is vulnerable to injury."[33]

Prayers and offerings were an important part of this protection. Medicine men and workers made sacrifices of *ntł'iz* (white shell, turquoise, abalone, and jet) to the earth, mountains, and mesas in sacred spots before entering the mines. They also said prayers to and for their equipment, that it would be wrapped within a shield of protection to prevent harm.[34] The form of these prayers followed a pattern. For example:

> You say Mother Earth and then you say First Man and then Mountain Woman. These three are in a group. You say, "Here I am making an offering to you. From here you will be my shield. With this I will live long. You will remember me, and you will hold off the monsters [sickness and death] from me." You would do this to rocks that had slid towards you. In this way it is a protection prayer. It is the same with mining when you are working with rocks.[35]

John Holiday understands the efficacy of prayer. When he was a young man, he worked in many of the small mines in Monument Valley. At one work site, he had an experience he would never forget.

> When mining, I usually left my sacred corn pollen pouch at home. It had rained that workday, and I was on my way to get some water from a tank located at the mine when I suddenly saw my pollen pouch on the ground before me. I had a dream the night before, in which I was told to make an offering of pollen to the steep cliff beside the mine area. It will be dangerous if you don't,

something told me. It was strange, but I picked up my pollen pouch and headed for the cliff as soon as I brought back the pail of water. I went to make my offering as I had been told to do in my dream. I prayed for my safety on the job among other things, then I went home to cook supper. I met my father-in-law on the way home, and he asked me if there were any job openings at the mine. I told him yes, and so the next day we went to the supervisor and got permission for us to work together. . . . We blasted the area close to the cliff in my dreams and hastily cleared the muck with large coal shovels. As soon as we took out the last load, I scooted closer to the tunnel, then suddenly, with a loud crash, the whole roof collapsed where we had been working just minutes before. Somehow my pollen pouch had followed me here and enabled me to perform the sacred offering. If I had not done so, I would not be alive today. I miraculously survived and crawled through the narrow passage outside. Everyone was surprised and amazed to see me. They kept asking me how I had survived. . . . The close relationship you have with the holy ones pays off throughout your life. They take care of you and keep you from harm and danger.[36]

More formal ceremonies also helped to encircle a miner with protection. Blessing Way rites allowed a person to live in harmony in some of the most dangerous circumstances. Sometimes the rituals were performed at the job site but more often in the seclusion of a hogan. The medicine man invoking these powers named all of the sacred mountains in his songs and prayers. The prayers were continued in the home even after the man had gone to work. "We have to pray for everything, wherever we may go, and whoever we are." Shone Holiday even went to a Hopi practitioner who ritually removed small stones from his body. He described them as "oblong in shape—like the ones the drillers get with their drills." He continued, "I too would have died by now if I had not done this, or said my sacred 'forgiving prayers.'"[37]

Navajo medicine men and women also have knowledge of plants that can effect a cure. Although the specific name of the plant has not been identified, it grows on top of Dibé Ntsaa (Hesperus Peak, Colorado) and is said to cure both cancer and tuberculosis. The juice from the roots of the plant is drunk, acting either as an emetic or passing from the bowels as it carries the sickness with it. The cure is credited with saving some miners' lives.[38]

Given the different worldviews of the two cultures, one may ask how Anglos and Navajos got along with one another. In general, Anglos and Indians appeared to have a harmonious relationship. John Meadows supervised the work crews because he had been raised at a trading post and spoke the language. He felt that the Navajos were excellent workers, often more dedicated than some of his white charges. The Navajos had confidence in themselves. They undertook tasks about which they knew little but completed them surprisingly well. Unlike the Anglo employees, however, they occasionally requested release time to attend ceremonies. Meadows understood their importance and made arrangements for the men while maintaining the necessary crews. On the weekends many of the workers returned home to their families, sheep, cattle, and "old sand-blown outfit."[39]

Not all of the supervisors were as understanding as Meadows. Fred Yazzie complained that he had been pushed to his physical limit by hard labor with barely a chance to rest. He said that the workers were constantly being told, "'Hurry and dig that out; hurry and fill this up.' . . . So we were in constant motion with our work. . . . The idea was to dig it up fast and give no thought to the workers."[40] But even with all of the hurry, at least some Navajos took time to draw with the soot from their carbide lamps on the smooth rock faces of the mine walls. Pictures of horses, men, and daily life dotted the surfaces and reminded the laborers of life above ground.[41]

Some of the Navajo workers already spoke English, while others learned it on the job. According to tradition, they bestowed names on their fellow workers and supervisors, regardless of race. The selection of a name might depend on a person's physical qualities or something he had done. For instance, Meadows's name was Big Eyes' Boy, because the Navajos remembered his trader father. Another person might be called Big Tooth, No Finger, or White Hair. One unfortunate Navajo miner received his title at the Mexican Hat post. He saw a man eating a can of pineapple and asked where he could get some. The diner explained where it was in the store, then watched the man disappear into the building. Once inside, the Navajo went to the place, selected a can that looked like the type the other man had, paid for it, then opened it. Much to his dismay, he had purchased a container of sauerkraut and was known by that name from then on.[42]

From the Navajo point of view, some of the white men at the mines were making a lot of money without doing much work: "The white bosses came inside the mines only once in a while. They feared the mines and so came at the beginning of a shift long enough to give instructions, then leave."[43] Some felt that the whites were cheating them because they could not read. And the supervisors demanded greater amounts of ore be wrenched from the earth. Others believed that they were not told of the dangers and that the work would "start to kill them in the future. . . . They would hide all of this dreadful information because they wanted [men] to work."[44] Some workers justified the destruction of the earth because the white men told them to do it. Shone felt that he should not be involved in mining but justified it this way: "[S]ince I did it according to the white men, then it is not my doing."[45] His prayers of forgiveness were sufficient to protect him. Still others, even today, appreciated the employment. One man said, "[It allowed me to] walk my way through life being paid for what I did."[46]

Not all of the blame for problems was fixed on the Anglos. True, in Navajo thinking, the white man has special powers and gifts that the Diné do not have. Anglos go to school where they learn about something that allows them to make a lot of money. They could take the things out of the earth, make millions of dollars, and give little in return. But it was the government in Window Rock that approved the transactions without consulting the people. Fred Yazzie believes that the tribal government "should have thought of us when they made these decisions." "But," he said, "they always sided with the Anglos. . . . We forgot to use our songs and prayers and so we were just taken advantage of. . . . They took the plate of food away from us. We have nothing. The Window Rock people believe we are not worth a thing."[47]

One of the important reasons, besides money, that the Navajos dug uranium was because of their patriotism. During the early days of mining in Monument Valley, World War II raged; in the late 1940s and 1950s, it was the cold war, with its attendant missile race, that provided the impetus. The bones of Yé'iitsoh, destroyed with lightning arrows, were being unearthed for the stunning power trapped within, waiting to be released. Uranium, conceived through war in the myths, was needed for new conflicts.

Two other stories illustrate the relationship between war and uranium. One tells of the white man's god, The One Who Wins You as a Prize, who gambled and won the earth and all of its people.[48] As he rested on Sleeping Ute Mountain, a holy being, jealous of his wealth, stunned him with a rainbow, seized his powers, and, among other things, created Walking Rock Monster. As the newly formed creature started to move about, it suddenly exploded; its body parts, and its power, seeped into the earth where it is found today as uranium and petroleum.

At this same time the Sun's lightning arrows, rays, and other deadly weapons were placed in the underworlds beneath this one. "It is said that if anybody should reinvent these deadly weapons, there will be more enemies." The white man's god spoke four times and said, "I will return some day to win back your language, your mind, your plans, your songs and prayers—everything." He has returned.[49] Thus the exploitation of uranium in arms development is linked to current events that are affecting the Navajos today.

Scanty information exists about the second story, but the general idea known as *béésh nilashí* concerns the same war-making ability that the Anasazi and some Navajos held at the beginning of the world. There were actually two applications of this power—that which was used by man to destroy and that which lay latent in the earth's crust or in the four cardinal directions. The Anasazi learned how to control and fight with electricity and other supernatural forces. When a person digs in the earth, he releases these types of powers that can wreak havoc unless prayers are invoked for protection. Death and destruction penetrate the person's supernatural defense system as a self-inflicted punishment, because he did not show proper respect to these forces.

Long ago the gods took this knowledge and control away from the Anasazi and some Navajos and placed it in the four directions, where it has remained latent until recently. Now the Anglos have learned how to use it—in the form of electricity, nuclear fusion, nuclear fission, and particle beam lasers. These weapons are synonymous with what the Twins used as lightning arrows, rainbow arrows, sunbeam arrows, and sheet lightning arrows. These powers had been resting. "When they come together, they will destroy us. Now they are calm and observing us. But they are being used by the Anglos. For this reason they [Anglos] can walk anywhere. They dig up the earth, walk underwater, walk in the heavens, and go up to the moon. For us [Navajos], we cannot do this. . . . This will kill us all in future times."[50]

Thus Navajo mythology explains the role that uranium and other minerals play in the wars of today. Many of the miners understand that their efforts underground were part of a plan for protection against foreign enemies. The government praised them because they "did their share of work to help keep their freedom in the United States."[51]

In 1943 Harry Goulding wrote a letter to Dwight D. Eisenhower, general commander in chief of Allied forces. The trader, hoping to counter German propaganda that the Navajos hated the Anglos and refused to support the war effort, had thirty-five miners place their thumbprints on a letter stating how they hoped vanadium would make the "guns and airplanes and munitions . . . strong to help win the war." Eisenhower responded with gratitude. Goulding said, "Ay gosh, the dust was aflying out of the smoke hole coming out of that mine after that!"[52]

Navajos responded to the sense of urgency in the war against the "metal hats" (Germans). The dangerous conditions in the smaller mines were excused because the war was in progress. "[The government] wanted bullets to be made, . . . so everything was done fast. . . . We went in there [the mines] to retain freedom for our people. . . . It was for the young men and women that we did this and also for our land."[53]

The long-term effects of the uranium industry were felt in two ways by the Navajos—economically and physically. Mining brought to the reservation a boom-and-bust economy that served as a catalyst for development. Navajos and Anglos worked side by side to build new roads stretching over miles of desert where none existed a few years previously. Some were built in almost inaccessible places, good only for a specific mine, while others served as main arteries that are still used today. The roads to Mexican Water, through Comb Ridge, down the Moki Dugway, and over the new steel bridge at Mexican Hat and those branching out through the Oljeto and Mexican Hat areas are examples of improvements made in the transportation network of southeastern Utah because of the uranium industry. Texas Zinc, for instance, paid about $3 million in 1956 for thirty-three miles of road that stretched from the Natural Bridges area to four miles north of Mexican Hat so that their newly established mill could process off-reservation uranium.[54]

Money poured into the trading posts in Oljeto, Starlight, Monument Valley, and Mexican Hat and the stores at Bluff, helping to move the Navajo economy from pawn to cash. The posts extended more credit to their Navajo customers, then waited for payday to receive their due. Mining companies also allowed borrowing against a worker's paycheck to purchase nails, boards, hammers, shovels, and other hardware.[55] Wages slowly increased from $100 every two weeks to $200 to $300, to keep up with growing demands and rising prices. Workers bought their own food, provided their own lodging, and still had enough to invest in a car or a truck for personal transportation. The Navajos moved ever deeper into America's cash economy.

With between one-third and one-half of all the nation's uranium reserves located in the Four Corners region, it is not surprising that the Navajo tribe worked closely with the Atomic Energy Commission, which purchased all high-grade uranium until 1970.[56] The economic boom brought by uranium mining is illustrated in the tribalwide figures over a four-year period. In 1950 the Navajo Nation garnered $65,755 from the industry; in 1954 the sum jumped to $650,000.[57] This was a significant amount added to the tribal coffers; however, Utah Navajos felt that they received few direct benefits. And although Texas Zinc built its processing mill at Halchita in 1956, an estimated 90 percent of its ore came from off-reservation mines. The mill, with its 775-ton-per-day capacity, did not cease operation until 1969, but by the mid-1960s, the relative prosperity associated with Navajo mining started its downward spiral.[58]

Of equal concern is the price in workers' health exacted by mining. Historically, the Navajos were introduced to uranium long before the first ore truck roared out of Monument Valley. People used to go to the Monument Two area to collect finely powdered red ochre to mix in fat for a sunburn cream called *chííh*. Later, Geiger counters recorded high levels of radioactivity near the sites where the red ochre was found. Other colored earths—white, yellow, and black—were used in ceremonies in sand paintings and as body paints. Whether the materials were radioactive is left to conjecture, but it is probable that some of them were toxic.[59]

Ada Black tells of how Navajo families used to eat a white clay found in diggings near Comb Ridge. Yellow rocks from other uranium mines were also brought home, boiled in water, ground to powder, and added as a food extender. The people also drank the water left over from this process. She explains, "At that time, we did not know the yellow rock was dangerous . . . and now all those people are dead. . . . I offered my prayers to the rocks where the mine is; this way it does not bother you. We [Ada and her husband] both reached old age even though we really ate it."[60]

Men drank the cool, clear water they found below ground as they ate their lunch with uranium-covered hands. Some miners put pipes in the walls to conduct the water to a certain location, making drinking easier. Pumps also pushed the water out of the mines, where it collected in pools from which sheep and goats drank, contaminating the meat eaten later. Ironically, at one point in its operation, Monument Two had such a contaminated water supply from nonradioactive sources that people feared an outbreak of typhoid fever. Instead of improving the system, health officials just immunized the workers.[61] Even during after-hours, the miners suffered from a different type of pollution—overindulgence in alcoholic beverages made available by cash in the pocket and a ready supply of vendors in towns surrounding the reservation.

Another type of attrition occurred through workplace accidents. One man barely survived and was crippled for life when a large rock slid down on his lower back and hips. Another miner died in a cave-in. His supervisor quickly whacked together a coffin, laid the corpse inside, and nailed the box shut. A bulldozer dug a hasty grave, the workers buried the body, and the mine was closed. The family received no compensation. One miner was standing near a large oxygen tank when its cap blew off. The pressure threw him several feet before he landed at the entrance of another tunnel with "hundreds of gravel stones etched under the skin all over [his] body."[62]

Some men worked so hard that they injured their health. John Holiday, for example, drilled 280 holes and loaded them with explosives and fuses during his graveyard shift. His supervisors were astonished at his accomplishment but transferred him to another part of the operation because they feared that he was overexerting himself. He next worked at the mouth of the mine, breaking large boulders, until one day he blacked out and awoke paralyzed. Eventually his normal range of motion returned, but he ceased work under doctor's orders. He said, "My job had failed me, and now I could not work like that again."[63]

Yet perhaps the most debilitating effects of mining came in its aftermath. Fred Yazzie, when asked to comment about what he said to his wife when he returned home from work, replied, "'Oh, my head, my eyes hurt. I am going deaf.' . . . It was dangerous and gave us terrible headaches; the pain would go into our eyes. . . . Many men died; it bothered their vital organs."[64] He also mentioned sores that covered men's bodies, from which they eventually died. His lesions have now turned to scabs, but others were not as fortunate. Little wonder that cancer, in Navajo, is translated as the "sore that never heals." A few men received partial compensation for these ills but found it too difficult to live on such a small sum and went back to the mines against their physicians' orders.[65] The choice for some was to work and eat or sit by and hope to survive.

All Navajo miners today mention how many of their fellow workers and relatives associated with the industry are now dead. Very few good quantitative studies have been done on the thousands of men—Anglo and Navajo—who worked in the mines. The toll uranium took on health, however, can be found in the 1982 hearings held by the Senate's Committee on Labor and Human Resources to determine radiation exposure compensation. During this meeting, Harry Tome, a member of the Navajo Tribal Council's Environmental Protection Commission, painted a representative picture from a survey of sixteen miners. At the time of this hearing, the men were relatively young—an average age of 54.4 years old—with an annual income of $5,184. Fourteen of the sixteen men had averaged fifteen years in the mines, sometime between the 1940s and 1950s, and thirteen of them suffered from "serious medical problems." Only four had medical insurance, and many were too young to receive Social Security benefits, Medicare, and Medicaid.[66]

Perry Charley, who worked for the tribe's Division of Health Improvement, testified from personal knowledge of twenty deaths directly associated with uranium mining. Fourteen of these men had died from lung cancer, five from respiratory failure, and one from "another type of cancer." He also stated that his agency had "documented that 50% of the miners examined, who are living within the Shiprock Agency, have clinical and radiological evidence of chronic lung disease."[67]

These Senate hearings bore fruit very slowly. In 1990 the U.S. Supreme Court determined that it could not hear the case since the uranium industry was immune from suit from the 1940s to the 1970s because of its governmental status. However, Congress passed the Radiation Exposure Compensation Act, stipulating an award of up to $100,000 to deserving miners, widows, or children if the parents were deceased. President George Bush signed the law, and Congress eventually appropriated funds for the compensation.[68]

The wheels of progress have moved slowly. Although there have been some positive moves, such as completing the burial of the tailings at the Mexican Hat mill in 1994, individual Navajos have still had problems.[69] Briefly, each year millions of dollars are allocated to help miners and their families. By 1996 a total of 324 of 788 Navajo families who had filed received payments.[70] The filing process has proven lengthy. The U.S. Department of Justice has the responsibility to determine if an individual qualifies for compensation. Couples who had traditional weddings and lacked a marriage certificate find it difficult to prove their marital status and subsequent eligibility. Lawyers' fees gobble up 10 percent or more of what could have gone to the victims, and documentation of mining careers is sometimes hard to obtain. Many Navajo miners have trouble understanding and have little faith in this bureaucratic system.

In 1998 the *Navajo Times* still carried articles on the lawsuits, one of which, "Miners Finding Compensation Hard to Collect," summarizes the frustration with the legal process. One miner put it this way: "The Navajo people kept their word and produced the uranium. Now the United States needs to deliver on the promises it made to us."[71]

In summarizing the Navajo experience in Monument Valley, it is valid to criticize the errors of the past, although some of them were unintentional. No doubt big business and big government prospered at the expense of the "little man"—both Indian and Anglo—during this era. Certainly greater care should have been taken, even considering the limited knowledge available, to protect and help the Navajos, whose only insurance was prayer.

Mining was dangerous, and many workers came away having been crippled or sickened with different kinds of cancer. There is little that can truly compensate for the tragic losses. Many of these miners worked hard and were motivated not only by the desire to earn money but also by the desire to protect their country. Just as the Twins proved their sincerity and skill to Johonaa'éí before being entrusted with powerful tools of destruction, so too did these miners prove their ability to work long and hard under dangerous conditions. And as Monster Slayer remarked, echoing sentiments that resonated during the cold war, "We cannot suffer in combat while we have weapons such as these." Once the Twins had killed Yé'iitsoh and his bones lay across the land, they returned to their mother, Changing Woman, and proudly reported their deed. So also can Navajo miners be proud of what they have accomplished, as they leave the remaining bones of Yé'iitsoh to lie in the earth for a long time to come.

CHAPTER TEN

POVERTY, POLITICS, AND PETROLEUM

The Utah Navajos and the Aneth Oil Field

Yé'iitsoh's bones were not the only things left behind during this time when the land was "soft," still going through its creative process. Other monsters inhabited the land, searching out and destroying the Diné. Many of these creatures assumed different forms and powers: one killed with its eyes; another pushed unsuspecting travelers off cliffs; another skewered its victims with its large horns; still others flew in the air, carried off their prey, and smashed them on the jagged peak of Shiprock, New Mexico.

The Twins, Monster Slayer and Born for Water, set about ridding the People of these monsters. The remains of the vanquished foe—dinosaur tracks and fossils—still dot the landscape. The sands of Red Mesa, Arizona, were stained with the blood of a monster that killed with its breath, and remnants of other creatures are found in the igneous and sandstone rock formations that cover Navajo land. Each serves as a reminder of the battle once waged to free the People from destruction.

Some of the monsters and their body parts survived in different forms to eventually help the Navajo. For instance, flint came from the armor of Yé'iitsoh. From the flying monsters came the eagle that provides bones for whistles and feathers for ceremonies, the owl that prophesies man's future, and small birds to beautify the earth. Tracking Bear Monster gave from his body yucca fruit for nourishment, soap from its roots, plus needle and thread from its spines.[1] The list goes on.

Monster Slayer allowed some less harmful creatures, personified abstract qualities, to exist. Cold Woman, who brings freezing temperatures, survived because otherwise the earth would become too hot, the springs would dry, and the trees would die. The Twins did not kill Hunger, Drowsiness, and Old Age, because they helped one to appreciate different aspects of life. Poverty, portrayed as a filthy old man and woman dressed in rags with little to call their own, were spared. "If we were to die, people would wear the same clothes day after day and year after year. . . . They would have no reason to replace anything, no cause to improve upon the tools they are accustomed to using."[2]

The blood of the monsters killed in various parts of the reservation seeped into the cracks and fissures of the earth and settled in the rock strata. Remaining in its liquid form, it is known today as oil. The power that had once given life to the monsters lay at rest in the ground, as did many of the body parts buried by Monster Slayer at the end of the conflict. Until the first quarter of the twentieth century, oil on Navajo lands remained largely undiscovered and untouched.

Poverty, however, did not rest and had no trouble surviving. Especially on the Utah portion of the Navajo Reservation, considered peripheral to most of the tribe's activity, there never seemed enough of anything to go around. Even in the 1960s and 1970s, a time of apparent abundance, when oil flowed freely from pumps in the Aneth region, there were too many factions, too much political maneuvering to overcome the monster.

This chapter examines the actors, many of whom appeared to be well intentioned yet at odds with each other, and the events that came into play in the development of natural resources on tribal lands. While history may not repeat itself, the Aneth oil field raises concerns that other Native American groups might contemplate in economic development.

As this story unfolds, one of its most prominent motifs is complexity. Unlike the Twins, who were tested and triumphed through supernatural aid, the various groups acting in the 1960s and 1970s were not fortunate. There was no set of clearly defined champions to assist and protect the People. There was not even agreement on the goal and how to obtain it. Instead, each faction—federal, tribal, state, and local—had its own agenda for change and its own philosophy on how to solve some very real problems. Although most of the participants were well meaning, the end result was disappointing to the People. Self-defeating political maneuvers blunted or deflected the lightning arrows of significant change.

The Utah portion of the Navajo Reservation was initially carved from the public domain because of expanding population and livestock pressures. President Arthur created this Utah Strip by executive order in 1884, hoping to quell a contest for grazing rights between Navajos and white settlers. With the additions of the Aneth–Montezuma Creek area in 1905 and the Aneth Extension–Paiute Strip in 1933, the stage was set for future economic growth.

One important understanding that came from the 1933 negotiations was that the tribe allow oil exploration and leasing of the land in the Aneth Extension, with 37 1/2 percent of the royalties coming from the oil and gas being paid to the state of Utah. These funds would subsequently be used for "Navajos and such other Indians" living on this section, with the remainder going to the tribe.[3] The money was to go toward education, road construction, and the general benefit of the Navajos. The law expanded in 1968 to include all Navajos living on the Utah portion of the reservation.

Starting in 1953, Humble Oil and Shell Oil initiated agreements with the tribe and the state of Utah to exploit the rich petroleum reserves locked beneath the Aneth lands. By February 1956 the Texas Company (predecessor of Texaco) was hard at work in Aneth. In its first full year of production, the field yielded nearly 1.3 million barrels of oil, which increased to over 30 million barrels by 1959. Rapidly the area became known as the "giant" Aneth field.[4]

Beginning in November 1956, the Navajo Nation officially opened its doors to general bidding on the 230,000 acres of oil-rich reservation lands in southeastern Utah. An estimated 500 to 600 oilmen attended the first session in Window Rock, Arizona. Two days later they left behind more than $27 million in lease money and an agreement that the Navajos and Utah would receive rentals plus 12 1/2 percent of the gross value of any oil produced.[5] Thus concluded what the Bureau of Indian Affairs termed the largest sale in its history. Surely now the mythical creatures called Poverty would be driven from the reservation.

In 1956 alone, long before its peak, the Aneth oil field yielded $34.5 million in royalties to the tribe.[6] With a population of more than eighty thousand members, the Navajo Nation decided against making a per capita distribution of the money, which would amount to an estimated

$425. Instead the leaders invested the royalties in services such as education and economic development. Much of this money, however, remained on the central part of the reservation and not in the periphery where the oil wells producing the wealth were located.

The Utah Indian Commission (later the Division of Indian Affairs) and the Utah State Legislature entered the picture in 1959 when a three-member board received responsibility to contract for services for the Utah Navajos based on oil royalties of $632,000. On July 27 Governor George D. Clyde attended the first meeting and charged the group to carry out the law. The commission, composed of a chairman who was a member at large, an Indian member, and a citizen from San Juan County, undertook the awesome task of improving conditions across the Utah reservation that eventually encompassed the lands from Aneth to Navajo Mountain.[7]

What appeared to be a huge sum of money rapidly diminished as it was dispersed over a vast, isolated region. While road development, health clinics, economic endeavors, and education filled the agenda of the committee, each geographic area had its own requirements, so numerous and diverse that a full-time administrative organization was necessary. In 1971 the Utah Navajo Development Council (UNDC), with an all-Navajo board, sprang from a previously established organization, the San Juan Resource Development Council, to meet the growing urgency of delivering necessary services. From a fledgling organization, UNDC expanded rapidly. At its height it administered funding from forty-five sources, but the most visible to the public was oil royalties.[8] UNDC appeared to be meeting the needs of many.

The disbursement of funds by the Navajo Nation and state administration handling the funds for the Utah Navajos now followed a clearly defined pattern. The tribal government received income from oil in three ways: first, the oil companies paid a bonus for the privilege of leasing oil lands; second, annual rentals of $1.25 per acre were paid on leased areas; and third, royalties were paid on the value of production. While lease-signing bonuses could provide a sudden windfall for the tribe, such as in 1957 when oil companies paid $33 million in bonuses, royalty payments were the most stable and significant source of income from oil production.[9]

The exact amount of income received from Aneth royalties is difficult to determine, as there are wide discrepancies in the available literature. The Utah Navajo administration averaged $1,352,821 from royalties between 1960 and 1991.[10] According to tribal sources, the royalty money from oil and gas rapidly became the "backbone" of tribal income, contributing from 50 to 80 percent to the annual income.[11]

The Utah Navajos, however, benefited very little from the increased tribal expenditures. The Navajo government believed that the royalty money the state of Utah received on behalf of the Utah Navajos was ample for those people. In fact, tribal officials felt they should control all of the funds, and they viewed the royalties paid to Utah with envy. Consequently, they spent only a small fraction of the oil revenues in the Utah communities. This deepened a chasm in the Navajo Nation that existed before the discovery of oil at Aneth. The Utah Navajos had long felt neglected, as they lived outside mainstream Navajo society in Arizona and New Mexico. The tribal council's conscious act of omitting them from the oil benefits only deepened the Utah Navajos's mistrust of the tribal government.

To make matters worse, most of the Utah Navajos believed that they did not benefit from the funds administered by the state of Utah. In fact, an investigator reported in 1961 that the Utah Navajos' economic aspirations, which had greatly increased because of the oil, now had declined because the people felt that the state of Utah had deprived them of their benefits. Some individuals considered litigation against the state to correct the situation. In essence, the Utah Navajos believed that neither the tribe nor the state was helping them to receive what they deserved from the oil.[12]

Production peaked in 1960. The next year the oil companies began injecting water into the wells to enhance recovery, but the decline continued. By 1972 the removal of Aneth's oil had dropped by 74 percent, down from a high of 32.4 million barrels in 1960 to 8.3 million barrels, and the tribe's royalty income was cut in half, from $10 million in 1961 to $5 million in 1972.[13] Despite this decrease, Aneth remained the largest oil field in Utah, with businesspeople still referring to it as "huge." In an effort to conserve the oil and prolong the life of the field, the Conservation Commission established eighty-acre spacing for the wells. This also prevented the area from becoming crowded with equipment as in other oil fields.[14]

The oil embargo imposed by the Organization of Petroleum Exporting Countries (OPEC) in 1973 dramatically changed the nation's energy picture and conditions at Aneth. As the United States searched for energy, it placed new emphasis on locating and producing domestic resources. Reservations became natural locations to look. Although the Aneth field had been declining, oil companies now increased their pumping and drilling there, so that between 1973 and 1975 the production of oil and gas increased by about 25 percent. Greater production and skyrocketing oil prices caused the Navajo royalty payments to more than double.[15]

The drive for energy development on reservations across the nation motivated Indian leaders to form the Council of Energy Resource Tribes (CERT). Founded in 1975, CERT's goals were to obtain data, share expertise, and help the native peoples protect their rights. Of special significance to the Navajos was the election of their tribal chairman, Peter MacDonald, as leader of CERT in 1976. A sophisticated and adroit spokesman on behalf of Indian rights, MacDonald was determined to assert Indian self-determination. He announced that he would make CERT a "domestic OPEC."[16]

From the time he was elected chairman of the Navajo Nation, in 1971, MacDonald emphasized Navajo control of Navajo resources.[17] He stressed that "products of energy development will be made available for use within the Navajo Reservation by Navajos," and "[Navajos] will be given opportunities to participate in and control energy developments."[18] Behind MacDonald's stern words, two facts confronted him and the People. First, expenditures had increased as a result of tribal involvement in resource development and the leasing processes.[19] Second, MacDonald's activism on behalf of the tribe and CERT had caused a drain on the treasury.[20]

For all of the hyperbole about new wealth, no dramatic increase in revenue had resulted, unlike in the 1950s, when oil inflated the budget of the Navajo Nation. Resources were not being developed on the reservation for several reasons. MacDonald and the Navajo leadership wanted to take a more active role in this type of economic growth. To do so, they stopped the leasing of new oil lands in 1974 and examined alternatives for better returns and more control. The tribe began considering joint venture agreements, not only for oil, but also for uranium and coal exploitation.[21]

Suddenly, MacDonald was the man in the middle. He acted in opposition to the large energy companies, preventing them from exploiting

Peter MacDonald, backed by protesters, signs the agreement ending the protest. The Save Mother Earth poster captures the spirit of the 1970s and one of the themes of the sit-in. Photo from Utah Navajo Development Council.

Navajo resources, but he also wanted to promote development. Income from Aneth had increased at the start of the energy crisis primarily because of price advances, even though production was still declining. Yet here was one location where the tribe could hope for further development. Because Aneth already had long-term leases in place and was located in a sparsely settled part of the reservation, the tribal offices believed that here was an opportunity to involve the oil companies in expanding drilling operations. More development ensued, while oil well spacing decreased from one per eighty acres to one per forty acres.[22]

This change initially increased production but then stabilized. The drilling did not result in the discovery of new oil but only drained the resource faster than the original development scheme. In fact, the tribal offices admitted that the future for Aneth oil looked "dismal." But they had no recourse, since, as they consistently mentioned in their economic reports, tribal income depended on this oil field.[23]

The people of Aneth were not oblivious to these events. They witnessed firsthand the developments in their backyards. They watched oil company workers, accompanied by tribal representatives, locating new well sites. They also heard MacDonald's protestations and understood his message: first, that they should be given the opportunity to participate in control of energy development; and, second, that the results should benefit the Navajos. The people at Aneth saw neither of these occurring. As they had not been consulted before drilling, they viewed the new development activity as one more act of an "imperialistic tribal government."[24]

To compound the friction, some Navajos sued the Utah Navajo Development Council for misappropriating trust funds. Since its incorporation in 1971, the UNDC had evolved into a large organization, operating several businesses, including a building supply warehouse and a puppet manufacturing enterprise. A group of San Juan County Navajos brought the lawsuit against the UNDC because they felt that these expenditures did not benefit them. They accused board members of using the resources for personal enrichment.[25] These complaints were similar to those registered twice in the early 1960s by Utah Navajos, when they talked of suing to prevent the state of Utah's administration of the funds.

Furthermore, because UNDC located its office in Blanding, Utah, and employed several white workers, the Navajos felt their interests were not adequately defended. Just as in oil development, the Utah Navajos believed more power should be given to them in determining the use of the money. One letter to the editor in the *Navajo Times* said, "The grassroots people in Utah are those dissatisfied with UNDC's self-dealing, conflict of interest. . . . [M]ore power should be given to the Navajo people . . . in how their money should be spent."[26] To summarize the political concerns facing the Utah Navajos, they felt ignored when it came to determining oil development policy and left out in the disbursement of the benefits.

There were also social issues that bothered the Navajos, especially those who had to live in the midst of the boom and bustle of the oil field. The improvements made in roads and the addition in 1958 of a $300,000 bridge across the San Juan River still did not make many of the people feel more congenial toward what they considered white interlopers.[27] Some Navajos complained that they did not know that they had "oil under [their] feet" and that the land had been "given out at [their] leader's office [in Window Rock]."[28] One man explained the exploration by companies in the oil field this way:

They came and it just happened. For ninety-nine years they would drill for oil and pump it out. . . . The Anglo put up ribbons to outline what they were going to do. They were driving all over the place in automobiles and drilling . . . but no one bothered them. Then we found out it was not a good thing. . . . It was after this that the water was not good anymore. They drilled and let whatever came out drain into the wash. Then the horses and sheep drank this water. It was from this time that things started to go bad. It was because of this that there were gripes against the drilling of oil.[29]

Another person remembered how beautiful the land had been, with vegetation in abundance, before all of the destruction started.

The prairie dogs stood on their hind legs and chattered as the tall grass made waves in the breeze. It was a beautiful sight. Then came the oil wells. Bulldozers tore up the land. . . . We could not get a drink of cool, unpolluted water anywhere without getting sick. It [pure spring water] did not cause heart problems, bone disease, headaches, or cramps like it does today. All these health problems began when the oil wells were put up. It has all been polluted and ruined.[30]

In addition to ruining the springs, pools, and vegetation, sacred sites on the mesas could no longer be used as places to pray for rain, plants, and livestock. Fumes permeated the air, "galloping" pumps dotted the land where horses once trotted, and machines sucked oil or "life" from the earth's bowels. At night the "grinding" noise of the pumps kept people awake, there were fears that the carbon dioxide injected into wells added to the general contamination, and the livestock suffered from continuous incursions on the ranges.[31] All of this was taking place at the local people's expense, while the government at Window Rock and the oil companies appeared to be getting rich.

Out of these conflicts and others on the reservation arose a self-styled champion for the People known as the Coalition for Navajo Liberation. The organization defined itself as an advocate for the "rights of the grassroots people." It proclaimed a desire to foster "the protection of our natural resources against white corporations, the protection of our Mother Earth, and the protection of individual rights."[32] The Coalition also felt responsible for shielding the people against an unresponsive tribal government, although this remained an unspoken tenet. As for resource development, the organization saw white corporations as exploitive at the expense of the People, who did not want it.[33] While not everyone in the Aneth–Montezuma Creek area necessarily subscribed to the activist agenda of the Coalition, many wanted answers about who was responsible for the problems in the oil field and what could be done to solve them.

Although not officially linked with the Coalition for Navajo Liberation, the American Indian Movement (AIM) also became an active presence on the reservation. Like the Coalition, AIM is an Indian rights movement, but it takes a more militant stand to make its point. AIM fought against a system it felt dominated the people and that was incapable of reform from within. The organization acquired fame nationally through such events as the siege at Wounded Knee, South Dakota, in 1973.[34] AIM activists on the Navajo Reservation operated out of an Albuquerque office to assist local people with Indian rights matters but specialized in problems resulting from energy projects.[35]

To an outside observer, the Utah Navajos' world seemed embroiled in battles between the conflicting interests of those with and those without power. The more influence MacDonald appeared to have, the more the Coalition seemed to resist his actions. If the tribal council wanted to control the revenues from the natural resources, the Coalition believed the earnings should be disbursed among tribal members. If the tribal leadership wanted to initiate resource development, the Coalition wished to prevent it. Often these disputes came down to fights between MacDonald and the Coalition leadership backed by AIM.[36]

A branch of the Coalition had formed in the Aneth area in late 1977. During January, it staged its first sit-in at the Blanding social services office. The activists protested a staff that they believed did not treat the Navajos as well as other clients. According to a spokesman for the Coalition, the protesters were next going to target the oil companies to advance their own organization among the Navajo people.[37]

Years of petty and not so petty annoyance and contention had accumulated to a boiling point. The Navajos believed that the oil companies were insensitive to the realities of reservation life and only cared about negotiations with the tribe. While Native Americans on other reservations captured the media spotlight of the 1960s and 1970s with their protest movements against social inequalities, government malpractice, and historic injustices, the Navajos never seemed to stir. Now, however, a simple incident struck a spark, igniting the fumes that hovered over the Aneth field. The ensuing conflagration delivered enough light to clearly illuminate, on a regional level, the issues and parties involved.

Ella Sakizzie remembers it well. Her problems with the oil companies went back to the 1950s. Like many local people, she had not been informed about the tribe's or the oil companies' intentions. Suddenly there were trucks cruising over the rangelands, drilling rigs punching holes in the earth, and "smoke stacks popping up here and there." The white workers became very "careless" and "ignorant," running over dogs, goats, and sheep in their vehicles. At one point, a driver plowed through part of Ella's herd and the goats "came rolling out from under the truck like balls." Another time she went toe to toe with a bulldozer operator, who was clearing rangelands near her trailer for another oil pump pad. She told him, "This greasewood pasture is where I take my sheep every morning, but now look at what you have done! You have completely stripped my land. Turn that bulldozer off right this instant! I'm not kidding you."[38]

But the final, unpardonable sin occurred when an oil field worker "shot at" Ella's son-in-law while he was herding the sheep. Hanging onto the bucking horse for all he was worth, the frightened man galloped home. The family went to investigate. Empty shell casings and a cartridge box at the scene were enough proof to fuel Ella's trip to a "main office" to recount her grievances. She told of how the oil company workers did not listen, "notice," or respect the people: "You could care less if you killed one of us; you are carrying on as you please, . . . and now with this most recent shooting incident against my son-in-law, I definitely will not let you get away with that."[39]

According to a later report by Chairman MacDonald, the protest came in response to a number of indignities, culminating when "a Navajo sheepherder tried to stop one of the oil company employees from stealing his sheep, only to have the employee turn and start shooting at him."[40] The story became embellished with retelling. One version has three oil company workers torturing a goat, and when confronted by a Navajo youth on horseback, they threatened his life and shot at him as he tried to leave.[41]

On March 30, 1978, a group of forty to fifty Navajos, reportedly numbering in the hundreds, took control of the Texaco pumping unit at the Aneth oil field on the Navajo Reservation. Using jargon reminiscent of Indian war stories, the *Western Oil Reporter* stated that the Navajos "swooped down on the field" and "barricaded" the facilities "in what appeared to be an elaborately planned operation."[42] Press sources more sympathetic to the Indian cause called the action a demonstration against "two and a half decades of oil company ruthlessness and arrogance."[43]

According to Coalition ideology, the discontentment of the Aneth community had surfaced and several hundred more Navajos from there joined the fray. The occupants of the pumping station issued a number of complaints, addressing a variety of concerns. The people stated that the underground wealth had not meant a better or easier life. In fact, it had killed their cattle and sheep, destroyed their environment, and disrupted their lives. The environmental concerns included the emission of noxious gas fumes and the pollution of waters by spilled petroleum. The economic complaints included the companies' low employment of Navajos, questions about how much money was made off "our land," where that money went, and what UNDC did with its share of the money.[44]

Although not mentioned in the *Navajo Times*, the *Arizona Republic* consistently pointed out that the Utah Navajos wanted the royalty money going to the tribal office to be disbursed to them in per capita payments. In a formal petition to the oil companies, the occupiers added new demands by asking for the oil leases to be renegotiated, for assistance in health, housing, and education, and for the establishment of a local environmental compliance office. The petition also asked the Navajo tribe to extend more services to the Aneth area.[45]

MacDonald and the tribal government did not react immediately to the takeover. In fact, the event took them by surprise. The Navajo Minerals Department admitted that it had "very little knowledge of the situation at Aneth," while the *Arizona Republic* reported the day after the takeover started that one of the basic goals of the insurgents was to discuss grievances with MacDonald.[46] Apprehensive about the protesters' mood, MacDonald delayed supporting the efforts until he realized that the Aneth community had joined the movement. Then the tribe began supplying food and other necessities to the protesters. MacDonald, however, delayed further action until he personally visited Aneth. According to the *Navajo Times,* once he did, and heard the stories of the people, he took what appeared to be a decisive step; he closed the Aneth area to all non-Navajos. This action came about ten days after the initial takeover and in reality had little impact on the field. Three days after the occupation started, all of the oil companies in the field had voluntarily shut down their operations and left.[47]

The protesters and residents of Aneth felt that MacDonald acted late and indecisively. He told the Utah Navajos that the tribal government stood behind them; the people responded that he was their leader, he should "stand in front."[48] Instead, MacDonald's primary goal seems to have been to deflect the demands coming from the occupiers and change the nature of the dispute. As national publicity grew, he wanted to keep the attention on the oil companies and off of any intratribal problems. Although the protesters had raised the question of financial concerns several times, MacDonald repeatedly told the press that "money is not the issue." He believed the conflict centered on respect for the Navajos and sounded the popular cry that oil workers had been "molesting Navajo women; had brought alcohol and drugs into the hogans; had stolen sheep and livestock; had dug up grave sites; had desecrated hallowed ground and fed the remains of [his] people's ancestors into rock-crushing machinery."[49]

While MacDonald told the press that money was not the concern, he told the people at Aneth that the revenues from the field could not be altered. He agreed that the contracts were dated and in need of revision but said it would be difficult to renegotiate them. MacDonald certainly had reason to avoid the money issue; in the same news piece that contained the diatribe against the oil workers, the Navajo tribal attorney told the press that oil and mineral royalties "make up about 40% of the tribe's income." The *Arizona Republic* later reported that the tribe was losing about $30,000 a day from the shutdown.[50]

Although MacDonald stood in a tenuous position, between supporting the takeover and losing the tribe's oil revenues, he benefited greatly from the publicity. Coincidentally, the Native American Treaty and Rights Organization conference was held during the takeover. Before the congregated tribal leaders in Window Rock, MacDonald presented the image of an Indian leader guiding his united people in a protest against the exploitive whites. At one session he arrived late because he had been "coordinating negotiations between the Indians and the four oil companies." The image of unity transcended the differences he had with AIM, the Coalition for Navajo Liberation, and the Utah Navajos. He called the people at Aneth "heroes," drawing what the *Republic* called "war whoops and cheers" from those assembled.[51]

Through all of the events in the Aneth field, the oil companies seemed to distance themselves from the battle. When the protesters entered the Texaco facilities, the company's employees offered little resistance, then departed. Texaco promptly shut down its operation, followed by the other three companies in the field—Phillips, Superior, and Continental. About thirty-five tribal police gathered a few miles away from the Texaco facility the day after the takeover and were willing to arrest the protesters for trespassing, but a police spokesman reported that the companies "declined" to file complaints.[52]

When asked about the takeover, one official said his company had been aware of "some dissatisfaction" but "had no warning of any action." He went on to deny that the operations were causing any harmful effects. All of the oil producers were firmly convinced that the dispute centered on the disbursement of the royalties, with the Utah Navajos believing that individuals should receive the money instead of the tribe. The spokesman for Conoco, however, made the company's position quite clear to the *Arizona Republic*: "Our agreement is with the Interior Department and the Tribal Council. We can't change it to pay an individual."[53] The oil companies also felt that they could not submit the leases for renegotiation. As for environmental complaints, the companies responded that they were within federal regulations and the stipulations of the leases. They did, however, announce the formation of a complaint review committee to consider some of the environmental grievances.[54]

The oil companies refused to negotiate directly with the occupiers but agreed to form a committee with tribal officials and representatives from the U.S. Geological Survey. This organization entered the picture because the Navajos accused it of failing to properly monitor the oil operations. The Geological Survey group met several times in early April, and as negotiations developed, MacDonald announced that the oil companies seemed to be ready to agree on several of the points. In an apparent attempt to deflect attention from the Coalition, he commented that one reason for the apparent success "stems from the fact that the demonstration is being led by residents of the community."[55]

The final step in the negotiations was not easy, however. After representatives from the various factions drew up a tentative agreement, they were to take it before the protesters at the Texaco facility. Here the divisions among the Navajo participants became quite evident. Clyde Benally, a San Juan School District employee, served as translator and moderator as both sides discussed each point of the agreement. Before much progress had been made, members of the Coalition seized the floor and began berating the oil company officials. The situation became tense, and "both company and tribal representatives were afraid that nothing would be accomplished."[56] Ultimately a representative from the Department of the Interior gained control of the debate, asking the oilmen to respond to specific demands. The session concluded with the Aneth residents agreeing to sign the settlement. The Coalition did not concur and asked the oil company representatives to come back the next day.

The Coalition and the Aneth residents did far more than just disagree. Benally later placed the meeting in context by calling it the "famous Friday night." He believed the Coalition wanted to "sacrifice somebody" to gain national attention. In fact, a few days before a leader from AIM drew a knife on a Texaco official, implying that decisive action needed to be taken. In light of these developments, and after the meeting with the oil company representatives, the community members announced that they planned to withdraw from the occupation. They were now satisfied with the accord and realized that the Coalition had its own agenda.[57]

The tribal office supported the people of Aneth and told the Coalition that it had promoted the original action because its officials "had assumed that they [the Coalition] were seriously interested in correcting the problems in the area." Instead, it appeared "that the Coalition was more interested in drawing attention to itself."[58] The activists initially stood fast, replying that without a renegotiation of the oil leases, the agreement was a sellout.

Realizing that they had the support of the community, the oil companies became defiant and set a deadline. They notified the tribal representative that if the agreement was not signed by 6:00 P.M. the next day, they would go to federal court to have the protesters evicted. As the deadline approached, the Coalition remained firm, until members of AIM said that with two more provisions they would agree to the settlement. First, the Navajo Tribal Council must pass a resolution supporting the occupation. The tribal representatives agreed. Second, they wanted amnesty for everyone involved. That caused more of a problem. One of the AIM protesters had received amnesty after a previous incident with the stipulation that he would not participate in any further takeovers. He had obviously broken these terms. The matter remained unsettled until Robert Billie, the councilman from Aneth, and Everett Thomas, one of the Coalition's driving forces, agreed to sign the settlement—essentially ending the takeover.[59]

The signed compromise addressed eighteen of twenty demands. It covered community and social problems, environmental concerns, respect for the Navajos, employment, and education. Salient points included guarantees of more jobs for Navajos, promises not to bring alcohol onto the reservation or to bother livestock, a provision for funding college scholarships, and tighter environmental controls. Tribal officials also agreed to work with the Navajo Tribal Utility to extend power and gas to all areas. The main concerns of revenue disbursement and lease renegotiations were not settled. The companies said that those discussions must be between the Navajo tribe and the federal government.[60]

The agreement brought mixed results for the Utah Navajos. As signed, it altered the basic relationship between them and the oil businesses. According to Benally, it forced the companies to cooperate with the Navajos and be more sensitive to local needs. To this end, Superior Oil hired Benally to assist in implementing the agreement. Similarly, Texaco employed Aneth councilman Robert Billie as "Community Relations Advisor." While Benally believed that the agreement only provided the "nuts and bolts" of a possible working relationship, Billie became an enthusiastic supporter of the Texaco cause. Through the pages of the *Navajo Times*, Billie highlighted Texaco's efforts on behalf of the Navajos. The companies also began to hire more Navajos for work in the oil field. Texaco increased the number of Navajo employees from seven in a crew of thirty-eight in 1974 to twenty-four in a crew of thirty-seven in 1983. Finally, the companies began to settle land and livestock damage claims.[61]

While the agreement appeared to improve the relationship between the Utah Navajos and the oil companies, the relationship with the tribe had only shifted partway. The administration in Window Rock became more aware of the Utah portion of the reservation. Whereas tribal representatives had seldom been seen in Aneth, they now began to appear more regularly. Relations were still tenuous, however. Benally believed that the tribal government "shot the Aneth residents in the back." The Council failed to pass the promised resolution supporting the Aneth takeover, and as soon as the excitement of the moment ended, it returned to assisting oil field development without consulting the Aneth community.[62]

In August 1978 antagonisms erupted again as representatives from the tribe went to Aneth to assist in locating new sites for wells. The local people responded by throwing rocks to drive the workers away. Tribal officials stated that they were afraid to go to the area, and a group of Utah Navajos reportedly beat one person from the tribal land office, stating: "We don't want any MacDonald dogs around here."[63] Some residents promised to use guns if any new drilling started. The people argued that according to the agreement signed in April, the community needed to be consulted before any new mineral development was undertaken. In November a group of Utah Navajos staged a 250-mile walk from Montezuma Creek to Window Rock to protest the "broken promises" of the Aneth accord, as they asked again, "who is benefiting?"[64]

Questions about UNDC's ability to deal effectively and fairly with the Utah royalties were raised again in 1991. Backed by accusations similar to those made in 1977, the Utah legislature ordered an investigation of the organization. The resulting audit showed that the main organization had performed its task impartially and effectively but that its subsidiaries, Utah Navajo Industries (UNI) and First Native American Corporation (FNAC), operating under a separate board, had "massive numbers of irregularities and questionable expenditures."[65] Oversight review for the two subsidiaries was to have been provided by the state, not UNDC, but the process failed to materialize. Deliberations about its proceedings are discussed in the concluding chapter.

As for the oil field development at Aneth, a new company, Chuska Energy Corporation, has entered the area in recent years. Although it signed an agreement that returns 2 percent of the royalties directly to the Aneth chapter, the concerns of the residents remain the same. The people complain that they are not consulted before development and that they are not receiving enough money from the operations. In June 1991 individuals from Aneth advocated forcing Chuska to renegotiate the lease.[66]

According to the elders who have watched the unfolding of events and couched their understanding in religious values, the problems have still not been solved: "Because of this mist of gas that hangs over us, the good rain clouds do not come over us any more. . . . I feel like our place [represents] the total destruction of 'Mother Earth.'"[67] Dozens of interviews with the older people in Aneth paint the same picture. Polluted air and water, lost vegetation, sickly animals and people, and impoverished human relations have been the main product derived from the oil field. From their perspective: "The oil wells have killed our land."[68] The monsters' blood placed in the earth at the time of creation has done little to drive off Old Man Poverty and his mate.

What, then, are the lessons to be learned from these events? There are elements in this story that will probably not be repeated. The polemics of the 1960s and 1970s have abated. No longer do visions of wealth inspire action, although receiving a proper return on resource development is still a major concern. The initial motivating forces behind the takeover, the Coalition for Navajo Liberation and AIM, are no longer militant agents on the reservation. And Peter MacDonald's bid for political power and land control in other areas eventually led to his downfall. Indeed, perhaps the only constants over the past forty years are the problems.

Yet there are four important factors that have emerged from the events surrounding the Aneth oil field. The first is the nature of the Navajo tribe's economy. At present, the most profitable resources—coal, petroleum, and related products—are still not under the direct control of the tribe. Outside corporations, in spite of the new Energy Policy drafted in 1991, remain the moving force behind mineral extraction. The investment capital that could be used to move Navajo economic independence forward is either nonexistent or used to run government programs ranging from police protection to distribution of commodities. This encumbers the flow of money in a system trying to meet unlimited needs while at the same time not generating new economic possibilities.

This lifestyle cannot persist. The Navajo Nation General Fund Revenues for fiscal year 1994 reveal a people heavily dependent on the nonrenewable mineral industry. Oil, gas, and mining accounted for 69 percent of the money feeding into the budget, with 28 percent more derived from taxes. All other sources combined make up the remaining 3 percent.[69] These figures obviously do not include federal payments, but the point is clear: the more than 220,000 Navajo people both on and off the reservation are going to place increasingly heavy demands on a tribe whose main source of income can only diminish. Alternatives must be sought quickly.

The second point, and a direct function of the first, is that the Navajo Nation must nurture friendly relations on a local, grassroots level. Feelings of mistrust, anger, and betrayal surfaced quickly in the Aneth incident. While the oil companies became the target, the proposed solution to the problems rested in renegotiation of the contract by the tribe and the companies for the benefit of the local people. The tribe has historically made business agreements that have hurt entire communities for the sake of economic growth. The price has at times been high in anguish and low on the scale of benefit when compared to what other regions involved in comparable activities received financially.[70]

Of equal importance are the more intangible feelings of anxiety and resentment between the core (Window Rock) and the periphery (Aneth and other communities). This is a common problem found wherever political power exists—eastern states (or California) versus western states, federal versus state government, county versus state government, and so on. Extra efforts must be made by the more powerful entities to include in a meaningful way the "little man" in the decision-making process as well as in the execution of the plan. To ignore this process only invites a reaction, and the third point of discussion.

Militancy is a two-edged sword that must be wielded carefully. Too much force exacts strong retribution that can be counterproductive to gaining the primary goal. Take, for instance, AIM's involvement at Wounded Knee in 1973. By the time the rioting on and off the reservation had run its course, the tribe had been split into warring factions (Dick Wilson's "goon squads" vs. the "traditionals" and members of AIM), people had been killed, and enough pressure had been brought by federal agencies to stamp out any productive change contrary to an established way of operating.

In the Aneth case, one might argue that not enough force had been used since only a few things changed. Perhaps dynamiting some oil wells, cutting pipelines, or a more aggressive fight would have sent a stronger message with more lasting results. But it did not work at Wounded Knee and would probably not have worked at Aneth. The Navajos walked the fine line of civil disobedience and were able to get generally positive media coverage without a strong backlash from opposing sides. Why did they not succeed?

The fourth and final point suggests an answer. All of the various groups involved held a different political agenda. Threads of agreement and collaboration wove throughout their efforts, but there was not sufficient cooperation to cinch strong enough ties for significant change. If the People's position had solidified every faction from the local Coalition and AIM through to the tribe, then the political posturing would have given way to more than a Band-aid solution. Because of the ad hoc nature of the protest, the political foundation of cooperation toward a unified goal was never achieved.

When Monster Slayer and Born for Water walked the earth killing monsters, they achieved success because of supernatural aid and a unified goal. Their plan was clear. Now a different monster has entrapped the people of Aneth and the results from the 1970s offer little promise for the future. As one elder described the relationship of tribal and federal government with the oil companies, "This whole 'system' holds us prisoner; we cannot speak for ourselves. I cannot stand to live here in this polluted land."[71] Based on the struggles and results of the past, supernatural intervention may be required once more.

CHAPTER ELEVEN

FROM DEZBA TO "JOHN"

The Changing Role of Navajo Women in Southeastern Utah

In 1939 Gladys A. Reichard published *Dezba: Woman of the Desert*, a fictional account based on the author's sixteen years of anthropological work among the Navajos. The events and feelings portrayed in the book show great understanding of the struggles of a "traditional" mother. Shocked at the younger generation's adaptation to Anglo-American culture and their growing unfamiliarity with Navajo customs, Dezba remains outwardly passive yet emotionally torn and frustrated as she watches the old lifestyle disappear before her eyes. Reichard, through Dezba, outlines this dissolution: "A reservation mother had no means to cope with white man's customs which led girls first to change dress and personal appearance. Next, children began to scorn social customs and became fastidious about food and the Navajo custom of sleeping on the ground. At worst, they took to drinking and became loose in morals."[1] Since Dezba's time, this process of change has intensified and taken new directions, as contact with the dominant society has increased. Perhaps it was not by chance that this important character was named Dezba, "Going to War."

Reichard was writing about the Navajos in the 1930s, seventy years or approximately three generations ago, when the most serious inroads of acculturation had just started. What has happened since that time on at least one part of the reservation is the subject of this chapter. While there has been some commentary about transitions in specific communities and general trends among female Navajos, little attention has been paid to the Navajo women of southeastern Utah.[2]

Before starting, however, there are three important points that need to be clarified. The first centers on the term "traditional." Because culture is always changing, what is new and innovative at one time may be considered old and traditional a few decades later. This creates the need to establish a baseline from which change can be measured. For my purposes, the Navajo woman's lifestyle of the 1930s serves as a point of reference.[3] By this time the culture adopted many material objects and some values of Anglo society, but it was not until stock reduction and the increasing availability of motorized transportation that the floodgates of change opened. Before that period Navajo culture was primarily matrilineal, the women controlling much of the wealth and local resources.

The second point is the difficulty of pinning down the slippery eel of change. The question quickly becomes, not whether there was change, but the direction it took and the rate at which it occurred. Obviously, change is not a homogeneous movement that sweeps through a population overnight, as governmental, geographic, local, and individual factors either speed or slow the process. Also, it is difficult to determine when a majority of people have accepted a certain practice, as records of this nature are not systematically kept. Therefore, I make use of four censuses—1931, 1960, 1980, and 1990.[4] The last two, because of computerization, provide the most detailed outline of existing circumstances in the Navajo Nation, while the former two give only a baseline of information. For instance, when the tribe took the 1931 census, the reservation was divided into districts. Southeastern Utah was lumped together with the Shiprock, New Mexico, area, and so while the data give some detailed information, the geographic area includes part of the reservation that is not my concern here.

The third point concerns gaining a qualitative dimension. To add a human face to the statistics, I derived questions from the numerical data and then presented them in formal interviews to Navajo women from the area. Because these women were of varying ages and from different parts of southeastern Utah, it is difficult to say that they were representative, although general patterns emerged.

Many of the interviews were collected in 1984 and have been corroborated over the past sixteen years. Because of the personal nature of this material, all informants remain anonymous unless they have been identified already in a published source. There are obvious problems in comparing data over time; some of the data do not distinguish between Navajo males and females and are derived from different parts of the Navajo Nation. Where possible, I have made distinctions. What becomes clear, however, is that there is a move away from the Dezbas of the 1930s to two broad classifications of younger-generation Navajo women in the 1990s: those who are "progressive" and those who are "Johns," young people caught between traditional and modern ways. How this has come about is the point of departure.

Utah's Navajo population is concentrated in San Juan County, whose southern third is part of the reservation. According to the 1990 census, the county population can be divided roughly in half, 5,501 whites and 6,859 American Indians; 261 blacks, Hispanics, and Asians comprise the remainder. There is a small Ute community (approximately 350 people) outside of Blanding, but the vast majority of American Indians are Navajos, 80 percent of whom live on the reservation and 52 percent of whom are female. The importance of this demographic profile lies in the clarity it offers for comparative purposes. Living conditions, employment, and education are defined with precision in the census. Thanks to the detailed information now collected by means of computers, the changing role of Navajo women has become more apparent.

The stock reduction of the 1930s eliminated many of the traditional forms of wealth and livelihood. As the Navajos could no longer depend on animals as their major source of wealth and because motorized transportation provided greater accessibility to the wage economy, the 1940s and 1950s saw an influx of Navajos into the San Juan region in search of jobs. Natural increase also pushed the population figures upward. These trends have continued to the present, giving rise to many of the predominantly Navajo towns on the fringe of the reservation. The discovery of oil and uranium on the Navajos' land plus the opening of Peabody Coal Mine, just south of the Utah border in Arizona, drew those looking for work. The result has been a steady increase in the Indian population in San Juan County.

A look at the demography of the Navajos in this region illustrates this dramatic growth. In 1960 there were 2,668 Navajo residents; in 1970, 4,740, an increase of 77.7 percent; in 1980, 5,622, an increase of 110.7 percent; and in 1990, 6,859, an increase of 157 percent. The earlier reports showed that the Navajos, as is the case with many underdeveloped and rural groups in the world, were a youthful population with few middle-aged and old people. The age distribution of males and females, according to the censuses from 1931 to 1960, shows that 68.9 percent of the population was below the age of twenty-four. According to the 1990 census, this trend is starting to change. That year only 56 percent of Navajos were under the age of twenty-four, underscoring the trend of a people in transition.

Still, the small proportion of those older than sixty (8 percent) accentuates the impact that cultural change will have on the young. As the last viable repositories of the traditional lifestyle, the elders play an increasingly critical role in passing along the older Navajo worldview. When they are gone, a different set of standards will emerge. Whereas in the 1930s the forces that brought about a transition were present but diluted due to isolation and the adherence to traditional culture, in the 1990s forces reach far beyond the reservation and Navajo custom to inculcate a different orientation among the youth.

Another concern in this process of change is the family, which in Navajo society revolves around women. Gary Witherspoon, in *Navajo Marriage and Kinship*, sees the role of motherhood as a central theme expressed in everything from ceremonies to dwellings and from language to deities.[5] Although he may overstress the female principle, few deny that in a traditionally matrilineal society the mother played an important role in social and economic affairs. In 1942 Solon T. Kimball and John H. Provinse studied Navajo social organization and summarized the woman's responsibilities as follows:

> The hogan and its vicinity represents her major locale of action. She is responsible for the preparation, serving and cooking of food; for the cleanliness of the hogan and her children; for the making of clothing, and for the general comfort of the members of her family. . . . Just as her husband seldom interferes in the domestic arrangements except where there is gross neglect, she too avoids interference in the duties and privileges of her husband. Though primarily engaged in household duties, her contribution to the economic welfare of the family is as great as that of any other member of the family. The most direct contribution comes from the weaving and sale

of rugs, but she is equally competent in the care of the sheep and goats and assists her husband in the light work in the fields when necessity arises.[6]

In 1931 Navajo families were essentially self-sufficient, growing crops and herding sheep and cattle for their livelihood. Today, wage work has drawn those who can compete for the jobs to towns or places where commuting is practical. Those who are not fortunate enough to live near a job site maintain their extended family structure with aunts, uncles, grandparents, and so on, in the same house or settlement, but this is done at the expense of economic independence. Unemployment, welfare, and part-time jobs are the result. Young people who want to earn a steady income must give up the social comfort of being near their next of kin and adapt to a nuclear family structure.

This conflict creates ambiguity among younger Navajo women concerning where their allegiance should lie. Formerly, a Navajo usually resided with or near the wife's family. There is no doubt that young women still desire to help their parents with economic and moral support, but the need to earn a living often dictates where young couples live. One woman, when asked where she wanted to settle in relation to her parents, said, "I could go back and teach computers, but it is important to live close to my parents. Perhaps I could get a job there [near home], but if not, then I would go where the job is. I will need the money, but I will still visit my parents as much as I can."[7]

As many young women move from the security of extended family and the assurance of a traditional economy, they become more dependent on their husbands, who, according to Anglo values, were the breadwinners. In Navajo culture the woman has always been the stable, dominant force, and although a husband may come and go, the wife remained to shoulder many of the economic and familial responsibilities. Now the wife who has moved away from kin must either live on what her husband has earned, provide it herself, or return to her family and hope that they can support her. The 1990 census indicates that only 53 percent of Utah Navajo women sixteen years of age or older are in the labor force, while 30 percent of the household owners on the Utah reservation are female and have no husband present. This, of course, would include older women whose husbands have died as well as women in various

Processing wool and weaving are traditional Navajo skills that have been an important part of the Navajo economy for four hundred years. Although there are still many talented weavers, the skill and craft remains only one generation away from extinction. Photo from Navajo Nation Museum, currently unlisted.

circumstances other than divorce, but it also does not include those who have returned to their parents. At any rate, 30 percent is a significant proportion of females feeling the force of economic pressures. Many do so without extended kin to cushion problems that arise.

Another way of looking at the issue of marital status is to point out that 79 percent of the people who fit into the census category "separated, widowed, and divorced" on the Utah part of the reservation are women. While there are many cultural and economic reasons for this disparity, it is obviously easier for a male to find companionship than it is for a female.[8]

A primary concern of Navajo religion and beliefs has always been health. Traditionally, physical and spiritual harm came to those who broke the taboos and transgressed divine laws as proscribed by the gods. Another side of Navajo health was concerned with using plants and minerals to heal the sick. Very few women serve as chanters in the long, complex ceremonies, but many medicine women have a vast knowledge of healing through plants and other natural remedies. This strictly physical healing, which shares some of the tenets of Western society's medicinal practices but is deeply rooted in mythology, was not as concerned with spirits and the maintenance of harmony.

Following the introduction of the Indian Health Service (IHS) on the reservation, a growing desire to use both traditional and Western medicine arose among the Navajos. Because health care facilities were located in the more developed areas of the reservation, such as Shiprock and Kayenta, many of the Utah Navajos were forced to travel long distances for help, to enroll in expensive Anglo hospitals, or to do without medical attention.

The solution to this problem was the creation of a Navajo-controlled and -operated organization in San Juan County that either provided or contracted to provide services in health, education, agriculture, and housing. The Utah Navajo Development Council, incorporated in 1971, provided

> for the health, education and general welfare of the Navajo Indian residing in San Juan County. Planning for such expenditures shall be done in cooperation with the appropriate departments, bureaus, commissions, divisions and agencies of the United States, State of

Utah, the County of San Juan in Utah, and the Navajo Tribe inso-
far as it is reasonably practicable to accomplish the objects and
purpose of this act.[9]

UNDC's programs started in 1971–72, and while they were designed to
help the Navajos in general, many of the health services were especially
applicable to women. Operating from three clinics located at Navajo
Mountain, Montezuma Creek, and Oljeto, nurse practitioners offered programs such as health education, well-baby clinics, prenatal and post-
partum care, family planning, and special clinics for screening cancer,
treating tuberculosis, and teaching handicapped children. The results
were impressive. In fiscal year 1971–72, Navajos made 8,421 visits to the
three clinics; by 1983 this figure had doubled, to 16,845.[10] UNDC instituted a program that further decentralized services and brought health
care into the hogans of some of the remotest camps. Navajo community
female health nurses traveled over rutted dirt roads in the backcountry,
visiting homes and bringing medicine and advice to those not able to
reach the clinics. In 1982 these nurses reached a peak of 2,700 visits.[10]

The clinic at Navajo Mountain expanded its capacity in an innovative
program in summer 1983. Assuming the name "Hogan Heroes," the
full-time health personnel trained female Navajo high school and college students, home for the summer, to give instruction to the old, the
disabled, and the housebound on subjects as varied as first aid, fitness,
drug use, and accident prevention. As a result, 122 of the 135 families
the clinic identified as needing such help were contacted and instructed,
giving rise to a final report that boasted, "Every family now has someone who can take a temperature."[11] Thus even the most rural residents
of the reservation have received health care, and tuberculosis and infant
mortality are no longer the scourge they once were.

The single most important tool of change that affects Navajo women
today is education. While traditional society had its methods for encul-
turating its members, there is a sharp contrast between the way the
older people were raised and the way younger women are raised today.
For the former, the use of example and informal methods stressed the
individual's need to choose and accept Navajo practices. One older
woman explained it this way:

They [mother and father] were the only ones to teach me these things. They said this is the way you walk through life. I found out it was true. "I will sit here and set examples for you," she [my mother] said, "until you can stand up. With my breath of life [for I gave you life] you will be like that throughout your years." I think sometimes that this is true. I always hang on to the old words said by her.[12]

Yet, according to the treaty of 1868, the government was to provide formal education through schools and teachers sent to all parts of the reservation. This program got off to a slow start, but by the mid-twentieth century large numbers of Navajo children were enrolled—either willingly or by force—in some type of educational program. Three general types of schools were available—the federal boarding school, the Navajo community boarding school, and the Anglo or Navajo community day school. To serve Utah residents, the BIA located boarding schools in Shonto, Navajo Mountain, Kayenta, Shiprock, and Aneth.

There are no complete studies of these institutions, but information compiled on their impact is instructive. In 1976 Ann Metcalf reported,

> [N]early every Navajo child born on the reservation after 1940 has spent some time in federal boarding school. During any given year, approximately 50% of all Navajo children are living in dormitories. The Bureau of Indian Affairs (BIA) estimates that 83% of the elementary pupils in federally operated boarding schools are Navajo.[13]

Metcalf pointed out that although many parents encouraged their children to go to school to get a "good education" and later a "good job," many of the students were ill prepared for the trauma they encountered when Anglo clothes, hairstyles, and language were forced on them. One woman said that her experience was so bad that she had blocked it out of her mind. Recently, when she was asked to write her life history, she broke down in tears as she forced herself to remember some of those experiences. This response may not be the rule, but it also is not the exception; and although Metcalf's informants resided in Oakland, California, and were limited in number, there is abundant anecdotal evidence on a local level that supports the idea that many Navajo women found their boarding school experience difficult, if not traumatic.

Metcalf saw other ill effects from the boarding school experience. Among the twenty-three women she interviewed in an urban setting in 1970–72, she found that those who attended these schools had higher anxiety than other Navajo parents, were less decisive, had lower self-images, were more likely to seek help from "experts," and manipulated their children more.[14] For many, boarding school did as much harm as good.

Another option available for Navajo children was the Placement Program of the Church of Jesus Christ of Latter-day Saints (LDS). Because Utah was predominantly Mormon, many of the Indian children remained in the state with LDS families and attended school in the Salt Lake area; others went to California for their education. The program was strictly voluntary, yet it was selective, based on ability and church membership. It is difficult to measure the impact of the program as the LDS Church has not released information on its success or failure, but Alexander Leighton and Dorothea Leighton's general observation, made in 1945, may be useful. They believed that 95 percent of the Navajo students who left the reservation to go to school returned to their old way of life and that it had proved more of a handicap than an aid to them.[15] Since that time the program became increasingly smaller and more selective, and by 1990 the LDS Placement Program had largely ended. Again, no statistics are available.

Still another option for the Navajos was not to attend school at all. A study conducted in 1969 found that for one reason or another many Navajo parents had chosen not to have their children formally educated. Whether they were caught in the web of familial responsibilities, blocked by transportation problems, or simply lacked the desire, these parents avoided sending their children off to an experience they had never had. The study points out that of the Navajo students attending San Juan High School, 40 percent of their fathers and 59 percent of their mothers had no formal education. Only 5 percent of these parents completed twelve years of school and only 2 percent of the fathers and 1 percent of the mothers held college degrees.[16] According to the 1990 census, 35 percent of the Utah Navajo population twenty-five years or older now hold a high school diploma and 4.4 percent have a bachelor's degree or higher.[17]

The increased emphasis on education among the Utah Navajos did not always come easily. The northern two-thirds of San Juan County contains the majority of the white population as well as private businesses, state and federal agencies, and schools. For those Navajos living on the reservation, the alternative to boarding schools and the LDS Placement Program—especially for high school students—was to travel to Blanding for an education.

Busing was the only reliable, daily means for getting students to school, but it came at a terrible price. Indian children, depending on which part of the reservation they lived on, were transported from 80 to 166 miles (round trip) each day to get to school.[18] Translated into travel time, this could mean as much as five or six hours by the time they had walked or been driven by parents out to their bus stop. Interviews with women who endured being bused confirm that it was a trial to get chores done, eat breakfast, and reach a pick-up point to meet their transportation, not to mention the effect this schedule had on extracurricular and after-school study activities.

In 1975 parents took steps to help the more than two hundred students who found themselves in this situation. Believing these children were products of educational and racial discrimination, forty-eight individuals, many of whom were women, filed notice with the Dinébe'iiná Náhiilna Be Agha'diit'ahii (roughly glossed as "Winning a Case for the People's Rights"), or DNA, office in Mexican Hat. The DNA, an agency that provides legal aid for the Navajo people, in turn filed suit, *Sinajini v. the Board of Education*. Jimmie Sinajini was just one of the students, but his case represented both the Oljeto and Red Mesa chapters' fight against the school district. Navajos read pertinent documents at chapter meetings, ensuring local involvement.[19]

Representatives of the San Juan School District sat down with lawyers from both sides and discussed emotionally charged issues. The committee pointed out that as late as 1958 only 4.4 percent of the students in the district, or 120 students, were American Indian and that the BIA schools had responsibility for the others. By 1974 the figure had changed dramatically. Indian students now numbered 1,235, or 46.5 percent, 431 of whom were involved in secondary education and 220 of whom were being bused. Studies showed that the high schools were located so that the average Navajo student traveled four times as far as his or her white counterpart. Many Navajo children spent the equivalent of 120 school days sitting on a bus just to attend classes for 180 days. For students at the end of the longest bus routes, these figures rose to 30,000 miles each year and an equivalent of 240 school days on a bus.[20]

The school district eventually came to terms. Both parties agreed that what was needed was a high school in Montezuma Creek and one in Monument Valley. The former opened in 1978, the latter in 1983, and each has had a larger attendance than the 150-person enrollment initially anticipated. The school district also improved the three elementary schools on or near the reservation in Bluff, Mexican Hat, and Montezuma Creek and initiated bilingual-bicultural programs at each institution. The Utah Navajo had claimed a partial "place in the sun."

The significance of these events is highlighted by information from the 1990 census. San Juan County has never had so many Navajo students enrolled in elementary and secondary education—1,600 on the reservation alone—while 332 others attended college. These figures support the general trend established in 1980 of dramatic increases that spiral upward toward more and higher education.

Fluency in speaking English is another important indicator of the effects of formal education. Unfortunately, the 1960 and 1970 censuses do not give detailed information on languages spoken in the home and proficiency in English, but the 1980 and 1990 censuses show that about one-third of the people speak only Navajo and that the large majority are bilingual and can communicate in English on at least an elementary level. A 1992 study of the Head Start program completed by the Navajo Division of Education found that 54 percent of the 682 children observed were monolingual English speakers, 18 percent were monolingual Navajo speakers, and 28 percent were bilingual.[21] The preschool teaching staff, composed predominantly of women, spoke primarily English even though most were bilingual. Thus younger generations of Navajo women and children are becoming more fluent in the language of the dominant society. In the future they will become ever more competitive in the job market but often at the expense of their native tongue.

On a more personal level, Navajo women, both old and young, seem to favor the effects of education. An interview in 1977 with Nedra Tó dích'íi'nii, an elderly woman who spoke little English, elicited the following response: "I always wish that my children would handle these things that you call papers, strong papers of higher education. This also pertains to everybody, boys and girls. The boys will start thinking about women. If you think of a woman, think of one who is well educated and has had a lot of schooling."[22]

A more recent interview revealed that a traditional mother was very much in favor of education. She told all her sons that they had to go to school to learn all they could. She warned, "If you don't get educated, it is like being deaf because you cannot live in a world where everybody is going in the direction of the white men." She had never been allowed to go to school because she had to stay home to herd sheep and weave. She realized now that education was important for her children to become self-sufficient in a changing world. "Navajos have to learn the Navajo way and use the white man's way. If we lose our way of life, it is something we will have to live with, but we are handicapped if we don't know English."[23]

Younger Navajo women express similar sentiments about education, as they feel an urgency to change their situation. The values of the dominant culture are infused in their philosophy; education is equated with upward social mobility and material wealth. One woman, who counseled high school students in Monument Valley, believes that women are more aggressive because of their cultural heritage, which places them in a position of power. The following statement sheds an interesting light on younger Navajo females' attitudes, as reflected by this counselor.

> I find that the women are more eager and they take a challenge more than the men do. The men are more unstable. Maybe that is because of the culture. The women can identify with their role, but as far as the men, what's their role? A long time ago they were the hunters; they were the providers, but now a lot of that is taken away. So where do they stand now? . . . Ladies around here have more guts, are more determined, will step out and say I'll take it. . . . They are tired of feeling like they have not accomplished anything.[24]

The desire to accomplish has been translated into the values of Anglo society—jobs, money, and influence. In the 1930s wealth was counted in sheep, rugs, and silverwork; today it is signified by pickup trucks and technology as much as by food and employment. Navajo women are aware of the material wealth around them that can be purchased to provide comfort and ease, yet many are frustrated by their inability to obtain it. This is particularly evident when one considers the unemployment and poverty of the Utah Navajos.

To place the economic situation of Navajo women in perspective, one needs to look at the general Utah employment scene. According to the 1983 "Report to the Governor: Poverty in Utah," "San Juan residents with incomes seventy-five percent of the poverty level comprise a larger proportion of the county population than in any other county in Utah."[25] The same is still true in the 1990s.

The report also mentions that "[a] Utah American Indian's chance of being poor is nearly four times that of a white individual."[26] In terms of Navajo employment, this means that because of isolation, lack of job training, barriers in English, and unfamiliarity with Anglo work values, many older men and women are cut off from gainful economic employment. Statistically, 52 percent of the reservation Navajos in southeastern Utah in 1990 were below the poverty level, surviving on an average family income of $11,732. Of those people sixteen years of age or older, 55 percent of the men and 57 percent of the women capable of entering the labor force were unemployed. Chances of economic prosperity for many Navajos in the near future look remote.

In an interview with members of the State Employment Office in Blanding, the director reflected on his twenty-three years of working in job placement with Navajos and offered the following impressions.[27] First, many of the statistics generated by state agencies are not accurate because of the definition of eligibility for unemployment and welfare. In Utah, if a family has an employable father, he is not able to receive state welfare, yet if he is a Navajo, he is eligible for tribal welfare. This has the effect of keeping those who cannot find work, on the reservation and away from employment agencies.

Second, job service statistics are based on those who come in and apply for work. After being turned down for employment a few times, it is unlikely that a person will travel many miles to keep trying, thereby reducing the number of registered applicants in comparison to those who actually need work. Navajos who have not worked for at least five months in a year are not eligible for unemployment insurance and so cannot call on this source of income. In addition, many Navajos are not adequately prepared to compete for employment, lacking the education and skills needed in the job market. Those who do find work often start at minimum wage.

Third, Navajo women are more stable and responsible on the job than men, which the interviewee attributed to their cultural role of controlling much of the economy. A BIA workforce profile showed almost one and a half times as many women being employed as men.[28]

As a result of unemployment, the material condition of the Utah Navajos is impoverishment. A brief yet depressing synopsis of living conditions on the Utah reservation follows: houses with one or fewer bedrooms, 61 percent; houses with four or more bedrooms, 2 percent; no bathrooms, 69 percent; homes heated with wood, 70 percent; houses without a telephone, 80 percent.

What, then, do Navajos do with the little money they have? A study conducted in 1974 showed they spent 23 percent of their income on food and 23.5 percent on transportation, a lifeline on the reservation.[29] Hauling water, wood, and groceries is a matter of survival. The Navajos have always been a mobile people, and with the expansion of the reservation and the shift from herding to wage work, the pickup truck has grown in importance. Yet transportation is only part of what is needed to solve the problems of unemployment, poverty, and cultural barriers.

Moving toward a synthesis in understanding the Navajo woman of today, one finds there are three general types. The first is the "Dezba" of Gladys Reichard's day. She will be found in any community on the reservation, herding sheep, weaving rugs, and running her homestead with decisiveness. She understands little English and practices Navajo customs: sings, squaw dances, and herding activities play an important part in her life. The "Dezbas" are respected by young and old and are often viewed, along with medicine men, as the repository of the old ways. Their lifestyle and their beliefs have changed little; they are traditional.

At the other end of the spectrum are the young Navajo women who have become increasingly aware of the Anglo world and its materialism. From an outsider's point of view, they are "progressive" in that modern values have a prominent place in how they view the world and what they want to obtain from it. Many of these women have been to boarding school or in the Placement Program or have attended day schools where they learned to appreciate the physical comforts of white society. Television, radio, movies, videos, books, and magazines advertise seductive lifestyles with an accompanying promise of wealth and prestige that cannot be found on the reservation. A nice home, a good job, an education—these are the things young women seek. Independence, not familial ties, is its fruit.

In response to the question, "Would you be happy with a large herd of sheep, your sisters living nearby, and a fine loom outside your hogan?" one "progressive" woman replied,

> I probably would be if that is all I knew—if I didn't have anything else to do or had not been exposed to books and the world. But that is not the case now. You've got to do more; there is no life in that. You can't get anything out of herding sheep and a loom. From the time I used to watch my mother weave up until now, her rugs used to cost maybe $300. Now they cost $50. It's a zero; you can't market in that or get anything out of that. Most people's view is that they [Navajos] live on the res in a hogan, they don't pay their taxes and rent, . . . but I can do it myself. . . . I want to get places and I want to do it how everybody else is doing it. I want to get an education and go out there and do it and not have it done for me. I want to be somebody.[30]

It would be inaccurate to give the impression that this woman, or hundreds like her, disparage the old ways. Many of them say they would either like to return, or at least would not mind returning, to the reservation to help their people. They expressed respect for and even delight in traditional ways, although many of the women had only a rudimentary knowledge of customs and beliefs. Mothers and grandmothers are the ones who are consulted if a question about tradition arises.

One girl, when asked if she would like to learn more about the Navajo way, replied, "Maybe someday I would, but right now I have college. Maybe after that I could look back into it." When asked what she would do to hold on to her culture, she said, "Well, I am now holding a title of Miss Northern Navajo and I think that will be a kind of traditional thing, like weaving, and that will really help to keep my traditional background. Also, language is important."[31] It is ironic that securing a title from a contest can be compared with traditional beliefs, but for some Navajo women, it has become synonymous. Dezba would probably only grimace.

Another woman commented on her future marital plans. She was adamant that she did not want to marry a Navajo because she perceived Navajo men as generally unstable and undependable when it came to earning money and raising a family. In her words, "Marrying into your tribe is like falling back down or a step down instead of going up. That's what I think. . . . It seems like things would never change for you in life. Marry an Anglo, that would be a really neat change, I think."[32] She subsequently did.

While these attitudes may not be representative of many Navajo women, there often appears a certain discontent with how Navajo men act. This is a feeling and thus difficult to quantify, but many years of working with Navajo women have given me the strong impression that they feel the men do not shoulder responsibilities on the home front with the same fervor that women do. Recently, a woman commented,

> We [Navajo women] were there all the time with our mothers, getting lectured about our responsibilities. The boys had too much freedom and were off herding sheep or doing other things. . . . We were always lectured about having a place for our children and that if we were stupid, dumb, and lazy, we would have to live off other people, which is not the right way. I want to find a man who cares and thinks about tomorrow. Many older women say the same thing.[33]

Education has been accepted as the key to social and economic improvement. Career planning, which had not been a thought for some as late as the 1960s, is now a major consideration for many. A study completed in 1974 stated, "Neither the Navajo or the Papago are accustomed to thinking in terms of 'careers' or jobs. Most work is viewed as a temporary activity for the purpose of raising money quickly. There are few jobs on the reservation; many of these are temporary or seasonal."[34] At least in Utah, this statement is only partly true.

Today, more than ever, young Navajo women are taking the education and training offered on or near the reservation and using it to lay a foundation for careers. Many Utah Navajos attend the College of Eastern Utah (CEU), San Juan Campus, for their first two years of higher education.

Using statistics from the fall quarters of 1992 and 1993 for an average, one finds that 76 percent (303) of the Navajo student body (399) was composed of women.[35] Many of them later go away to school and receive four-year degrees. As one Navajo graduate said,

> I'm a real career person. I want to get ahead because I've seen too much tragedy right down here in a relationship between man and wife. I'm a survivor. I want to accomplish what I want. If I'm going to survive, it is going to be me that puts me through. I never had the attitude of relying on anybody. . . . I have a mind and it is up to me to develop it, to learn as much as I can; it is my responsibility. Just like anything else, you exercise your mind like you exercise your body. . . . So it is very important to me to learn to get ahead. Education helps you get in a lot of places and get good jobs and a good life. I don't like to be anybody's underdog. I like to voice my opinion and be a little important—at least be recognized—to say, "I have an opinion and I want to be heard."[36]

Much of what this student said is substantiated quantitatively. In spring 1991, 60 percent (66 females and 33 males) of the Navajo student population on the CEU–San Juan Campus answered a fifty-seven-response questionnaire concerning lifestyle and work aspirations.[37] A brief summary of their replies shows how these "progressives" feel. In three different categories, 92 percent of the Navajo women felt it was either very important or extremely important to advance to higher-level positions in a job, be paid well enough to live comfortably, and work with and meet new people. Only 24 percent believed it important to live near relatives and 39 percent to stay home; 17 percent wanted to do the same thing most of the time, while 80 percent wanted to be creative and have work that required skill; 65 percent felt it very/extremely important to work with computers. When asked, "If by chance you had enough money to live comfortably without working, do you think that you would work anyway?" 100 percent said yes compared with 66 percent of the Anglo females. Whether traditional or progressive, Navajo women have a strong work ethic that is still very much a part of their values.

Many of the old people are ambivalent toward the young "progressive" Navajo who obtains skills and aggressively seeks change. In one respect the elders encourage this idea of receiving an education in order to improve life on the reservation, but they are sad to see the traditional lifestyle die and unnerved by the lack of respect for tradition and self-discipline. One woman, reflecting on the differences between past and present, said, "Nowadays, things are a lot different. The younger generation is too lazy because it did not have a severe struggle to survive. They [young people] have had too many conveniences. But in those days, the kids were well disciplined and obeyed their parents and that was part of the Navajo way."[38] While this view may be attributed in part to the "good old days" syndrome, there is still a large measure of truth to it, since survival required greater rigor and self-control than is necessary today.

The old ways also present barriers to achieving a career. Clyde Kluckhohn branded these obstacles "leveling mechanisms."[39] Redistribution of wealth, confining social attitudes, and the threat of witchcraft were all ways of keeping tribal members on a relatively equal economic and social plane. These practices still hold people back. For instance, one woman said that her neighbors became jealous when she and her sisters were in college. Indications of witchcraft started to occur, with one incident of a skinwalker taking place as well as the discovery of sorcerer's materials near their home. Her father had an increasingly hard time economically and socially, and when he died of a heart attack while hunting, the family attributed it to witchcraft.[40]

Another woman provided a less dramatic but equally instructive view:

> Our family is known for its education. We are all known to have good schooling and to do well, so other Navajo people look at us and say we are not learning traditional ways and they get really jealous. . . . People in Blanding, especially the Navajo people, are kind of mean to our family; they don't want us to get ahead, so they put lies and rumors on us. It really makes our family upset and frustrated. Sometimes I don't want to go home because of all that conflict down there. I don't want to face it.[41]

Not all young Navajo women have the desire to become acculturated to Anglo ways. Many are not thinking of careers but are content with being wives, with finding part-time or full-time employment in service industries on or off the reservation, or with herding the family livestock.

These women used to be the majority, but given the increasing number and types of programs now available on the reservation, many have found change more desirable.

A term has been coined by "progressive" Navajos to describe those on the reservation who are caught between two worlds. The word "John" denotes either a male or a female who speaks little English, is socially unskilled in an Anglo setting, remains on the reservation, and is more traditional than modern. While it usually carries a negative connotation, many older and younger Navajo people are not offended by its use but see it as an in-group name that describes a real, if not amusing, situation. The best single definition of "John" was given by a woman who prided herself on her ability to communicate in Navajo with old people, who knew the traditions, and yet who could operate in an Anglo world to earn a living and obtain an education. She was not casting aspersions on traditions per se but only poking fun at those who have not yet learned to operate in the dominant society.

> "John" is used the same way you would use the word "hick." It has that kind of a connotation to it. They are just reservation kids—Indians through and through. They have an accent, but it is not too bad. They wear old levis, cowboy boots, have never been away from the reservation, and go to town once in a while, but that is all they do. They don't have any other views of what the world is like outside, or opinions of any type—just their own little world. Somebody that has never been anywhere. They don't do much for themselves; they just live on the reservation, herd sheep, and eat mutton stew. They have no desire to travel or get acquainted with the outside world. They just live from day to day. . . . A "John" is a zero, I guess.[42]

The meaning of the term "John" is highly situational, depending on how and when it is used and who uses it. For instance, if a friend, relative, or peer uses it, the person being referred to would not take offense but would view it as a joke. If an Anglo uses the word to describe someone he does not know, or if a Navajo uses it to denote superiority, then it becomes offensive. In the latter case, the offended person might think to himself or herself, "Where did this person come from? He is just as John as I am. He probably came from worse conditions than I came from—he probably came from a hogan too."[43]

It is interesting that older, traditional women are regarded with respect and deference for their following of the Navajo way, but when younger women stay home on the reservation and herd sheep, they are regarded by some as "Johns." The importance of this lies in the fact that education, material wealth, and values have entered into the Utah Navajos' views, creating internal pressure for group modification. In the past change has been foisted on the Navajos by outside sources—the government, the BIA, and the state. Now there are pressures for change from within as women—the core of economic and social control in traditional culture—shift their emphasis to accepting more of mainstream American culture.

Women returning from school are no longer satisfied with a family of six living in a one-room home that has no plumbing, no central heating, and no telephone. One might ask if these women will even return to the reservation. Many may not, but my impression from talking with many Navajos over a twenty-year period is that family ties are important enough to encourage these women to either live on the reservation or close enough to it so that they can visit their relatives frequently. Jobs in schools, industry, oil companies, and government services are available to those who are qualified; it is for these jobs that an increasing number of Navajos are training.

Thus the shift from "Dezba" to "John" is only a transitional stage, part of the movement away from traditional society into a crucible of change. As the desire for material wealth and social mobility increases, many of the old bonds that held the people to Navajo culture will loosen and, in turn, strengthen the growing internal pressures to enter mainstream Anglo culture. When this happens, there will be a dramatic shift, both quantitatively and qualitatively, toward the modernization of the roles of Navajo women in southeastern Utah.

CHAPTER TWELVE

CONCLUSION

A Glance at the Present, a Glimpse of the Future

As the Utah Navajos step into the twenty-first century, they can look back at the last years of the twentieth century and discern patterns of what lies ahead. Not surprisingly, many of the same issues that have been both a help and a hindrance in the past remain concerns in the present, although they take a new form. Central to these concerns are the land, Navajo culture, and the People's relationship to the dominant society. Yet, unlike the past, the battle for control of resources and self-determination is being played out in the courts, the schools, and other institutions of local, state, and federal jurisdiction. Some of these issues are not limited to the Utah Navajos or even tribes in the Southwest but are faced by Indian groups throughout the United States. The Utah Navajos provide an excellent window for understanding issues in Native America today.

Generally, there are four areas, all of which are intertwined, that both help and challenge the Utah Navajos: economic development, lawsuits, education, and political power. As the People become increasingly adept at maneuvering on these playing fields, they have obtained some important results; the final outcome of others is still pending.

One of the most significant of these issues surrounds the Utah Navajo Trust Fund, money generated from royalties paid for oil from the Aneth Extension. Since 1959 the Utah Division of Indian Affairs (UDIA) has had the fiduciary responsibility for supervising the expenditure of these funds that are earmarked for the benefit of the Utah Navajos. A large portion of this money eventually was used by the Utah Navajo Development Council, a private nonprofit organization, and its subsidiary, Utah Navajo Industries, a for-profit organization. UNDC played an important role in delivering services not offered in Utah by the Navajo tribe, which focused most of its support in Arizona and New Mexico. Large amounts of money, estimated at $61 million between 1961 and 1991, flowed through UNDC and UNI over the years.[1] Toward the end of this thirty-year period, clouds began to loom on the horizon.

In the late 1980s people familiar with the operation of these organizations perceived what they believed to be financial irregularities. An investigation completed in November 1991 confirmed at least some of these suspicions. The auditor general, Wayne L. Welsh, reported, "The three-board system (UDIA, UNDC, and UNI) has diluted oversight responsibility to the point that effective policy direction and accountability have not existed."[2] Among the findings were charges that (1) UNDC was poorly managed, increasing its budget expenditure when reserves were dwindling; (2) every UNI enterprise had ended in failure; (3) state buildings such as the Edge of the Cedars Museum, the Social Services Building, and two buildings for the College of Eastern Utah, as well as state roads off the reservation were paid for, at least in part, with trust money; (4) UNI made payments for various reasons to people in high political places that could influence their decisions; and (5) there was extremely poor management and accountability of funds.[3] Example after example followed, raising the eyebrows of even the most casual observers. The big question soon became how these lost funds could be recouped.

Following the audit, all existing funds ($10 million) were frozen to prevent future misspending. Jake C. Pelt and four other Navajos filed a class action lawsuit (*Pelt et al. v. Utah*) that charged the state with wasting and losing millions of dollars through mismanagement. Lawyers for the state tried to dismiss the suit but to no avail. San Juan County commissioners suggested joining the Navajos, expressing a desire to "protect the money and who is responsible to deal with Native Americans in Utah."[4] Governor Michael Leavitt met with the commissioners and importuned them not to make the suit any more costly, but he also suggested in a joking manner that perhaps the Navajo tribe at Window Rock should administer the funds. One of the county commissioners, Mark Maryboy, a Navajo, reacted quickly, indicating that action would be highly undesirable.[5]

On June 22, 1995, U.S. District Judge David Sam ruled on behalf of the state of Utah that the Navajo Nation did not have a right to sue for mismanagement of trust money. The judge said that "because the fund was created by the federal government, the State of Utah is not a legally obligated trustee of the fund."[6] In a local meeting held in Bluff, one Navajo elder expressed the sentiments of many Utah Navajos: "The State of Utah knows how to deceive us. The benefits we are supposed to get do not come to us. They go somewhere else—we do not know."[7]

Utah's position in the lawsuit was that the blame for the mishandling of funds sat squarely on the shoulders of the Navajos. The state's position was that UNDC and UNI spent 83 percent ($41 million of the $49 million in royalties between 1971 and 1991) of the money at issue. Over the twenty years in question, the state had given the funds to these organizations so that they could better serve the Navajos of southeastern Utah. Once distributed, the funds were under the control of the leaders and advisory councils. Thus *they* should be held accountable by the Utah Navajos if there were problems with how the money was spent.[8]

The legal fight continued. On December 31, 1996, the Tenth Circuit Court of Appeals in Denver overturned Judge Sam's ruling and allowed the Utah Navajos to pursue their suit. Governor Leavitt decided that it might be cheaper and easier to settle out of court, although estimates of the moneys that were lost ranged between $52 million and the seemingly impossible figure of $200 million.[9] Both sides sailed back into the maelstrom, as Utah waited to have certain stipulations met before making available its data on how much money, if any, was actually misspent. The state tried to claim a four-year statute of limitations to avoid going too far into the past. Judge Sam ruled against that argument and ordered the state to pay $2,450 for withholding the records collected from UNDC and others to support its case.[10] The judge thus established the state's potential liability, by extending the period of accountability to over thirty years. At present, the lawsuit drags on indefinitely into the future.

In spite of the ongoing lawsuit, oil royalty funds are available for use. In 1992 the state created the Utah Navajo Trust Fund (UNTF), directed by a three-member board of trustees (consisting of the state treasurer, the director of finance, and a member selected by the governor) to oversee the fair disbursement of funds. There is also a nine-member Dineh committee representing the seven chapters (Oljeto and Aneth, because they have larger populations, have two representatives; all other chapters have one). UNTF money is used for health, education, and chapter projects.

Although the Trust Fund is not directly involved with health services, it owns the Montezuma Creek Clinic, contributes to the cost of its maintenance, and continues to provide health care for the Utah Navajos through arrangements with San Juan Health Services. In the field of education, the UNTF dispenses funds for college scholarships, tutorial assistance, student enrichment, and a vocational-tech support program. Chapter projects help to promote better living conditions, including making home improvements, extending power lines to isolated communities and individual homes, and paying for chapter purchases and repair programs.[11]

A few examples of how UNTF money is being used demonstrate its importance. An estimated 15 percent of the Utah Navajos still do not have electricity in their homes. As the twenty-first century begins, the number of families without power is being decreased by a project that uses federal grants, UNTF money, and tribal funds. The cost—an estimated $300,000—will provide a service that is taken for granted everywhere else in the country.[12] The provision of health care, a second issue, is still frustrated by long distances and the scattered population. Since the Monument Valley Hospital closed in 1996, only an outpatient clinic provides services to this area. Serious emergencies usually require at least a two-hour drive—to Tuba City or Chinle, Arizona, to Shiprock, New Mexico, or to Monticello, Utah. Patients may also be airlifted to Flagstaff, Arizona (150 miles away) or Salt Lake City, Utah (approximately 400 miles).[13] And the Montezuma Creek Clinic renders basic aid to those in need. There never seems to be enough UNTF money (an average of $1.7 million per year) to accomplish everything.[14] Prioritizing projects can lead to disputes, but many Utah Navajos feel that now the funds from the oil fields are at least coming home to the people who deserve them.

Still, the problems associated with the oil field in the Montezuma Creek–Aneth area have not abated. In December 1997 an explosion at a Mobil pumping station once again raised the issue of the oil company's relationship with the people who live nearby. Reminiscent of the 1978 "takeover" that closed eight hundred wells for two weeks and the 1993 blockade of a road used by another oil company to drill on a nearby mesa, the protesters set up a tepee in the parking lot of the Mobil offices near Aneth. Their concerns, echoes from past demonstrations, centered on environmental degradation, health problems, employment opportunities, and renegotiating leases.

Mobil Oil reacted calmly. It set about reopening the sixty-three wells closed at the insistence of the demonstrators. There were other people just as anxious to see the closure end. With five hundred oil wells on the Utah Strip producing millions of dollars for the Utah Navajo Trust Fund and $1.5 million in San Juan County property taxes, many area residents—both Navajo and Anglo—wished to have the problems resolved quickly.[15] Albert Hale, president of the Navajo Nation at the time, played an important part in the negotiations.

Seventy-two hours after the talks started the various factions had signed a thirty-two-point agreement. In addition to paying partial salaries for two Navajo public liaison specialists, Mobil pledged to follow Navajo hiring practices and to settle further issues in the tribe's "peacemaker" courts, which operate according to a community-level conflict resolution format. Hale promised that more of the tribe's royalties would go to the Utah Navajos.[16] With that, the Aneth oil field resumed normal business.

However, it was just a matter of time before new problems arose. In March 1998 the federal government filed lawsuits against Texaco and Mobil for polluting the San Juan River. Oil spills of various sizes had been recorded since 1991, with the bulk of the charges specifying violations of the Federal Clean Water Act. Improper procedures and faulty or missing equipment made up the remainder of the complaints. Because of these errors, Texaco is charged with leaking 85 barrels, or 3,570 gallons, of oil during this period; Mobil has had 73 spills, losing 2,000 barrels of contaminated "production water" (used to pump oil out of the ground) and 450 barrels of oil.[17] The government is seeking fines of $25,000 per day for each violation. From Mobil's and Texaco's perspective, the claims are groundless.

Utah Navajos face other issues as well. Hundreds of miles of dirt roads, particularly on the western portion of the Utah Strip, present an obstacle to travel in inclement weather. An estimated $50 million would be required to meet most of these needs, but that kind of money is not available. At present, a $3 million federal program will either gravel or pave routes used by school buses.[18]

Improved roads bring more tourists. Recently, two important bills have appropriated money that will bring greater financial opportunities to the reservation. The U.S. Congress authorized construction of a visitors' center at the Four Corners boundary marker, enticing more travelers to stop at the comfortable facilities and vendors' booths. Even more impressive is the $3.7 million Monument Valley Rest Area and Vendor Village that will include a 14,000-square-foot museum and welcome center, sixty booths for Navajo artisans, an outdoor amphitheater, and extensive parking facilities. Utah, the Navajo Nation, and San Juan County will add their money to the $2.8 million provided by the Arizona Department of Transportation to fund the project.[19]

While these issues are economic in nature, there are others that revolve around cultural concerns. One of the most interesting questions to be raised recently is the status of Indians in prison. Since 1970 there have been more than fifty lawsuits nationally addressing this issue.[20] Utah has had more than its share of the controversy. Starting in 1986 when the correctional facility in Draper denied nineteen Navajo inmates access to a sweat lodge, the prison system has been under fire. The protesters invoked their rights under the Native American Religious Freedom Act of 1978, claiming that the government denied their entitlements and had not consulted with traditional practitioners as it should. These denied rights came in many forms—not providing space to hold ceremonies, an absence of sweat lodges, forbidding prisoners to grow their hair long, restricting paraphernalia necessary for ceremonies in the prison, and treating Indian religious leaders who performed the ceremonies differently than ministers from other faiths.[21]

Advocacy groups continued to form. Beyond a national network of protesters, there developed a number of organizations that represented Indians in Utah: the Native American Brotherhood Organization, Aboriginal Uintah (Ute) Nation of Utah, Navajo Inmate Spiritual/Social Development, and the Navajo Nation Corrections Project. In 1993 the U.S. Congress passed the Religious Freedom Restoration Act, which encouraged litigation on behalf of Native American inmates if their rights were not honored during incarceration. In lay terms, what this means is that (1) prisoners have equal access to Native American religious ceremonies that are comparable to what is allowed Judeo-Christian practitioners; (2) prisoners can wear their hair according to tribal customs; (3) there can be no discrimination against those who practice these

226   A GLANCE AT THE PRESENT, A GLIMPSE OF THE FUTURE

beliefs; and (4) non-Indian workers in the penal system must receive training to increase sensitivity to these rights and their obligations.[22]

In 1996 Utah passed Senate Bill 128, Indian Worship at Correctional Facilities, which guaranteed the state's commitment to equality. One section itemized some of the objects permitted for use in ceremonies: cedar, corn husks, corn pollen, cornmeal, eagle and other feathers, sage, sweetgrass, willows, drums, gourds, lava rock, medicine bundles, bags or pouches, staffs, pipes, and tobacco.[23]

The last item has raised the eyebrows of some prison officials. Tobacco is contraband and cannot be used by certain inmates. The fear now is that it will become a black market item and that allowing it shows favoritism to a small sector (in 1996, 1.4 percent were Indian) of the state's prison population.[24] Native Americans counter that tobacco is an integral part of traditional practices and is used in the rehabilitation process to combat substance abuse. Leonard Foster, director of the Navajo Nation Corrections Project, argued, "Approximately 95% of those Native Americans incarcerated are serious substance abusers and under the influence of alcohol while committing a crime and this rate is 30–50% higher than that of other ethnic groups in the institutions."[25] He indicated elsewhere that when Indians participate in indigenous religious rituals while in prison, only 7 percent become repeat offenders, compared to the 30 to 40 percent repeat offenders among those who do not participate.[26]

There is still controversy over the contents of medicine bundles, the type of tobacco to be used, and whether pipes or cigarettes are acceptable. Guards have interrupted some ceremonies to perform accountability or contraband checks, thus killing the spirit of the rite. And often spiritual advisers are not consulted when an interpretation of what is or is not acceptable is made by prison officials.[27] While conditions have improved for Native American inmates, there is room for progress.

At the bottom of this religious conflict lay race relations. Examples of mistrust that colors Anglo-Indian relationships were found in discussions about splitting San Juan County into two entities. The division, if accepted, would have created an Indian (primarily Navajo) and a non-Indian county. The friction that has existed on both sides for many years came to a head through the deliberations over whether this split was feasible. The contention focused on myriad issues but can be summarized as two social, economic, and political philosophies at odds with each other.

The root of the conflict is Navajo tribal sovereignty, which created problems that the county could not solve by itself. Who should pay for services on the reservation, support the schools, define school district policy, care for the roads, and determine the jurisdiction of tribal courts and law enforcement? Some of these questions have been satisfactorily answered, but others have not. In 1996 Navajo Nation president Albert Hale signed a memorandum of understanding to work with Utah's newly established Native American Legislative Liaison Committee to try to find solutions.[28] Founded in 1995, this organization's purpose was to work with reservations throughout the state to formulate answers to problems and then propose appropriate bills to the Utah legislature.[29] While the splitting of the county was a huge issue, similar problems of sovereignty existed with most of the Utah tribes.

Fundamental to this political issue is an economic issue. In San Juan property owners felt they had paid and would continue to have to pay taxes to solve reservation problems. Since Navajos living on the reservation do not pay county property taxes, it did not seem fair to the white minority (by a small percentage) that they should support the growing Navajo population.[30] Some people expressed the feeling that everyone should be treated equally and that the special status of the reservation should be done away with entirely.

This was the environment that the Center for Public Policy and Administration, an independent arbitrator from the University of Utah, stepped into. Its task was to form a blue ribbon committee to study the issue and then present its findings. That was in 1995. By 1997 the final report was available to county residents but held nothing surprising. It stated that if the split were carried out, the southern (Indian) county would have a difficult time meeting its financial obligations, since most of the businesses are in the north. The report did not recommend any specific course of action, but a petition would need to be signed by 25 percent of the voters of San Juan County to get the process under way.[31] The issue died a natural death. What is important, however, are the feelings engendered by the trust relationship and special status of reservations. Similar questions and feelings have existed since the beginning of the federal government's program of establishing enclaves for Indian people.

The special status afforded Native Americans has led to other questions on the state, local, and tribal levels. For instance, a Navajo man, Loren Crank, filed a lawsuit against the Seventh District Court, claiming that the number of Indians represented on juries was far below what it should be. The court claimed that because of a reservation Indian's special status, he or she could not be required to serve on a jury the same way other people could. The court's findings indicated that jury lists should be expanded to include those living on the reservation; the tribe agreed to help enforce the ruling.[32] In December 1998 the Third District Court reviewed the progress in this case and determined that the county was in full compliance with jury selection procedures. Lists, generating Navajo jurors, were based on information provided by the tribe and represented the 52 percent Navajo population in the county. David Wright, attorney for the Utah Judicial Council, hailed this positive result as an "unprecedented agreement" that showed the county's efforts to cooperate with the Navajo Nation.[33]

Legal decisions have also played an important part in education, long considered a crucial component of cultural change. Litigation led to a court order requiring the San Juan School District to build a small high school (at an estimated cost of $4.1 million) for students living in the isolated Navajo Mountain area. Although there were only thirty-five enrollees in October 1997, the county and the state committed to supporting this outreach project to eliminate busing and boarding students.[34] In a special election held on May 6, 1997, voters (who were predominantly white) favored by a ratio of three to one the building of the school.[35] The construction of the facility and the growing attendance not only have been a boon to the community, but an example of favorable racial relations.

The San Juan School District has been embroiled in some type of legal dispute for almost thirty years. In 1993 new allegations, resurrecting old concerns, charged that federal funding designated for Navajo students was being spent on white children in the northern schools. With approximately fourteen hundred children in the south, this was a serious charge. In the blunt words of the Navajos' attorney, Eric Swenson: "The San Juan County School District has and continues to discriminate against Native American students on the basis of their race."[36]

Investigations followed, as did exorbitant legal costs. Three years after the lawsuit started, the district's superintendent determined that for every child in school, $58 were being spent on legal fees. Four months into the fiscal year only 10 percent of the district's legal budget of $100,000 remained.³⁷ The plaintiffs, however, did not find the gross prejudicial treatment they had expected. In terms of educational technology, libraries, facilities, and other concerns, the school district had been fair, and in some cases, the schools in the south were in better shape than those in the north. In April 1997 the disputing parties reached a settlement in the long-standing dispute. The major provisions of the agreement were that the state of Utah would contribute $2 million toward construction of the Navajo Mountain school, the Navajo Nation would help to reduce the cost of utilities, and committees of educators would review and revise the curriculum, bilingual education, and special education.³⁸

While this last point has not generated a new lawsuit, it has become a divisive issue among teachers, administrators, students, and community members. Throughout the nation bilingual education has been a political football. All sides have research to support their point of view. Regardless of how individuals felt, the San Juan School District, because of legal agreements, was committed. Statistics from the district showed beyond a doubt that there was a need. In September 1997 there was a total enrollment of 3,642 students (pre-kindergarten through grade 12), 49 percent of whom were Navajos. Of the total number of potentially English-proficient (PEP) students, 1,275 (95 percent) were Navajos, who were 84 percent more likely to drop out of school than their fully English-proficient peers.³⁹ The elementary and high schools in the south, with a predominantly Navajo population, averaged 80 percent PEP, based on standardized test results obtained in 1997.⁴⁰ The Stanford Achievement Test (SAT) "shows that a school's test scores drop proportionately as the percentage of PEP students enrolled rises."⁴¹ Put another way, San Juan's academic test scores are at the bottom of the heap when compared to the rest of the state of Utah.

No one disputed these facts, but there was a great deal of argument about how a change could be brought about. The district proposed a number of solutions that centered on introducing Navajo literacy and a dual-language program. In elementary schools where enough Navajo students attended, a subject would also be taught in both Navajo and English. In high schools Navajo language would be offered as an elective into which ninth- and tenth-grade PEP students would be automatically enrolled; in grades eleven and twelve, a content class would also be taught in Navajo. Traditional culture and curriculum would be available on all levels. While this plan was implemented in various stages in 1998, there are some people who still voice complaints. They argue that the system hinders the acquisition of English-language skills for those who need the help the most; that the whole plan is politically and legally motivated and does not consider the welfare of the children; that the Navajo tribe, which has a voice in the adoption of curriculum, is foisting family responsibility for teaching language and heritage onto the schools, where it does not belong; and that there are not enough staff to implement a true bilingual model. After listening to these arguments, a Navajo man serving on the school board countered: "I think we should withdraw every Navajo student from the San Juan School District. That's when you will be happy. Take care of it once and for all. Just sweep the floor and go home. You have no interest in educating Navajo students in the San Juan School District."⁴² Eventually, tempers settled and a plan was agreed on. At this point the district is using a combination of teaching strategies that include English as a second language, sheltered English, cooperative learning, bilingual instruction, and traditional methodology.

There are many people who view the school district's bilingual and bicultural program favorably. A two-hundred-page report titled *A Study of the Educational Perceptions and Attitudes of the Four Stakeholder Groups in the San Juan School District in 1998*, by Carolyn M. Shields, a consultant from British Columbia, examined teachers', students', and parents' views of the educational system. This extensive study examines each school's environment and makes a comparison between those that serve primarily Navajo students and those that serve Anglos. A few statistics provide a clear evaluation of the parents' perspective on the bilingual program's success. The report indicates that 73 percent of the Navajo parents in the district are either reasonably or very satisfied with the bilingual program; that 64 percent are happy with the teachers' expectations in that program; that 86 percent support Navajo language being taught in the schools but only 48 percent believe it should be a graduation requirement; and that 69 percent believe that the schools have values similar to the parents'.[43] There appears to be substantial agreement on the direction the district is taking to meet cultural expectations.

The "Consensus Committee Monitoring Report," issued in April 1999, evaluated the program's strengths and weaknesses in the classroom. On the positive side, staff and faculty exhibited both awareness and acceptance of the goals established by the district. However, there was a need for improved teaching methodology and more facility with the Navajo language. The report warns:

> Some [teachers] are fairly successful in staying in Navajo the whole [class] period. Some switch back and forth between English and Navajo. . . . Relatively few seem to have been able to help students communicate meaningfully in Navajo. . . . Teachers have done well to get things going this year. But we have to say that if teachers are doing the same things this time next year, then this program is likely to crash.[44]

The implementation of a bilingual program, especially for a language that does not have a history of being written, is an uphill fight at best. When introduced into a dominant English-language environment, it becomes even more difficult to preserve the native tongue.

What has been playing out in southeastern Utah is only part of a larger debate in the state and the nation. In 1997 the state legislature received an English-only bill late in its session. The politicians took no action before adjourning, but news of the bill spread to various ethnic minority communities, Navajo included. The next year saw one thousand people marching in opposition to the bill. Among them was Samuel Billison, a tribal education leader and president of the Navajo Code Talkers' Association. Predictably, he recounted how his language had been an important ally during World War II, saving lives on the battlefields of the Pacific as it dumbfounded the Japanese, who could not understand the language or break the code. Billison later went on record, saying, "The holy people gave us this language, and only they can take it away."[45] Although the bill never intended to do away with any of the 120 languages spoken in Utah but only to decrease the printing costs of government publications by using only one language, many minorities did not perceive it in that light. On January 22, 1999, the legislature cast a forty-three to thirty-one vote defeating the bill.[46] Although it did not pass, this legislation once again raised the importance of language as an ingredient of cultural identity, as a cultural symbol, and as a potent force on political battlegrounds.

Yet these battlegrounds and issues are shifting, in some instances, to different terrain. As people think of the Utah Navajos, they often envision life on the reservation: elders huddled around a wood-burning stove, youngsters herding livestock on horseback, and the ubiquitous pickup truck, hauling wood, water, or the family to town. While these are all very real images, they ignore a growing sector of Utah's Indian community. According to the 1990 census, the second-largest group of Native Americans (6,111) is in Salt Lake County, the largest group in San Juan County (6,859), and the third largest in Uintah County (2,335 Utes).[47]

What this means is that the urban Indian, 25 percent of the total Indian population, will play an important part, now and in the future, in determining the direction of Utah's Native American cultural heritage. While individuals may get lost in the sea of other cultures in the cities, a number of organizations have been established that make their presence felt.

There are two dozen Indian organizations in the most populated part of the region known as the Wasatch Front (from Provo to Logan, which includes Salt Lake City). Among these are Native American Community Services (Church of Jesus Christ of Latter-day Saints Social Services), the Indian Christian Center (nondenominational), the Utah Inter-Tribal Veterans Association, the American Indian Resource Center, the Intertribal Students Association (University of Utah), and Native American Educational Outreach (Brigham Young University). All of these groups help to bring Native Americans together to celebrate their unique heritage and to provide needed services.

Two of the organizations demonstrate the importance of this type of institution in fostering a Pan-Indian environment in an urban setting. The Indian Walk-In Center, which has been in existence for more than twenty years, is a nonprofit organization supported by the United Way Agency whose mission is to give material assistance, promote cultural values and heritage, and strengthen Native American families and communities. The volume and scope of the center's accomplishments are impressive. In 1996 more than eighteen thousand people, half of whom were under the age of eighteen, received help with emergency food.[48] While this service is available to all low-income families, members of all of the Utah tribes as well as the members of forty-three other tribes who live along the Wasatch Front were recipients of this aid. The center also provides counseling services, cultural enrichment programs for Indian youths, an elders program, and a rehabilitation program for alcohol abuse. Each month there is a powwow that draws an average of four hundred to five hundred participants. At Christmas, an average of six hundred needy people receive a Christmas dinner and toys for the children.[49]

To support many of these activities, the center sponsors a variety of fund-raising activities. For instance, it rents parking space for the Buzz baseball games, the fees from which go to its programs. Indian arts and crafts shows raise money while giving talented Native American artists an opportunity for public exposure. Local businesses and individuals are canvassed for support of special programs such as the Christmas dinner. Auctions bring in yet another group of contributors.[50] One reason that the center has remained viable for so long, when many similar programs blossom and die within a short time, is its ability to reach many different segments of both the Indian and the non-Indian community of Salt Lake City.

Five blocks south of the Walk-In Center is the Indian Training Education Center (ITEC), which has enjoyed similar success. This Utah-based, private nonprofit corporation, funded in part by a Title IV Job Training Partnership Act (JTPA) grant, was established in 1988 to provide short-term (usually three to nine months) job training and education for Native Americans. An applicant must be over the age of fourteen, economically disadvantaged, and living off-reservation in Utah. Programs available include adult basic education, GED preparation, high school completion, occupational skills training, and short-term college certificates or degrees.

ITEC conducted a study of its first five years (1989–94) of operation to determine who was using its services and what kinds of barriers and success they encountered. An interesting profile emerged, based on the 1,044 customers served during that time. The "typical" person who walked through the door was a Navajo (71%) male who was twenty-seven years old, supported a family of two, earned less than $8,000 per year, held a high school diploma but was unemployed, and who, at the end of the program, entered unsubsidized employment that provided a wage per hour increase.[51] Subsequent data confirm this profile.

What the new enrollee encounters is personalized counseling and placement that meets his or her needs. Monitoring of progress in the form of class attendance and satisfactory grades is tied to a monthly stipend for living expenses. At the end of the training, the participant is assisted in a job search and placement. During the past eight years, ITEC has achieved an 80 percent success rate, meaning that its graduates have either "finished their programs successfully and/or entered into the job market better prepared than when they started."[52] All through this experience, cultural sensitivity ensures open dialogue between student and counselor.

All of the contemporary issues discussed thus far relate in one way or another to political power. As the Utah Navajos enter the twenty-first century, they are seeing that most major decisions affecting their future revolve around such power. Recent agreements share power between both state and tribe. One of the most significant of these, which has opened a variety of doors, is the Memorandum of Understanding signed in 1996 by Navajo Nation president Albert Hale and Utah governor Mike Leavitt. Its purpose is to provide guidelines for state, county, and tribal governments to work together to solve common problems. Jurisdiction in law enforcement across shared boundaries, services for individuals, families, and communities, as well as firm procedures for dealing with gas and oil severance taxes are all part of the agreement.[53]

Two examples of the diversity that this type of understanding allows illustrate its importance. In January 1997 members of the Navajo Tribal Police and the San Juan County Sheriff's Department forged an agreement to purchase six vehicles, provide a housing unit, and share law enforcement responsibilities in the Aneth–Montezuma Creek area.[54] The importance of this decision became apparent a year later. In May 1998 the shooting of a Colorado police officer launched a three-county, two-state, and Navajo Nation manhunt for three individuals involved in the killing. One of the fugitives fled to the banks of the San Juan River, where he committed suicide; the other two were believed to have escaped in this same area. More than five hundred law enforcement officers, including local police, sheriffs, SWAT teams from Salt Lake City, members of the National Guard, Navajo police, and a specialized Navajo police tracking unit participated in the manhunt.⁵⁵ A year later and an estimated $2 million poorer, the searchers have left the country but respond to sightings reported by local people. (In 1999 the body of one of the fugitives was found by Navajo deer hunters in the rugged canyon country ten to fifteen miles from the river.) To defray their expenses incurred in the manhunt, the Navajo police presented a $700,000 bill to Utah's congressional team that was seeking special funds to pay for the search.⁵⁶ Cross-jurisdictional operations have proven to be expensive on both sides of the reservation boundary.

Less dramatic but longer lasting was an intergovernmental agreement signed by the state and the Navajo Nation to help abused children living on the Utah Strip. Since the previous agreement of 1996, state social workers have had the obligation to intervene on behalf of abused and abandoned children. A problem arose in removing these children from troubled environments, the Navajo courts often refusing to recognize the "Caucasian" workers' obligation to send the children to foster homes. Since very few families on the reservation could be found to take the children, they had to be placed in white homes in northern Utah. The agreement signed in June 1999 provided for four Navajo caseworkers to live and work on the reservation with the intent that they would be more successful in the Navajo court system protecting abused children. Thus the state of Utah now contracts with the tribe to provide this service.⁵⁷

The importance of this and other political agreements has not been lost on the Navajo people, who are becoming increasingly politicized. As the younger generation casts its lot in the legal and governmental arenas, its voice will be louder. The best example of this is the political activities of Utah Navajo Mark Maryboy, who over the past fifteen years has grown in power and influence on a local, state, and tribal level. In 1987 the people of San Juan County elected him the first ever Native American county commissioner in Utah. Since that time he has served as a Navajo Nation council delegate from the Aneth area and as chairman of the tribe's Budget and Finance Committee.⁵⁸ President Bill Clinton appointed him to the National Indian Education Advisory Committee in 1994 and asked him to deliver the opening prayer at the 1992 Democratic National Convention in New York City.⁵⁹ And finally, he has encouraged more political activity on the reservation by helping Navajos to register and vote in local, state, and national elections. Maryboy's activity serves as an example to the young people of the influence that can be wielded when one enters the political realm.

What does the future hold for the Utah Navajos? Using the past as a barometer for the future, it appears that decision-making power and change will be in the hands of an increasingly younger generation, as opposed to the traditional past when important decisions were made by the elders. Courtrooms, legislation, money, and influence—just as in the dominant society—will play an increasingly important role on the Utah Strip. And as education in school replaces the religious teachings and values previously provided by the elders, much of what is uniquely Navajo now will take on a different tone.

This is not to suggest that the Navajos will become carbon copies of the dominant society. They have always adapted to shifting circumstances, from the days of the trading post and the introduction of the car to those of uranium and dependence on oil. What becomes crystal clear as one looks at the past one hundred years of economic development and cultural change is that the Navajos will continue to be in charge of their destiny. From the time of the Twins to today, the People have always found solutions to the problems that confront them. Whether killing the monsters that roamed the earth in the "palm of time" or using their bones and blood to fight new battles, the Navajos have triumphed. They will continue to do so in the future.

NOTES

CHAPTER ONE

1. Ada Black, interview by author and Marilyn Holiday, October 11, 1991, transcript in possession of author.

2. Dozens of books have been written about the Navajo creation story. Two interesting versions are Father Berard Haile, *The Upward Moving and Emergence Way: The Gishin Biyé Version* (Lincoln: University of Nebraska Press, 1981), and Paul G. Zolbrod, *Diné bahane': The Navajo Creation Story* (Albuquerque: University of New Mexico Press, 1984).

3. Gary Witherspoon, "Navajo Social Organization," in *Handbook of North American Indians—Southwest* 10, ed. Alfonso Ortiz (Washington, D.C.: Smithsonian Institution Press, 1983), 524.

4. For more on mythological teachings about landforms in southeastern Utah, see Robert S. McPherson, *Sacred Land, Sacred View: Navajo Perceptions of the Four Corners Region,* Charles Redd Center Monograph Series, no. 19 (Provo: Brigham Young University Press, 1992).

5. See Leland C. Wyman, "Navajo Ceremonial System," in *Handbook of North American Indians* 10, ed. Alfonso Ortiz (Washington, D.C.: Smithsonian Institution Press, 1983), 536–57.

6. Harry Hoijier, "The Chronology of the Athapaskan Languages," *International Journal of American Linguistics* 22 (October 1956): 219–32.

7. Florence H. Ellis, *An Anthropological Study of the Navajo Indians* (New York: Garland, 1974), 3; see also George E. Hyde, *Indians of the High Plains* (Norman: University of Oklahoma Press, 1959); Morris E. Opler, "The Apachean Culture Pattern and Its Origins," in *Handbook of North American Indians* 10, ed. Alfonso Ortiz (Washington, D.C.: Smithsonian Institution Press, 1983), 382.

8. Clyde Kluckhohn and Dorothea Leighton, *The Navaho,* rev. ed. (Cambridge, Mass.: Harvard University Press, 1974), 33; David M. Brugge, "Navajo

Prehistory and History to 1850," in *Handbook of North American Indians* 10, ed. Alfonso Ortiz (Washington, D.C.: Smithsonian Institution Press, 1983), 490.

9. See McPherson, *Sacred Land, Sacred View*, 77–127.

10. Alan D. Reed and Jonathan C. Horn, "Early Navajo Occupation of the American Southwest: Reexamination of the Dinetah Phase," *Kiva* 55, no. 4 (Fall 1990): 297.

11. J. Lee Correll, *Through White Men's Eyes: A Contribution to Navajo History* 1 (Window Rock, Ariz.: Navajo Heritage Center, 1979), 27, 45.

12. S. Lyman Tyler, "The Yuta Indians before 1680," *Western Humanities Review* 5 (Spring 1951): 160; Correll, *Through White Men's Eyes*, 30.

13. Fray Angelico Chavez and Ted J. Warner, *The Dominguez-Escalante Journal: Their Expedition through Colorado, Utah, Arizona, and New Mexico in 1776* (Provo: Brigham Young University Press, 1976), 9.

14. David M. Brugge, "Vizcarra's Navajo Campaign of 1823," *Arizona and the West* 6 (Autumn 1964): 237.

15. Ibid., 237–39.

16. Ibid., 242–44.

17. Charles Kelly, "Hoskaninni Begay," interview, August 13, 1938, Charles Kelly Papers, Special Collections, Marriott Library, University of Utah, Salt Lake City, Utah, 1, 11.

18. David Meriwether to George Manypenny, January 1, 1857, Record Group 75, Letters Received by the Office of Indian Affairs, New Mexico Superintendency, 1857, National Archives, Washington, D.C.

19. For this period of Navajo history, see Lynn R. Bailey, *If You Take My Sheep: The Evolution and Conflicts of Navajo Pastoralism, 1630–1868* (Los Angeles: Westernlore Press, 1980); *The Long Walk* (Los Angeles: Westernlore Press, 1964); Bailey, *The Navajo Reconnaissance* (Los Angeles: Westernlore Press, 1964); Lawrence C. Kelly, *Navajo Roundup: Selected Correspondence of Kit Carson's Expedition against the Navajo, 1863–65* (Boulder, Colo.: Pruett, 1970); Frank McNitt, *Navajo Wars, Military Campaigns, Slave Raids and Reprisals* (Albuquerque: University of New Mexico Press, 1972); Clifford E. Trafzer, *The Kit Carson Campaign* (Norman: University of Oklahoma Press, 1982).

20. James S. Collins, "New Mexico Superintendency," October 8, 1861, *Report of the Commissioner of Indian Affairs* (Washington, D.C.: Government Printing Office, 1862), 124–25; Andrew Evans to Acting Assistant Adjutant General, October 28, 1861, Record Group 98, Records of the United States Army Commander, Department of New Mexico, 1861, National Archives, Washington, D.C. (hereafter Letters Received—Army); William Arny to William Dole, 6 January 1861; Testimony of James H. Carleton, July 3, 1865, Record Group 75, Letters Received by the Office of Indian Affairs, New Mexico Superintendency, National Archives, Washington, D.C. (hereafter Letters Received—N.M.)

21. Asa Carey to Assistant Adjutant General, May 10, 1864; Eathan Eaton to Benjamin Cutler, February 8, 1865, Letters Received—Army.

22. U.S. Congress, *War of the Rebellion*, ser. 1, vol. 48, pt. 1, Carleton to No Addressee, February 15, 1865, 864–65; John Ayers to Cutler, March 20, 1865, Letters Received—Army.

23. Carleton to Julius Shaw, March 23, 1865; Shaw to Cutler, March 24, 1865; Edmond Butler to Assistant Adjutant General, January 18, 1866, Letters Received—Army.

24. Henry Bristol to W. R. Savage, June 23, 1866; Edmond Butler to Cyrus H. DeForrest, September 2, 1866, Letters Received—Army; Julius K. Graves to D. N. Cooley, September 28, 1866, Letters Received—N.M.

25. Fred Yazzie, interview by author, November 5, 1987, in possession of author; Francis Toledo, cited in *Navajo Stories of the Long Walk Period*, ed. Broderick H. Johnson (Tsaile, Ariz.: Navajo Community College Press, 1973), 144–45.

26. See the following testimonies in Johnson, *Navajo Stories*: Tezbah Mitchell, 252; Frank Johnson, 88–90; and Chahadineli Benally, 62–70. See also Sam Bingham and Janet Bingham, *Between Sacred Mountains: Navajo Stories and Lessons for the Land* (Tucson: Sun Tracks and University of Arizona Press, 1982), 127–35.

27. W. F. M. Arny to Legislative Assembly, Territory of New Mexico, December 16, 1865, Letters Received—N.M.

28. For a more detailed account of this period of San Juan and Navajo history, see Robert S. McPherson, *The Northern Navajo Frontier: Expansion through Adversity, 1860–1900* (Albuquerque: University of New Mexico Press, 1988), 5–19.

29. Kelly, "Hoskaninni Begay," 1–2, 8–9.

30. For more on the ties between protection ceremonies and the land that were created during this time, see Karl W. Luckert, *Navajo Mountain and Rainbow Bridge Religion* (Flagstaff: Museum of Northern Arizona Press, 1977).

31. U.S. Congress, House, *Report of the Commissioner of Indian Affairs*, New Mexico Superintendency, 1864, 185.

32. Sherman in council on May 28, 1868, cited in Correll, *Through White Men's Eyes*, 133.

33. For fuller treatment of this topic, see McPherson, *The Northern Navajo Frontier*, 63–78.

34. U.S. Congress, House, *Report of the Secretary of the Interior*, "The Navajoes," H. Ex Doc. 1, pt. 5, 52d Cong., 2d sess., 1892, 876.

35. For the scope and events of this gold rush, see Robert S. McPherson and Richard Kitchen, "Much Ado about Nothing: The San Juan River Gold Rush, 1892–1893," *Utah Historical Quarterly* 67 (Winter 1999): 68–87.

36. Frank Silvey, "Stampede for Placer Gold," unpublished manuscript, April 10, 1936, Utah State Historical Society, Salt Lake City, 3–4.

37. *Salt Lake Tribune*, January 17, 1893, 1.

38. Antes to President Theodore Roosevelt, April 18, 1904, cited in David M. Brugge, "Navajo Use and Occupation of the Area North of the San Juan River in Present-Day Utah," unpublished manuscript in possession of author (hereafter NUOL).

39. Kate Perkins to Commissioner of Indian Affairs, January 15, 1900, NUOL.

40. Ordinance, Minutes of County Commission of San Juan County, Utah, April 26, 1880–March 1900, Court House, Monticello, Utah, 245.

41. Hayzlett to Commissioner of Indian Affairs, July 28, 1903, NUOL.

42. "Navaho Reservation, Utah—Cancellation of Lands Set Apart in Utah," Executive Order 324A, cited in Charles J. Kappler, *Indian Affairs—Laws and Treaties* (Washington, D.C.: Government Printing Office, 1913), 690.

43. Levi Chubbuck to Secretary of the Interior, December 31, 1906, Record Group 75, Letters Received by Office of Indian Affairs, 1881–1907, Bureau of Indian Affairs, National Archives, Washington, D.C., 30.

44. Walter Runke to Commissioner of Indian Affairs, September 19, 1909, J. Lee Correll Collection, Tribal Archives, Navajo Tribe, Window Rock, Arizona (hereafter Tribe); Runke to Commissioner, April 23, 1915, Tribe.

45. E. B. Merritt to Paradise Oil Company, June 4, 1921, Tribe; Merritt to Byron A. Sharp, December 28, 1922, Tribe; C. Hauck to Sharp, March 24, 1922, Tribe.

46. Elsie Holiday to Secretary of the Interior, November 27, 1922, Tribe; Holiday to Secretary of the Indian Department, November 28, 1922, Tribe; A. W. Leech to Commissioner of Indian Affairs, May 18, 1923, Tribe.

47. C. L. Walker to Commissioner of Indian Affairs, December 6, 1928, Tribe.

CHAPTER 2

1. For examples of this current interest in Native American relationships with the land, see Gordon M. Day, "The Indian as an Ecological Factor in the Northeastern Forests," *Ecology* 34 (April 1953): 329–43; Richard White, "Indian Land Use and Environmental Change," *Arizona and the West* 17, no. 4 (Winter 1975): 327–38; Dan Flores, "Bison Ecology and Bison Diplomacy: The Southern Plains from 1800–1850," *Journal of American History* 78 (September 1991): 465–85: William Cronon, *Changes in the Land* (New York: Hill and Wang, 1983); Timothy Silver, *A New Face on the Countryside* (New York: Cambridge University Press, 1990).

2. Calvin Martin, *Keepers of the Game: Indian-Animal Relationships and the Fur Trade* (Berkeley: University of California Press, 1978).

3. Ibid., 149.

4. Shepherd Krech III, ed., *Indians, Animals, and the Fur Trade: A Critique of Keepers of the Game* (Athens: University of Georgia Press, 1981).

5. Franciscan Friars, *An Ethnologic Dictionary of the Navajo Language* (Saint Michaels, Ariz.: Saint Michaels Press, 1910), 175.

6. Jim Dandy, interview by author, December 4, 1989, transcript in possession of author.

7. Karl W. Luckert, *The Navajo Hunter Tradition* (Tucson: University of Arizona Press, 1975), 27, 102.

8. Ibid., 103, 38–39.

9. Karl W. Luckert, *A Navajo Bringing-Home Ceremony: The Claus Chee Sonny Version of Deerway Ajiłee* (Flagstaff: Museum of Northern Arizona Press, 1978), 129.

10. Cecil Parrish, interview by author, October 10, 1991, transcript in possession of author.

11. Walter Dyk and Ruth Dyk, *Left Handed: A Navajo Autobiography* (New York: Columbia University Press, 1980), 33.

12. Luckert, *The Navajo Hunter Tradition*, 65.

13. W. W. Hill, *The Agricultural and Hunting Methods of the Navaho Indians* (New Haven: Yale University Press, 1938), 98–110; Buck Navajo, interview by author, December 16, 1991, transcript in possession of author.

14. Hill, *Agricultural and Hunting Methods*, 109–10.

15. Ibid., 111.

16. Buck Navajo, interview.

17. Luckert, *Navajo Bringing-Home Ceremony*, 191.

18. Billy Yellow, interview by author, November 6, 1987, transcript in possession of author.

19. John Holiday, interview by author, September 9, 1991, transcript in possession of author.

20. Hill, *Agricultural and Hunting Methods*, 102–3, 122; Sam Bingham and Janet Bingham, *Between Sacred Mountains: Navajo Stories and Lessons from the Land* (Tucson: Sun Tracks and University of Arizona Press, 1982), 42.

21. Bingham and Bingham, *Between Sacred Mountains*, 41.

22. Hill, *Agricultural and Hunting Methods*, 98.

23. Navajo Oshley, interview by Wesley Oshley and Winston Hurst, January 5, 1978, transcript in possession of author.

24. Luckert, *The Navajo Hunter Tradition*, 113–14.

25. Ibid., 115–16.

26. Ibid., 126.

27. Ibid., 107.

28. Navajo Oshley, interview; Luckert, 30, 49.

29. Francis H. Elmore, "The Deer and His Importance to the Navaho," *El Palacio* 60 (November 1953): 371–84; Hill, *Navaho*, 143–44.

30. Terry Knight, spiritual leader of the Ute Mountain Utes, interview by Mary Jane Yazzie and author, December 19, 1994, manuscript in possession of author.

31. Joseph G. Jorgensen, "The Ethnohistory and Acculturation of the Northern Ute" (Ph.D. diss., Brigham Young University), 330–32.

32. Edward Dutchie, Sr., interview by author, May 7, 1996, manuscript in possession of author.

33. Harold Lindsay Amoss, Jr., "The Ute Mountain Utes" (Ph.D. diss., University of California, Berkeley), 51.

34. See Robert S. McPherson, *The Northern Navajo Frontier: Expansion through Adversity, 1860–1900* (Albuquerque: University of New Mexico Press, 1988), for historic events in this region.

35. *Treaty between the United States of America and the Navajo Tribe of Indians* (Las Vegas: KC Publications, 1973), 22, 24.

36. Garrick Bailey and Roberta Bailey, *A History of the Navajos: The Reservation Years* (Santa Fe, New Mex.: School of American Research, 1986), 47–48.

37. Edmund S. Carlisle to W. M. Clark, October 1, 1884; Carlisle to Major Hall (Fort Lewis, Colo.), November 8, 1884; John F. Tapping to William Clark, December 16, 1884, Record Group 75, Consolidated Ute Records, Denver Record Center (hereafter Consol. Ute).

38. Carlisle to Clark, October 1, 1884; Carlisle to Hall, November 8, 1884, Consol. Ute.

39. P. T. Swain to C. F. Stollsteimer, November 26, 1885; L. Richardson to Indian Agent, September 1, 1886, Consol. Ute.

40. Frank Silvey, "History and Settlement of Northern San Juan County," n.p., n.d., Utah State Historical Society, Salt Lake City, 33.

41. Petition to Colonel P. T. Swain, December 16, 1886; Harold Carlisle to Stollsteimer June 12, 1887, Consol. Ute.

42. L. M. Armstrong to C. H. Stollsteimer, July 17 and August 19, 1887; F. W. Knoege(?) to Honorable Secretary Lamar, September 9, 1887, Consol. Ute.

43. T. J. Morgan to Charles A. Bartholomew, September 25, 1889, Consol Ute.

44. Bartholomew to Commissioner of Indian Affairs, October 26, 1889, Consol. Ute.

45. "The Southern Utes Not to Blame," *Durango Herald*, October 25, 1889, 1.

46. George M. Williams to Post Adjutant, December 11, 1889, Record Group 75, Letters Received by Bureau of Indian Affairs, 1881–1907, National Archives, Washington, D.C. (hereafter Letters Received—BIA).

47. Ibid.; Cornelia Perkins, Marian Nielson, and Lenora Jones, *The Saga of San Juan* (Salt Lake City: Mercury, 1968), 220; Silvey, "History and Settlement," 42.

48. Petition from Citizens of Grand and San Juan Counties to A. L. Thomas (Governor of Utah), August 14, 1890; Petition from Citizens of Monticello to Governor, August 14, 1890, Letters Received—BIA.

49. Bartholomew to David L. Shipley, October 13, 1890, Consol. Ute; Bartholomew "To the Navajo Indians," November 11, 1890, Letters Received—BIA.

50. Article (no title), *Creede Candle*, August 12, 1892, 1; Governor Davis H. Waite to President Grover Cleveland, May 9, 1893, Letters Received—BIA.

51. Bartholomew to Commissioner of Indian Affairs, May 16, 1893, Consol. Ute.

52. Walter Dyk, *A Navaho Autobiography* (New York: Viking Fund, 1947), 40, 75.

53. Dyk and Dyk, *Left Handed*, 35, 396–401.

54. Hill, *Navaho*, 135.

55. "Destruction of Game By Indians," *Report of the Commissioner of Indian Affairs*, 1894, Office of Indian Affairs, Department of the Interior, Washington, D.C., 66–67.

56. Petition from "Citizens and Taxpayers" to Secretary of the Interior, April 20, 1895, General History, Navajo Archives, Window Rock, Arizona (hereafter Archives).

57. Constant Williams to Commissioner of Indian Affairs, September 10, 1895, Archives.

58. George W. Hayzlett to Commissioner of Indian Affairs, February 24, March 19, and September 28, 1900; A. C. Tonner to Hayzlett, September 19, 1900, Archives.

59. R. C. McClure to Commissioner of Indian Affairs, November 17, 1900; Herman to Secretary of the Interior, November 28, 1900; Commissioner of Indian Affairs to Secretary of the Interior, December 3, 1900; Hayzlett to Commissioner of Indian Affairs, December 14, 1900; Commissioner of Indian Affairs to Secretary of the Interior, January 17, 1901, Archives.

60. Hayzlett to Commissioner of Indian Affairs, March 12 and April 27, 1901, Archives.

61. Commissioner of Indian Affairs to Western Navajo Agency, November 2, 1903; L. Pratt (Forest Supervisor) to Department of the Interior, January 31, 1903, Archives.

62. Franciscan Friars, *Ethnologic Dictionary*, 475.

63. Charles S. Peterson, *Look to the Mountains: Southeastern Utah and the La Sal National Forest* (Provo: Brigham Young University Press, 1975), 194–95.

64. William Riley Hurst, interview by author, January 23, 1992, transcript in possession of author.

65. Mildred Palmer, "Hanson Bayles: The Story" (published by the family, 1988), 104–5.

66. Sage O. Carlisle, "Caring and Sharing," *San Juan Record*, July 27, 1988, 7.

67. Hurst, interview.

68. Susan L. Flader, *Thinking Like a Mountain* (Lincoln: University of Nebraska Press, 1974), 39.

69. Ibid., 55–56.

70. Guy Wallace (Officer Division of Wildlife Resources–Monticello), telephone conversation with author, January 27, 1992.

71. Hill, *Navaho*, 101.

72. Frank Silvey, "Information on Indians," 1936, manuscript in Utah State Historical Society, Salt Lake City, 1.

73. Ibid.

74. Francis A. Hammond to Editor, January 8, 1887, *Deseret News*; Hammond to Editor, November 23, 1887, *Deseret News*, cited in San Juan Stake History, Historical Archives, Church of Jesus Christ of Latter-day Saints, Salt Lake City.

75. *Deseret News*, September 28, 1887, 9.

76. Peterson, *Look to the Mountain*, 93–94, 96, 100; Bryant L. Jensen, "An Historical Study of Bluff City, Utah, from 1878 to 1906," (M.A. thesis, Brigham Young University, 1966), 60–63; *Deseret News*, September 28, 1887, 9.

77. Albert R. Lyman, "History of San Juan County, 1879–1917," Special Collections, Brigham Young University, Provo, Utah, 15, 33.

78. Lyman P. Hunter, interview by Michael Hurst, February 21, 1973, Special Collections, Brigham Young University Library, Provo, Utah, 3–4.

79. Flader, *Thinking Like a Mountain*, 51.

80. Hurst, interview.

81. For more on the battle between whites and Indians for the public domain, see McPherson, *Northern Navajo Frontier*, 51–62; Robert S. McPherson, *A History of San Juan County: In the Palm of Time* (Salt Lake City: Utah State Historical Society, 1995).

82. McPherson, *Northern Navajo Frontier*, 40–43.

83. Wallace, telephone conversation.

84. Luckert, *The Navajo Hunter Tradition*, 65.

85. Long after this chapter had been written, I read Robert A. Brightman's *Grateful Prey: Rock Cree Human-Animal Relationships* (Berkeley: University of California Press, 1993), an excellent, detailed study in which the author arrives at similar conclusions for a different group of American Indians dependent on hunting. A few of his chapter titles indicate Rock Cree beliefs about animals and the hunting experience: "You Got to Keep It Holy," "The Same Respect You Give Yourself," "They Come to Be Like Human," and "The More They Destroy, the Greater Plenty Will Succeed." Simply stated, Brightman's complex thesis is that the Cree depended on the replenishment of game through their relationship with the gods involved in hunting.

86. John Holiday, interview.

87. Ibid.

88. Luckert, *The Navajo Hunter Tradition*, 54.

CHAPTER 3

1. Robert J. Foster, *General Geology* (Columbus: Merrill, 1988), 124.

2. W. W. Hill, *The Agricultural and Hunting Methods of the Navaho Indians* (New Haven: Yale University Press, 1938), 13–14; R. Clayton Brough, Dale L. Jones, and Dale J. Stevens, *Utah's Comprehensive Weather Almanac* (Salt Lake City: Publishers Press, 1987), 278.

3. Hill, *Agricultural and Hunting Methods*, 25.

4. Ibid., 26–27, 30.

5. T. J. Morgan, "The Navajo Situation," *Report of the Commissioner of Indian Affairs* (hereafter RCIA), 1892, Office of Indian Affairs, Department of the Interior, Washington, D.C., 125–26.

6. Odon Gurovitz, "Survey of the Navajo Reservation," November 17, 1892, cited in David M. Brugge, "Navajo Use and Occupation of the Area North of the San Juan River in Present-Day Utah," unpublished manuscript in possession of author (hereafter NUOL).

7. C. E. Vandever to Commissioner of Indian Affairs, March 4, 1890, NUOL.

8. E. H. Plummer to Commissioner of Indian Affairs, December 29, 1893, NUOL.

9. Constant Williams to Commissioner of Indian Affairs, December 11, 1894, NUOL.

10. Albert R. Lyman, "History of San Juan County, 1879–1917," unpublished manuscript, Special Collections, Harold B. Lee Library, Brigham Young University, Provo, Utah, 28.

11. Ibid., 28, 31, 34.

12. Ibid., pp. 42, 50, 58.

13. Williams to Commissioner of Indian Affairs, February 3, 1895; Mary Eldridge to Commissioner of Indian Affairs, n.d., NUOL.

14. W. A. Jones, "Irrigation," 1897, RCIA, 29–30.

15. "Annual Report of the Department of Indian Affairs," June 30, 1901, RCIA, 65–66.

16. George W. Hayzlett to Commissioner of Indian Affairs, January 16, 1903, NUOL.

17. Hayzlett to Commissioner of Indian Affairs, July 28, 1903; William T. Shelton to Commissioner of Indian Affairs, December 28, 1903, NUOL.

18. Shelton to Commissioner of Indian Affairs, April 30, 1904, NUOL.

19. Walter Dyk, *A Navaho Autobiography* (New York: Viking Fund, 1947), 62.

20. Shelton to Commissioner of Indian Affairs, July 24, 1905; Harriet Peabody to Commissioner of Indian Affairs, February 28, 1905; Holley to Shelton, February 20, 1905, NUOL.

21. Dyk, *Navaho Autobiography*, 86.

22. Ibid., 97–98.

23. Ibid., 101–3; Shelton to Holley, October 2, 1907, NUOL.

24. Dyk, *Navaho Autobiography*, 95.

25. Ibid., 99.

26. Ibid., 108, 121.

27. U.S. Congress, Senate, "Testimony Regarding Trouble on Navajo Reservation," S. Doc. 757, 60th Cong., 2d sess., March 3, 1909, 46–47, 51.

28. Dyk, *Navaho Autobiography*, 112–13.

29. William T. Shelton, "Report of Superintendent of San Juan School," 1906, RCIA, 280; Dyk, *Navaho Autobiography*, 127.

30. Shelton, "Statements from Navajos," 1909, NUOL, 142.

31. Dyk, *Navaho Autobiography*, 142.

32. Ibid., 145.

33. "Shiprock Has First Navajo Indian Fair," *Farmington Enterprise*, October 29, 1909, 1.

34. Ibid.

35. Dyk, *Navaho Autobiography*, 135.

36. Ibid., 156–57.

37. Shelton to Commissioner of Indian Affairs, June 14, 1912, NUOL.

38. Ibid.

39. Herbert Redshaw, autobiographical sketch, n.d., in possession of author; "Obituary," *San Juan Record*, December 11, 1946, 3–4.

40. Ray Hunt, interview by author, January 21, 1991; Robert Howell, interview by author, May 14, 1991; Kay Howell, interview by author, May 14, 1991; Helen Redshaw, interview by author, May 16, 1991, all in possession of author.

41. Hunt, interview; Margaret Weston, interview by author, February 13, 1991.

42. Hunt, interview; Jane Silas, interview by author, January 27, 1991, in possession of author.

43. Harvey Oliver, interview by author, May 7, 1991, in possession of author.

44. Ibid.

45. Whitehorse, interview; Silas, interview; Weston, interview; Mary Jay, interview by author, February 27, 1991; Ella Sakizzie, interview by author, May 14, 1991; Cyrus Begay, interview by author, May 7, 1991, in possession of author.

46. John Meadows, interview by author, May 30, 1991, manuscript in possession of author.

47. C. L. Christensen, "Tells of Strange Navajo Ceremonies," *(Moab) Times-Independent*, February 9, 1922, 3.

48. Evan W. Estep to Colonel Dorrington, September 3, 1922, Navajo Files, Edge of the Cedars Museum, Blanding, Utah.

49. Kay Howell, interview; Oliver, interview; Ray Hunt, personal conversation with author, July 1991.

50. Redshaw to Evan W. Estep, January 29, 1921, NUOL.

51. Estep to Commissioner of Indian Affairs, February 9, 1921, NUOL.

52. Estep to Commissioner of Indian Affairs, January 25, 1923, Navajo Files, Edge of the Cedars, Blanding, Utah; Oliver, interview.

53. Oliver, interview.

54. Redshaw, interview.

55. Ibid.

56. "Navajo Indians Plan a Mass Protest Meet," *San Juan Record*, May 5, 1938, 1.

57. "WIN Trainees Tap San Juan River," *San Juan Record*, January 21, 1971, 7; "UNDC, Navajo Build Biggest Irrigated Farm," *San Juan Record*, October 3, 1974, 10.

58. Ibid.; Tully Lameman, former director, Utah Navajo Development Council Division of Natural Resources, telephone conversation with author, August 13, 1996.

59. Lameman, telephone conversation.

60. "Overall Economic Development Plan 1992–1993," Navajo Nation Division of Economic Development, Window Rock, Arizona, 18.

CHAPTER 4

1. For works that stress the importance of trading posts in bringing about change, see, e.g., Garrick Bailey and Roberta Bailey, *A History of the Navajos: The Reservation Years* (Santa Fe, New Mex.: School of American Research, 1986); Frank McNitt, *The Indian Traders* (Norman: University of Oklahoma Press, 1962); H. Baxter Liebler, "The Social and Cultural Patterns of the Navajo Indians," *Utah Historical Quarterly* 30 (Fall 1962): 298–325.

2. Elizabeth C. Hegemann, *Navaho Trading Days* (Albuquerque: University of New Mexico Press, 1963), 267–68.

3. "Indian Traders," *Report of the Commissioner of Indian Affairs, 1903* (Washington, D.C.: Department of the Interior), 34; E. B. Merritt to William T. Sullivan, March 26, 1914, Record Group 75, Bureau of Indian Affairs, Western Navajo, National Archives, Washington, D.C.; Hegemann, *Navaho Trading Days*, 267–68.

4. See Robert S. McPherson, *The Northern Navajo Frontier: Expansion through Adversity, 1860–1900* (Albuquerque: University of New Mexico Press, 1988), 63–78.

5. LTC George Hunter to Adjutant General—Colorado, August 26, 1908, Record Group 393, U.S. Army Continental Command, 1821–1920, National Archives, Washington, D.C.

6. Fred Yazzie, interview by author, November 5, 1987, manuscript in possession of author; Charlie Blueeyes, interview by author, June 7, 1988, manuscript in possession of author.

7. J. M. Sherwood, "Notes Regarding Charles E. Walton," Utah Historical Society, Salt Lake City, 3; Fred Yazzie, interview; Martha Nez, interview by author, August 10, 1988, manuscript in possession of author.

8. Navajo Oshley, interview by Winston Hurst and Wesley Oshley, January 1978 (multiple interviews), manuscript in possession of author.

9. Rose Begay, interview by Bertha Parrish, June 17, 1987, in possession of author.

10. W. W. Hill, "Navaho Trading and Trading Ritual: A Study of Cultural Dynamics," *Southwestern Journal of Anthropology* 4 (Autumn 1948): 385.

11. Hegemann, *Navaho Trading Days*, 345; Arthur L. Chaffin, interview by P. T. Reilly, December 24, 1966, Utah State Historical Society, Salt Lake City, 3.

12. Blueeyes, interview; Martha Nez, interview by author, August 10, 1988, in possession of author; Slim Benally, interview by author, July 8, 1988, in possession of author; Hegemann, *Navaho Trading Days*, 272.

13. Cecil Richardson, "The Navajo Way," *Arizona Highways* (July 1948): 22.

14. Hegemann, *Navaho Trading Days*, 342; Blueeyes, interview; Nez, interview.

15. Hilda Wetherill, "The Trading Post: Letters from a Primitive Land," *Atlantic Monthly* 142 (September 1928): 289–90.

16. Richardson, "The Navajo Way," 24.

17. Kitty At'iinii, interview by Fern Charley and Dean Sunberg, July 13, 1972, California State University, Southern Utah Oral History Project, 21.

18. Genevieve Herrick, "Women in the News," *Country Gentleman* 46 (October 1939): 46.

19. For examples of daily life in a post, see Frances Gillmor and Louisa Wade Wetherill, *Traders to the Navajo* (Albuquerque: University of New Mexico Press, 1934); Hegemann, *Navaho Trading Days*; Hilda Faunce, *Desert Wife* (Lincoln: University of Nebraska Press, 1928); Willow Roberts, *Stokes Carson: Twentieth-Century Trading on the Navajo Reservation* (Albuquerque: University of New Mexico Press, 1987); Gladwell Richardson, *Navajo Trader* (Tucson: University of Arizona Press, 1986).

20. Mary Shepardson and Blodwen Hammond, *The Navajo Mountain Community* (Berkeley: University of California Press, 1970), 203.

21. Hegemann, *Navaho Trading Days*, 58–59.

22. Catherine Moore, interview by Jessie Embry, April 23, 1979, Charles Redd Center, Brigham Young University, Provo, Utah, 8–9.

23. "Traffic in Relics from Indian Ruins," *Report of the Commissioner of Indian Affairs* (Washington, D.C.: Government Printing Office, 1905), 29–30.

24. Hegemann, *Navaho Trading Days*, 366–68.

25. Gillmor and Wetherill, *Traders to the Navajo*, 130.

26. David M. Brugge, *A History of the Chaco Navajos* (Albuquerque: National Park Service, 1980), 166.

27. Faunce, *Desert Wife*, 238–40.

28. T. Mitchell Prudden, *On the Great American Plateau* (New York: G. P. Putnam's Sons, 1906), 172–74.

29. Alberta Hannum, *Spin a Silver Dollar* (New York: Ballantine Books, 1944), 24–26.

30. Ann Axtell Morris, *Digging in the Southwest* (Chicago: Cadmus Books, 1933), 167; Frank McNitt, *Richard Wetherill: Anasazi* (Albuquerque: University of New Mexico Press, 1957), 143, 165–68; see also Brugge, *History of the Chaco Navajos*, 155, 159–60.

31. Oshley, interview.

32. Walter Dyk, *A Navaho Autobiography* (New York: Viking Fund, 1947), 87.

33. Ibid., 95.

34. See George Wharton James, *Indian Blankets and Their Makers* (New York: Dover Publications, 1974); Gladys A. Reichard, *Navajo Shepherd and Weaver* (Glorieta, New Mex.: Rio Grande Press, 1936); Reichard, *Spider Woman: A Story of Navajo Weavers and Chanters* (Glorieta, New Mex.: Rio Grande Press, 1934); Marian E. Rodee, *One Hundred Years of Navajo Rugs* (Albuquerque: University of New Mexico Press, 1995).

35. Bailey and Bailey, *History of the Navajos*, 150–52.

36. Hegemann, *Navaho Trading Days*, 299.

37. Daisy Buck, conversation with author, August 18, 1989; Nakai Begay, interview.

38. G. W. Hayzlett to Commissioner of Indian Affairs, September 18, 1902, Record Group 75, Bureau of Indian Affairs, National Archives, Washington, D.

C.; "Navajo Blankets," Report of the Commissioner of Indian Affairs, Department of the Interior, vol. 2, 1914, Washington, D.C., 36.

39. F. E. Brandon, "Wool," Western Navajo, November 28, 1922, Record Group 75, Bureau of Indian Affairs, National Archives, Washington, D.C.

40. Sharp to Commissioner of Indian Affairs, March 1, 1923, Record Group 75, Bureau of Indian Affairs, National Archives, Washington, D.C.

41. "Shiprock Has First Navajo Indian Fair," *Farmington Enterprise*, October 29, 1909, 1; Dyk, *Navaho Autobiography*, 143; "Navajo Blankets," 36.

42. Bailey and Bailey, *History of the Navajos*, 152–54; E. Merritt to Walter Runke, April 4, 1919; Runke to Commissioner, March 12, 1919, Record Group 75, Bureau of Indian Affairs, National Archives, Washington, D. C.; Hegemann, *Navaho Trading Days*, 273.

43. Gillmor and Wetherill, *Traders to the Navajo*, 191; Hegemann, *Navaho Trading Days*, 274; Richardson, *Navajo Trader*, 49–57.

44. "Latest on Gallup Road," *Cortez Herald*, October 28, 1915, 1.

45. H. E. Williams, "Report on the Western Navajo Indian Reservation," July 31, 1929, Record Group 75, Bureau of Indian Affairs, National Archives, Washington, D.C.

46. C. L. Walker to Commissioner of Indian Affairs, August 8, 1927, Record Group 75, Bureau of Indian Affairs, National Archives, Washington, D.C.

47. Gillmor and Wetherill, *Traders to the Navajo*, 255.

48. Charles J. Kappler, *Indian Affairs—Laws and Treaties*, (Washington, D.C.: Government Printing Office, 1913): 3:407, 433, 491, 575.

49. U.S. Congress, Senate, "Report on the Necessity of a Bridge Near Tanner's Crossing, Navajo Indian Reservation, Arizona," S. Ex. Doc. 684, 61st Cong., 3d sess., 1910, 1–2.

50. U.S. Congress, Senate, "Bridge Across the Colorado River Near Lee's Ferry, Ariz.," S. Rpt. No. 111, 68th Cong., 2d sess., 1925, 1–2.

51. U.S. Congress, Senate, "Hearings Before a Subcommittee on Indian Affairs," *Survey of Conditions of the Indians in the United States*, pt. 6, 70th Cong., 2d sess., 1930, 2205–6; U.S. Congress, Senate, "The Navajo Indians of New Mexico," *Senate Congressional Record* 71, pt. 4, 71st Cong., 1st sess., 1929, 4484–85; C. L. Walker to Commissioner of Indian Affairs, July 6, 1929, Record Group 75, Bureau of Indian Affairs, National Archives, Washington, D.C.

CHAPTER 5

1. Fernando Alvarado Tezozomoc, in "Crónica mexicana," cited in Miguel León-Portilla, *The Broken Spears: The Aztec Account of the Conquest of Mexico* (Boston: Beacon Press, 1962), 13.

2. Ibid., 30–31.

3. Martha Nez, interview by author, August 10, 1988; Jane Silas, interview by author, February 27, 1991, in possession of author.

4. *Montezuma Journal*, July 9, 1908.

5. John Knot Begay, interview by author, May 7, 1991, in possession of author.

6. Fred Yazzie, interview by author, August 6, 1991, in possession of author.

7. Nakai Begay, interview by Bette Benally, February 24, 1991, manuscript in possession of author; Ben Whitehorse, interview by author, January 30, 1991, manuscript in possession of author; Robert W. Young and William Morgan, Sr., *The Navajo Language: A Grammar and Colloquial Dictionary*, 2d ed. (Albuquerque: University of New Mexico Press, 1987), 271.

8. Silas, interview; Mabel Jean Begay, interview by author, January 18, 1991, manuscript in possession of author.

9. Whitehorse, interview; John Bluesalt, interview by author, January 14, 1991, manuscript in possession of author.

10. Albert H. Kneale, *Indian Agent* (Caldwell: Caxton Printers, 1950), 368–69.

11. Young and Morgan, *The Navajo Language*.

12. Suzie Yazzie, interview by author, August 6, 1991, manuscript in possession of author.

13. Fred Yazzie, interview.

14. John Holiday, interview by author, September 9, 1991, manuscript in possession of author.

15. "Car Seats Blessed for Child's Use," *Navajo Times*, July 24, 1997, A3.

16. George Tom, interview by author, August 7, 1991, manuscript in possession of author.

17. Fred Yazzie, interview by author, August 6, 1991; John Holiday, interview; manuscripts in possession of author.

18. Mary Blueeyes, interview by Bette Benally, March 10, 1991; Ira Hatch, interview by author, May 30, 1991, manuscripts in possession of author; Mabel Jean Begay, interview; Bluesalt, interview.

19. Tony Nakai, interview by Bette Benally, March 3, 1991, manuscript in possession of author; Nakai Begay, interview; Hilda Nakai, interview by Bette Benally, March 3, 1991, manuscript in possession of author.

20. Hilda Nakai, interview; Nakai Begay, interview; Silas, interview; Mabel Jean Begay, interview.

21. Interviews with Hilda Nakai, Suzie Yazzie, Tony Nakai.

22. Ibid.

23. Ray Hunt, interview by author, January 21, 1991, manuscript in possession of author.

24. Suzie Yazzie, interview.

25. Nakai Begay, interview.

26. Curtis Zahn, "The Automobile Is Here to Stay," *Arizona Highways* 22, no. 6 (June 1946): 22–23.

27. Ibid.

28. Inteviews with Whitehorse, Meadows.

29. Interviews with Hilda Nakai, Meadows.

30. Hunt, interview.

31. "Navajos Demonstrate New Way of Starting a Ford," *(Moab) Times-Independent*, October 9, 1991, 8.

32. Cited in Garrick Bailey and Roberta Bailey, *A History of the Navajos: The Reservation Years* (Santa Fe, New Mex.: School of American Research Press, 1986), 168.

33. Clyde Kluckhohn and Dorothea Leighton, *The Navaho*, rev. ed. (Cambridge, Mass.: Harvard University Press, 1974), 71.

34. Bailey and Bailey, *History of the Navajos*, 267–68.

35. H. Baxter Liebler, "The Social and Cultural Patterns of the Navajo Indians," *Utah Historical Quarterly* 30 (Fall 1962): 299–325.

36. Navajo Nation, *1990 Census Population and Housing Characteristics of the Navajo Nation* (Scottsdale, Ariz.: Printing Company, 1993), 50.

37. David C. Williams, "Spending Patterns of Navajo Families," *New Mexico Business* 28, no. 2 (March 1975): 3–10.

38. Nakai Begay, interview.

39. Blueeyes, interview.

40. Ibid.; Nakai Begay, interview.

41. Harvey Oliver, interview by author, May 14, 1991, manuscript in possession of author.

42. Fred Yazzie, interview.

43. John Norton, interview by author, January 16, 1991, manuscript in possession of author; Nakai Begay, Blueeyes, Hilda Nakai, interview.

44. Suzie Yazzie, interview.

45. Whitehorse, interview.

46. John Knot Begay, interview.

47. Ada Benally, interview by author, February 6, 1991, manuscript in possession of author.

48. Bruce G. Trigger, "Early Native North American Responses to European Contact; Romantic versus Rationalistic Interpretations," *Journal of American History* 77, no. 4 (March 1991): 1214.

49. Joseph Campbell, *Myths to Live By* (New York: Bantam Press, 1984), 221–22.

CHAPTER 6

1. For more on the livestock reduction, see Kenneth R. Philp, *John Collier's Crusade for Indian Reform, 1920–54* (Tucson: University of Arizona Press, 1977); Richard White, *The Roots of Dependency: Subsistence Environment and Social Change among Choctow, Pawnees, and Navajos* (Lincoln: University of Nebraska Press, 1983); Ruth Roessel and Broderick Johnson, eds., *Navajo Livestock Reduction: A National Disgrace* (Tsaile, Airz.: Navajo Community College Press, 1974);

and L. Schuyler Fonaroff, "Conservation and Stock Reduction on the Navajo Tribal Range," *Geographical Review* 53, no. 2 (April 1963): 200–23.

2. Donald L. Parman, *The Navajos and the New Deal* (New Haven: Yale University Press, 1976): Lawrence C. Kelly, *The Navajo Indians and Federal Indian Policy* (Tucson: University of Arizona Press, 1968).

3. Slim Benally, interview by author, July 8, 1988, manuscript in possession of author.

4. Martha Nez, interview by author, August 2, 1988, manuscript in possession of author.

5. Charlie Blueeyes, interview by author, July 8, 1988, manuscript in possession of author.

6. Mary Blueeyes, interview by author, July 8, 1988, manuscript in possession of author.

7. Karl W. Luckert, *A Navajo Bringing-Home Ceremony: The Claus Chee Sonny Version of Deerway Ajiłee* (Flagstaff: Museum of Northern Arizona Press, 1978), 191.

8. Jim Dandy, interview by author, December 4, 1989, manuscript in possession of author.

9. Marilyn Holiday, interview by author, February 14, 1992.

10. Charlie Blueeyes, interview by author, June 7, 1988, manuscript in possession of author.

11. Buck Navajo, interview by author, December 16, 1991, manuscript in possession of author.

12. Luckert, *Navajo Bringing-Home Ceremony*, 174.

13. Ernest L. Bulow, *Navajo Taboos* (Gallup, New Mex.: Southwesterner Books, 1982), 52–53.

14. Ella Sakizzie, interview by author, May 14, 1991, manuscript in possession of author.

15. Joe Ben, interview by Lorraine Ben, March 16, 1986, permission granted to cite material received from Lorraine Ben on March 25, 1986, manuscript in possession of author.

16. Susie Yazzie, interview by author, August 6, 1991, manuscript in possession of author.

17. Ibid.

18. Pearl Philips, interview by Bertha Parrish, June 17, 1987; Sally Lee, interview by author, February 13, 1991, manuscripts in possession of author.

19. Richard Hobson, *Navaho Acquisitive Values*, Peabody Archaeology Papers 42, no. 3 (Cambridge, Mass.: Harvard University Press, 1953), 9-11.

20. Gary Witherspoon, "Sheep in Navajo Culture and Social Organization," *American Anthropologist* 75 (Winter 1973): 1441–47.

21. Hobson, *Navaho Acquisitive Values*, 25.

22. Annual Report, 1934, Bureau of Indian Affairs, Navajo Archives, Edge of the Cedars Museum, Blanding, Utah (hereafter Navajo Archives), 4.

23. Annual Report, 1930, Bureau of Indian Affairs, Navajo Archives, n.p.

24. Annual Report, 1934, Navajo Archives.

25. Ibid.

26. For an excellent explanation of the ecological and economic impact of livestock reduction, see Richard White's *Roots of Dependency*, 212–323.

27. Hite Chee, interview by Dean Sundberg and Fern Charley, July 20, 1974, cited in *The Navajo Stock Reduction Interviews*, Southeastern Utah Project, compiled by the Utah State Historical Society and California State University–Fullerton (hereafter cited *NSRI*), 1–17.

28. Ibid., 4–5.

29. Louise Lamphere, "The Navajo Nation: A Case Study," in *Economic Development in American Reservations*, ed. Roxanne Ortiz (Albuquerque: University of New Mexico Press, 1980), 82.

30. Cecil Parrish, interview by author, October 10, 1991, manuscript in possession of author; Chee interview, *NSRI*, 5.

31. Ernest Nelson, interview, cited in Roessel and Johnson, *Navajo Livestock Reduction*, 159 (hereafter *NLR*).

32. Ralph Grey interview, June 1974, *NSRI*, 6.

33. Pearl Philips interview, *NSRI*, 8.

34. Tall John, cited in James F. Downs, *Animal Husbandry in Navaho Society and Culture* (Berkeley: University of California Press, 1964), 20.

35. Nedra Tó dích'íi'nii interview, July 13, 1972, *NSRI*, 5.

36. Buck Austin interview, *NLR*, 22; Akinabh Burbank, *NLR*, 124.

37. Margaret Weston, interview by author, February 13, 1991, manuscript in possession of author.

38. Ben Whitehorse, interview by author, January 30, 1991, manuscript in possession of author.

39. Tó dích'íi'nii interview, *NSRI*, 5.

40. Jane Silas, interview by author, February 27, 1991, manuscript in possession of author.

41. Tó dích'íi'nii interview, *NSRI*, 17.

42. Ibid., 18–21.

43. Buck Navajo, interview.

44. Tó dích'íi'nii interview, *NSRI*, 5; Kitty At'iinii interview, July 13, 1972, *NSRI*, 5; Ben interview, 9.

45. Ibid.

46. Silas, interview; Ada Benally, interview by author, February 6, 1991; Sally Lee, interview by author, February 13, 1991, manuscripts in possession of author.

47. Stella Cly, interview by author, August 7, 1991, manuscript in possession of author.

48. Tó dích'íi'nii interview, *NSRI*, 4, 23.

49. Ada Black, interview by author, October 11, 1991, manuscript in possession of author.

50. Guy Cly, interview by author, August 7, 1991, manuscript in possession of author; Navajo, interview; Austin, interview, *NLR*, 17; Ason Attakai interview, *NLR*, 127; Sarah Begay, interview, June 20, 1974, *NSRI*, 9; Lamar Bedoni interview, June 30, 1972, *NSRI*, 2; Mary Tsosie interview by author, January 30, 1991, manuscript in possession of author; Sloan Haycock, interview by author, October 10, 1991, manuscript in possession of author.

51. Tsosie, interview.

52. At'iinii interview, *NSRI*, 4; Tó dích'íí'nii interview, *NSRI*, 20; Pete Sheen interview, *NLR*, 168.

53. At'iinii interview, *NSRI*, 9.

54. H. E. Holman (Navajo Service) to U.S. Attorney (Utah) with accompanying statements, June 11, 1938, Record Group 75, Navajo Service Personnel File, Denver Records Center, Denver, Colorado.

55. Tacheadeny Tso Begay interview, *NLR*, 111.

56. Capiton Benally interview, *NLR*, 33–37.

57. Austin interview, *NLR*, 17; Chee interview, *NSRI*, 8.

58. Tó dích'íí'nii interview, *NSRI*, 5, 21; Black, interview; Florence Norton interview by author, March 6, 1991, manuscript in possession of author.

59. Ben, interview, 17.

60. Benally, interview.

61. Chee interview, *NLR*, 10–11.

62. Katso interview with S. Moon, August 15, 1974, manuscript in possession of author; Bedoni interview, *NSRI*, 7; Parrish interview; Ben interview, 17; John Joe Begay, interview by author, September 18, 1990, manuscript in possession of author; Norman Nielson, interview by author, May 1, 1991, manuscript in possession of author.

63. Howard W. Gorman interview, *NLR*, 47.

64. Bedoni interview, *NLR*, 8.

65. At'iinii interview, *NSRI*, 6, 17.

66. White, *Roots of Dependency*, 312.

67. John Holiday, interview by author, September 9, 1991, manuscript in possession of author.

68. Zane Grey, *Tales of Lonely Trails* (New York: Harper and Brothers, 1922), 7.

69. Tó dích'íí'nii interview, *NSRI*, 23; Attakai interview, *NSR*, 129.

70. Deneh Bitsilly interview, *NSR*, 132; Ernest Nelson interview, *NSR*, 159; Chee interview, *NSRI*, 7–8; Canyon, interview; Tó dích'íí'nii interview, *NSRI*, 24; Cly.

71. Chee interview, *NSRI*, 13.

72. Holiday, interview.

73. Robert W. Young and William Morgan, *Analytical Lexicon of Navajo* (Albuquerque: University of New Mexico Press, 1992), 111.

74. Parrish, interview; Phillips, interview; Canyon, interview; Billy Bryant interview, *NSR*, 141; Navajo Oshley, interview by Winston Hurst, January and

February 1978, manuscript in possession of author; Begay, interview; Ben, interview, 9.

75. See Victor E. Frankl, *Man's Search for Meaning* (New York: Washington Square Press, 1946).

76. Begay, interview.

77. Canyon, interview.

CHAPTER 7

1. Bernard A. Weisberger, "You Press the Button, We Do the Rest," in *A Sense of History: The Best Writing from the Pages of American Heritage* (New York: American Heritage, 1985), 521–36.

2. Floyd Laughter, interview by author, April 9, 1992, manuscript in possession of author; an abbreviated version of this story is found in the Floyd Laughter interview in Karl W. Luckert, ed., *Navajo Mountain and Rainbow Bridge Religion*, (Flagstaff: Museum of Northern Arizona, 1977), 46.

3. Luckert, *Navajo Mountain*, 59.

4. Tom Dougi, interview by author, April 8, 1992, manuscript in possession of author; Buck Navajo interview, in Luckert, *Navajo Mountain*, 86.

5. For a broad treatment of the importance of Rainbow Bridge among different Native American groups, see Stephen C. Jett, "Testimony of the Sacredness of Rainbow Natural Bridge to Puebloans, Navajos, and Paiutes," *Plateau* 45, no. 4 (Spring 1973): 133–42.

6. Laughter, cited in Luckert, *Navajo Mountain*, 45.

7. Ernest Nelson, cited in Luckert, *Navajo Mountain*, 126.

8. Buck Navajo, cited in Luckert, *Navajo Mountain*, 86.

9. Luckert, *Navajo Mountain*, 9.

10. See "Statement of W. F. Williams," in James E. Babbitt, ed., *Rainbow Trails: Early-Day Adventures in Rainbow Bridge Country* (Page, Ariz.: Glen Canyon Natural History Association, 1990), 19–25.

11. For the most complete discussion and documentation of the discovery of Rainbow Bridge, see Stephen C. Jett, "The Great 'Race' to 'Discover' Rainbow Natural Bridge," *Kiva* 58, no. 1 (Fall 1992): 3–66; see also Babbitt, *Rainbow Trails*.

12. Frank McNitt, *The Indian Traders* (Norman: University of Oklahoma Press, 1962), 272.

13. Zane Grey, *Tales of Lonely Trails* (New York: Harper and Brothers, 1922), 6.

14. Ibid., 4.

15. The origin of the word *Nonnezoshe*, which Zane Grey and other writers of his time use for Rainbow Bridge, is not clear. It most likely comes from the Navajo word *honish'ooshii*, meaning "deep, dark canyon."

16. Grey, *Tales of Lonely Trails*, 7, 16.

17. W. D. Sayle, *A Trip to the Rainbow Arch* (Cleveland: Privately printed, 1920), 40.

18. Clyde Kluckhohn, *To the Foot of the Rainbow* (Glorieta, New Mex.: Rio Grande Press, 1967), 196.

19. Ibid., 205–6.

20. Winifred H. Dixon, *Westward Hoboes: Ups and Downs of Frontier Motoring* (New York: Scribner's Sons, 1930), 271, 273, 281.

21. Ibid., 271, 280, and 294.

22. Ibid., 291.

23. Ibid., 281.

24. Frank McNitt, *The Indian Traders* (Norman: University of Oklahoma Press, 1962), 274–76.

25. Gladwell Richardson, *Navajo Trader* (Tucson: University of Arizona Press, 1986), 33, 49–52.

26. Ibid., 52.

27. Ibid., 52–57.

28. Ibid., 41–42.

29. Maurice Kildare, "Builders to the Rainbow," *Frontier Times* 40 (June–July 1966): 51.

30. Ibid., 52; "Wilsons Leave Rainbow Lodge" *Arizona News,* June 13, 1952, 1.

31. Joe Manygoats, interview by author, December 18, 1991; Walter Smallcanyon, interview by author, April 3, 1993; Robert Chief, interview by author, April 16, 1993, manuscripts in possession of author.

32. Statistical Summary of Visitations to Rainbow Bridge, in "Rainbow Bridge—Land Exchange w/Navahos; Barrier Dam," Gladwell Richardson Collection, Special Collections, Northern Arizona University Library, Flagstaff.

33. "Rainbow Bridge—Rates and Other Information," Gladwell Richardson Collection, Special Collections, Northern Arizona University Library, Flagstaff.

34. Manygoats, interview.

35. Velta Luther, interview by author, April 8, 1992, manuscript in possession of author.

36. Chief, interview.

37. Floyd Laughter, interview by author, April 9, 1992, manuscript in possession of author.

38. Manygoats, interview; Chief, interview.

39. Luckert, *Navajo Mountain,* 12–25.

40. Manygoats, interview.

41. Barry Goldwater, interview by author, December 12, 1993, manuscript in possession of author.

42. Goldwater, interview; letter by Stan Jones, in "History—Rainbow Lodge," Gladwell Richardson Collection, Northern Arizona University Library, Flagstaff.

43. Paul B. Alexander, "Rainbow Bridge National Monument" (Grand Junction, Colo.: Trans-Mountain Surveys, 1971), located in Special Collections, Northern Arizona University Library, Flagstaff, 23; Chris Smith and Elizabeth

Manning, "The Sacred and Profane Collide in the West," *High Country News* 29 (May 1997): 1; Glen Canyon National Park statistics for 1999, located at the San Juan County Visitor's Center, Monticello, Utah.

44. Floyd Laughter, in Luckert, *Navajo Mountain*, 45, 56–57.

45. The information is from the following, all cited in Luckert, *Navajo Mountain*: Floyd Laughter, 45; Buck Navajo, 92; Ernest Nelson, 125; Buster Hastiin Nez, 133; Luckert, 33.

46. Keith Holiday, interview by author, April 9, 1992, manuscript in possession of author.

47. Buck Navajo, interview.

48. "Navajos Blockade Bridge during Tribal Ceremonies," *Deseret News*, August 12, 1995, B1; "Rainbow Bridge Closed for 'Cleansing Ceremony,'" *San Juan Record*, August 16, 1995, 1; "Rainbow Bridge Open after Four-Day Closure," *Navajo Times*, August 17, 1995, A5.

49. Smith and Manning, "The Sacred and Profane Collide in the West," 1–4.

50. Ibid., 4.

51. O. F. Oldendorph, "Monument Valley: A Navajo Tribal Park," *National Parks Magazine* 40, no. 227 (August 1966): 4–8; "2,000 Attend Valley Park Dedication," *San Juan Record*, May 13, 1960, 1; "Navajos Dedicate Tribal Park Gateway," *Denver Post*, May 9, 1960, 31; Marsha Keele, "Monument Valley Park Celebrates 25th Year," *San Juan Record*, July 28, 1983, 1; Statistics on file in San Juan County Economic Development Office, County Courthouse, Monticello, Utah.

52. Cecil Parrish, interview by author, October 10, 1991, manuscript in possession of author.

53. Guy Cly, interview by author, August 7, 1991, manuscript in possession of author.

54. John Holiday, interview by author, September 9, 1991, manuscript in possession of author.

55. Guy Cly, interview.

56. John Holiday, interview.

57. Stewart L. Udall, "More Tourists, Please," *Cross Currents* (July 18, 1997): 11–14.

58. Ibid., 13.

CHAPTER 8

1. For accounts of Goulding's role in the film industry, see Samuel Moon, *Tall Sheep: Harry Goulding, Monument Valley Trader* (Norman: University of Oklahoma Press, 1992), 144–63; Richard Klinck, *Land of Room Enough and Time Enough* (Layton, Utah: Gibbs M. Smith, 1984), 74–85; William R. Florence, "John Ford . . . The Duke . . . and Monument Valley," *Arizona Highways* (September 1981): 22–37; Todd McCarthy, "John Ford and Monument Valley," *American Film* 8, no. 7 (May 1978): 10–16.

2. "Will Advertise Desert Attractions," *Mancos Times-Tribune*, October 26, 1917, 1.

3. Fred Yazzie, interview by author, August 6, 1991, manuscript in possession of author.

4. Ibid.

5. Florence, "John Ford," 34.

6. Rusty Musselman, interview by author, November 6, 1991, manuscript in possession of author.

7. Seth Clitso, interview by author, January 20, 1992; Katso interview by Samuel Moon, July 25, 1974, manuscripts in possession of author.

8. Bud Haycock, interview by author, October 10, 1991; Ada Black, interview by author, October 11, 1991, manuscripts in possession of author.

9. Fred Yazzie, interview.

10. Musselman, interview.

11. Ibid.

12. Florence, "John Ford," 37.

13. Michael N. Budd, "A Critical Analysis of Western Films Directed by John Ford from *Stagecoach* to *Cheyenne Autumn*" (Ph.D. diss., University of Iowa, 1975), 436–79.

14. Guy Cly, interview by author, August 7, 1991, manuscript in possession of author; Fred Yazzie, interview.

15. Musselman, interview.

16. Moon, *Tall Sheep*, 160; Katso, interview.

17. Musselman, interview.

18. Harry Goulding and Joyce R. Muench, "When Tombstone Came to Monument Valley," *Desert Magazine* 11, no. 12 (October, 1948): 6–10; Yazzie, interview.

19. Pastor and Mrs. Walters, interview by Samuel Moon, September 12, 1973, manuscript in possession of author; Yazzie, interview; Haycock, interview; Cecil Parrish, interview by author, October 10, 1991, manuscript in possession of author; Clitso, interview.

20. Goulding and Muench, "When Tombstone Came," 8.

21. Haycock, interview; Clitso, interview; Yazzie, interview; Black, interview; Jack Sleeth, interview by Samuel Moon, July 15, 1974, manuscript in possession of author, 8.

22. Holiday, interview.

23. Ibid.

24. Ibid.

25. Bodie Thoene and Rona Stuck, "Navajo Nation Meets Hollywood," *American West* 20, no. 5 (September–October 1983): 43.

26. Clitso, interview; Moon, *Tall Sheep*, 161.

27. McCarthy, "John Ford," 16.

28. Holiday, interview; Musselman, interview.

29. Holiday, interview; Haycock, interview; Clitso, interview.

30. Thoene and Stuck, "Navajo Nation," 43.

31. See Moon, *Tall Sheep*; McCarthy, "John Ford"; Klinck, *Land of Room Enough*; and Florence, "John Ford."

32. Moon, *Tall Sheep*, 152–56.

33. Jim Dandy, interview by author, December 4, 1989, manuscript in possession of author; Hilda Wetherill, "The Trading Post: Letters from a Primitive Land," *Atlantic Monthly* 142 (September 1928): 293.

34. Holiday, interview; Parrish, interview; Haycock, interview.

35. Parrish, interview.

36. Ibid.; Moon, *Tall Sheep*, 156.

37. Bud Haycock, interview; Harry Goulding, interview by Sam Moon, July 25, 1975, manuscript in possession of author, 2.

38. Thoene and Stuck, "Navajo Nation," 39–40; Musselman, interview.

39. Bud Haycock, interview; Parrish, interview; Harry Goulding, interview by Samuel Moon, August 1, 1977, manuscript in possession of author, 2.

40. Thoene and Stuck, "Navajo Nation," 40–43.

41. Clitso, interview.

42. Musselman, interview.

43. Fred Yazzie, interview; Holiday, interview.

44. For information on Navajo sacred geography in the Monument Valley area, see Robert S. McPherson, *Sacred Land, Sacred View: Navajo Perceptions of the Four Corners Region*, Charles Redd Center Monograph Series, no. 19 (Provo: Brigham Young University Press, 1992).

45. Clitso, interview; Fred Yazzie, interview.

46. Clitso, interview.

47. McPherson, *Sacred Land*, 43; Clitso, interview; Yazzie, interview; Holiday, interview.

48. Sol Worth and John Adair, *Through Navajo Eyes: An Exploration in Film Communication and Anthropology* (Bloomington: Indiana University Press, 1972), 182.

49. Bud Haycock, interview; Holiday, interview; Clitso, interview.

50. Holiday, interview.

51. Informants remain anonymous.

52. Bud Haycock, interview; Yazzie, interview.

53. Clitso, interview.

54. Sloan Haycock, interview by author, October 10, 1991, manuscript in possession of author; Cly, interview; Bud Haycock, interview.

55. Florence, "John Ford," 34.

56. McCarthy, "John Ford," 16; Holiday, interview; Clitso, interview.

CHAPTER 9

1. Father Berard Haile, *The Upward Moving and Emergence Way: The Gishin Biyé Version* (Lincoln: University of Nebraska Press, 1981), 175–76, 190–92;

Washington Matthews, *Navaho Legends* (New York: Houghton Mifflin, 1897), 113–16, 234.

2. Albert B. Reagan, "Petrified Wood Myth," Albert B. Reagan Collection, Special Collections, Harold B. Lee Library, Brigham Young University, Provo, Utah.

3. For an excellent overview of the history of uranium mining in San Juan County, Utah, and the various uses of carnotite during the industry's developmental stages, see Gary L. Shumway, "Uranium Mining on the Colorado Plateau, in *San Juan County, Utah*, ed. Allan Kent Powell (Salt Lake City: Utah State Historical Society, 1983), 265–98.

4. Preston Redd, *From Horseback to Cadillac, I'm Still a Cowboy* (Tempe, Ariz.: Tavas Cash Press, 1988), 227–28.

5. William Chenoweth, "Early Uranium-Vanadium Mining in Monument Valley, San Juan County, Utah," *Survey Notes* 18, no. 2 (Summer 1984): 3, 19.

6. Ibid., 19.

7. Ibid.

8. Charles H. Dunning, "Arizona Uranium Rush," *Arizona Highways* 25, no. 8 (August 1949): 4–7.

9. Harry Goulding, "The Navajos Hunt Big Game . . . Uranium," *Popular Mechanics* (June 1950): 89–92.

10. Samuel Moon, *Tall Sheep: Harry Goulding, Monument Valley Trader* (Norman: University of Oklahoma Press, 1992), 175–81.

11. John Meadows, interview by author, May 30, 1991, manuscript in possession of author.

12. Moon, *Tall Sheep*, 180.

13. Ada Black, interview by author, October 11, 1991, manuscript in possession of author; Meadows, interview; Rusty Musselman, interview by author, November 6, 1991, manuscript in possession of author.

14. William L. Chenoweth and Roger C. Malan, *Uranium Deposits of Northeastern Arizona* (Grand Junction, Colo.: U. S. Atomic Energy Commission, 1973), 7.

15. Cecil Parrish, interview by author, October 10, 1991; George Tom, interview by author, August 7, 1991, manuscripts in possession of author.

16. Meadows, interview.

17. Ibid.; Bud Haycock, interview by author, October 10, 1991; Guy Cly, interview by author, August 7, 1991, manuscripts in possession of author; Parrish, interview.

18. Peter Iverson, *The Navajo Nation* (Albuquerque: University of New Mexico Press, 1981), 78–79.

19. Moon, *Tall Sheep*, 185.

20. Parrish, interview; Black, interview.

21. Meadows, interview.

22. Fred Yazzie, interview by author, August 6, 1991, manuscript in possession of author.

23. Ibid.; Parrish, interview.

24. Shone Holiday, interview by author, September 10, 1991, manuscript in possession of author.

25. Ibid.; Seth Clitso, interview by author, January 20, 1992, manuscript in possession of author; Cly, interview; Parrish, interview.

26. For a history concerning the dispute over government safety regulations in the mines, see Raye C. Ringholz, *Uranium Frenzy: Boom and Bust on the Colorado Plateau* (Albuquerque: University of New Mexico Press, 1989).

27. Meadows, interview.

28. Ibid.

29. For additional information on beliefs about sacred geography, see Robert S. McPherson, *Sacred Land, Sacred View: Navajo Perceptions of the Four Corners Region* (Provo: Brigham Young University, 1992).

30. Yazzie, interview.

31. Tom, interview.

32. Cly, interview.

33. Shone Holiday, interview.

34. John Holiday, interview; Parrish, interview.

35. Black, interview.

36. John Holiday, interview.

37. Bud Haycock, interview; Shone Holiday, interview.

38. Harvey Oliver, interview by author, May 14, 1991, manuscript in possession of author.

39. Meadows, interview.

40. Yazzie, interview.

41. Meadows, interview.

42. Ibid.; Shone Holiday, interview.

43. John Holiday, interview.

44. Harvey Black, interview by author, October 11, 1991, manuscript in possession of author; Yazzie.

45. Shone Holiday, interview.

46. Parrish, interview.

47. Yazzie, interview.

48. For additional stories about the Gambler, see McPherson, *Sacred Land*, 87–90.

49. John Holiday, interview.

50. Buck Navajo, interview with author, December 16, 1991, manuscript in possession of author; Yazzie.

51. Shone Holiday, interview.

52. Moon, *Tall Sheep*, 182–83.

53. Clitso, interview; Parrish, interview.

54. Doris Valle, *Looking Back around the Hat: A History of Mexican Hat* (Mexican Hat, Utah: Privately published, 1986), 49.

55. Bud Haycock, interview.

56. Philip Reno, *Mother Earth, Father Sky, and Economic Development: Navajo Resources and Their Use* (Albuquerque: University of New Mexico Press, 1981), 133–34.

57. Iverson, *The Navajo Nation*, 78.

58. Valle, *Looking Back*, 47–49; Jack Pehrson, foreman at Halchita, stated that the mill did not close until 1969, which differs from Valle's date of 1965 (conversation with author, June 20, 1992).

59. Yazzie, interview; Musselman, interview; Navajo, interview; Bud Haycock, interview.

60. Ada Black, interview.

61. Bud Haycock, interview; Parrish, interview; Mrs. Gwen Walters, interview by Samuel Moon, September 12, 1973, manuscript in possession of author, 17–18.

62. Black, interview; Bud Haycock, interview.

63. John Holiday, interview.

64. Yazzie, interview.

65. Bud Haycock, interview.

66. U.S. Congress, Senate, "Statement of Councilman Harry Tome . . . ," Hearing Before Committee on Labor and Human Resources, S. Doc. 1483, 97th Cong., 2d sess., April 8, 1982, 138–40.

67. Ibid., Perry H. Charley, U.S. Congress, Senate, "Statement of Councilman Perry H. Charley," Hearing Before Committee on Labor and Human Resources, S. Doc. 1483., 47th Cong., 2d sess., April 8, 1982, 142–43.

68. "Zah Vows to Battle for Due Payment," *Navajo Times*, August 22, 1991, 1.

69. "Radon Barrier Complete at Mexican Hat," *San Juan Record*, August 10, 1994, 1.

70. "Navajo Nation Supports $75 Million for Uranium Compensation Funds," *Navajo Times*, May 13, 1993, 2; "Families Receive Payments for Uranium Compensation," *Navajo Times*, March 28, 1996, 2.

71. "Miners Finding Compensation Hard to Collect," *Navajo Times*, January 8, 1998, 8.

CHAPTER 10

1. Paul G. Zolbrod, *Diné bahane': The Navajo Creation Story* (Albuquerque: University of New Mexico Press, 1984), 233–56.

2. Ibid., 267.

3. U.S. Congress, House, "Amending the Act of March 1, 1933 . . . as an Addition to the Navajo Indian Reservation," S. Report 1324, 90th Cong., 2d sess., 1968, 1–6.

4. Don Preston, ed. *A Symposium of the Oil and Gas Fields in Utah* (Salt Lake City: Intermountain Association of Petroleum Geologists, 1961), 8; Michael

Rounds, "Indian Sovereignty Issue Concerns Operators," *Western Oil Reporter*, June 1978, 19; Philip Reno, *Mother Earth, Father Sky, and Economic Development: Navajo Resources and Their Use* (Albuquerque: University of New Mexico Press, 1981), 127.

5. Robert W. Bernick, "Tribe Opens Bids Today on San Juan Oil Leases," *Salt Lake Tribune*, November 1, 1956, C; Robert W. Bernick, "Indian Land Buyers Term $27 Million 'Right Price,'" *Salt Lake Tribune*, November 3, 1956, sec C33.

6. Peter Iverson, *The Navajo Nation* (Albuquerque: University of New Mexico Press, 1981), 68.

7. "Minutes of Commission of State Indian Affairs," July 27, 1959, Navajo Files, Edge of the Cedars Museum, Blanding, Utah.

8. Cleal Bradford, Executive Director of the San Juan Resource Development Council and the Utah Navajo Development Council (1968–78), conversation with author, May 1, 1995.

9. Robert W. Young, ed. *The Navajo Yearbook, 1951–1961: A Decade of Progress*, Report no. 8 (Window Rock, Ariz.: Bureau of Indian Affairs, 1961), 265; Reno, *Mother Earth*, 125; Garrick Bailey and Roberta Bailey, *A History of the Navajos: The Reservation Years* (Santa Fe, New Mex.: School of American Research Press, 1986), 238. The biggest problem in determining revenue from royalties is that none of the figures add up. If the tribe receives $10 million from Aneth oil royalties, the 37.5 to 62.5% disbursement formula would mean that the total oil royalties should have been $16 million, but this is not borne out in the available data. Other factors are undoubtedly involved that are not mentioned in the sources, or perhaps the tribal total includes the Utah payment.

10. Notes from the 1991 legislative audit of the Utah Navajo Development Council and the Utah Division of Indian Affairs, summary chart in possession of author.

11. Office of Program Development, *Navajo Nation Overall Economic Development Program* (Window Rock, Ariz.: Navajo Nation, 1980), 31; Bailey and Bailey, *History of the Navajos*, 237.

12. Harvey C. Moore, "Culture Change in a Navaho Community," in *American Historical Anthropology: Essays in Honor of Leslie Spier*, ed. Carroll L. Riley and Walter W. Taylor (Carbondale: Southern Illinois University Press, 1967), 126–28.

13. Reno, *Mother Earth*, 125, 127; Steve Marks, "Navajos Seize, Occupy Utah's Huge Aneth Field," *Western Oil Reporter*, April 1978, 23.

14. Frank Cole, *Well Spacing in the Aneth Reservoir* (Norman: University of Oklahoma Press, 1962), vii; Moore, "Culture Change in a Navaho Community," 127, 129–30; Clyde Benally, telephone interview by author, April 30, 1992.

15. Reno, *Mother Earth*, 125, 127.

16. Peter Iverson, "Peter MacDonald," in *American Indian Leaders: Studies in Diversity*, ed. R. David Edmunds (Lincoln: University of Nebraska Press, 1980), 230.

17. Marjane Ambler, *Breaking the Iron Bonds: Indian Control of Energy Development* (Lawrence: University Press of Kansas, 1990), 91–92, 96; Iverson, "Peter MacDonald," 230, 237, 239.

18. Lynn Arnold Robbins, "Navajo Energy Politics," *Social Science Journal* 16, no. 2 (April 1979): 116.

19. Lynn Arnold Robbins, "Energy Development and the Navajo Nation," in *Native Americans and Energy Development*, ed. Joseph G. Jorgensen and Sally Swenson (Cambridge, Mass.: Anthropology Resource Center, 1978), 47.

20. "Indians Form Coalition to Aid Treaties Fight," *Arizona Republic*, April 15, 1978, B1; *Arizona Republic*, April 14, 1978, B1.

21. Office of Program Development, *Navajo Nation Overall Economic Development Program*, 27; Iverson, "Peter MacDonald," 230.

22. Carlton Stowe, *Utah's Oil and Gas Industry: Past, Present, and Future* (Salt Lake City: Utah Engineering Experiment Station, University of Utah, 1979), 11, 51.

23. Office of Program Development, *Navajo Nation Overall Economic Development Program*, 31.

24. Clyde Benally, telephone interview by author, April 30, 1992.

25. Wendy Feder, "Utah Agency Comes Under Fire," *Navajo Times*, January 12, 1978, A1.

26. Anonymous letter, *Navajo Times*, February 16, 1978, A13.

27. "Bridge Dedication Opens New Way across San Juan," *San Juan Record*, December 12, 1958, 1.

28. John Norton, interview by Baxter Benally and Robert McPherson, January 16, 1991, manuscript in possession of author.

29. Ibid.

30. John Knot Begay, interview by Baxter Benally and Robert McPherson, May 7, 1991, manuscript in possession of author.

31. Harvey Oliver, interview by Baxter Benally and Robert McPherson, March 6, 1991, manuscript in possession of author; Jane Silas, interview by Baxter Benally and Robert McPherson, February 27, 1991, manuscript in possession of author; Ben Whitehorse interview by Baxter Benally and Robert McPherson, January 30, 1991, manuscript in possession of author; Jerry Begay, interview by Baxter Benally and Robert McPherson, January 16, 1991, manuscript in possession of author.

32. "Coalition for Navajo Liberation: Spreading Out from Shiprock," *Navajo Times*, February 2, 1978, A2.

33. Casey Watchman, "Coalition Is Still Going Strong," *Navajo Times*, August 17, 1978, A13.

34. W. Richard West, Jr., and Kevin Gover, "The Struggle for Indian Civil Rights," in *Indians in American History*, ed. Frederick E. Hoxie (Arlington Heights, Ill.: Harlan Davidson, 1988), 290.

35. Robbins, "Energy Development and the Navajo Nation," 45.

36. "Coalition for Navajo Liberation: Spreading Out from Shiprock," *Navajo Times*, February 2, 1978, A2.

37. "Navajos Hold Sit-in at Texaco Oil Station," *Arizona Republic*, March 31, 1978, A2.

38. Ella Sakizzie, interview by Baxter Benally and Robert McPherson, May 14, 1991, manuscript in possession of author.

39. Ibid.

40. "Navajos Seize Field and Promise to Ban Oil Companies Until Tribe Is Respected," *Arizona Republic*, April 11, 1978, A1.

41. Al Henderson, "The Aneth Community: Oil Crisis in Navajoland," *Indian Historian* (Winter 1979): 33–34.

42. Steve Marks, "Navajos Seize, Occupy Utah's Huge Aneth Field," *Western Oil Reporter* (April 1978): 23.

43. Henderson, "The Aneth Community," 33–34.

44. "Inside Look at Aneth Occupation," *Navajo Times*, April 13, 1978, A1; Clyde Benally, telephone interview with author, April 30, 1992.

45. Ibid., "Indians Block Oil Station in Utah," *Arizona Republic*, April 1, 1978, A5; "Three More Oil Operators Closed in Indian Dispute," *Arizona Republic*, April 2, 1978, B24.

46. "Inside Look at Aneth Occupation," *Navajo Times*, April 13, 1978, A1.

47. Ibid.; "Navajos Hold Sit-in at Texaco Oil Station," *Arizona Republic*, March 31, 1978, A2; "Three More Oil Operators Closed in Indian Dispute," *Arizona Republic*, April 2, 1978, B24.

48. Clyde Benally, telephone interview.

49. "Navajos Seize Field and Promise to Ban Oil Companies Until Tribe Is Respected," *Arizona Republic*, April 11, 1978, A1.

50. Ibid.; Grant E. Smith, "Indians Are Determined to Alter Oil Firm Policies," *Arizona Republic*, April 16, 1978, A1.

51. "MacDonald Urges Delegates of the Native American Treaties and Rights Organization," *Arizona Republic*, April 14, 1978, B1.

52. "Three More Oil Operators Closed in Indian Dispute," *Arizona Republic*, April 2, 1978, B24.

53. "Navajos Seize Field and Promise to Ban Oil Companies Until Tribe Is Respected," *Arizona Republic*, 11 April 1978, sec A, p. 1.

54. "Inside Look at Aneth Occupation," *Navajo Times*, April 13, 1978, A1.

55. Ibid.; "Texaco Agrees to Examine Complaints," *Navajo Times*, April 6, 1978, A10.

56. "Texaco Occupation Ends: Agreement Reached," *Navajo Times*, April 20, 1978, A6.

57. Ibid.; Clyde Benally, telephone interview.

58. "Texaco Occupation Ends: Agreement Reached," *Navajo Times*, April 20, 1978, A6.

59. Ibid.

60. "Navajo Oil Field Siege Ends Today," *Arizona Republic*, April 17, 1978, A3; "Navajos End Oil-Field Takeover: Celebration Planned," *Arizona Republic*, April 18, 1978, A5.

61. Office of Program Development, *Navajo Nation Overall Economic Development Program* (Window Rock, Ariz.: Navajo Nation, 1983), 60; Office of Program Development, *Navajo Nation Overall Economic Development Program* (Window Rock, Ariz.: Navajo Nation, 1974), 22, 267; "Utah Councilman Signs on as Spokesman for Texaco Oil Company," *Navajo Times*, February 1, 1979; Clyde Benally, telephone interview.

62. Clyde Benally, telephone interview.

63. "Situation in Aneth Is Worsening; Tribal Officials Afraid to Visit," *Navajo Times*, August 10, 1978, sec. A10.

64. "Reasons for 'Montezuma Walk,'" *Navajo Times*, November 30, 1978, A18.

65. Bill Donovan, "Audit Shows Millions Wasted," *Navajo Times*, November 14, 1991, A1.

66. Bill Donovan, "Concerns of Aneth Residents Need to Be Heard Says EDC: Renegotiation of Contract Is Sought," *Navajo Times*, June 6, 1991, A1–2.

67. Jerry Begay, interview.

68. Cyrus Begay, interview by Baxter Benally and Robert McPherson, May 14, 1991, manuscript in possession of author.

69. Navajo Nation, "Overall Economic Development Plan, 1992–1993," Navajo Nation Division of Economic Development, Window Rock, Ariz., 1933, 12.

70. See Sam Bingham and Janet Bingham, eds., *Between Sacred Mountains: Navajo Stories and Lessons from the Land* (Tucson: Sun Tracks and University of Arizona Press, 1982), 230–39.

71. John Knot Begay, interview.

CHAPTER 11

1. Gladys A. Reichard, *Dezba: Woman of the Desert* (Glorieta, New Mex.: Rio Grande Press, 1939), 28.

2. See Christine Conte, "Ladies, Livestock, Land and Lucre: Women's Networks and Social Status on the Western Navajo Reservation," *American Indian Quarterly* 6 (Spring–Summer 1982): 105–23; Mary Shepardson and Blodwen Hammond, "Change and Persistence in an Isolated Navajo Community," *American Anthropologist* 66 (Fall 1964): 1029–50; Laila Hamamsy, "The Role of Women in a Changing Navajo Society," *American Anthropologist* 1 (February 1957): 101–11; Kendall Blanchard, "Changing Sex Roles and Protestantism among the Navajo Women in Ramah," *Journal for the Scientific Study of Religion* 14 (March 1975): 43–50; Mary Shepardson, "The Status of Navajo Women," *American Indian Quarterly* 6 (Spring–Summer 1982): 149–69.

3. See Dorothea C. Leighton, "As I Knew Them: Navajo Women in 1940," *American Indian Quarterly* 6 (Spring–Summer 1982): 34–51; Charlotte J. Frisbie,

"Traditional Navajo Women: Ethnographic and Life History Portrayals," *American Indian Quarterly* 6 (Spring–Summer 1982): 11–33.

4. The statistical information for this chapter is taken from federal government censuses derived from research done at the beginning of each decade. Copies of these are available in most research libraries; the closest microfilm collection available for my use is at Brigham Young University. Thus the following reels were consulted: Navajo Census—1931, Microfilm #579,714, Genealogy Library, Harold B. Lee Library, Brigham Young University, Provo, Utah; censuses—1960, 1970, 1980, Government Publications Section, Harold B. Lee Library, Brigham Young University, Provo, Utah. The 1980 and 1990 census materials came directly from the state capitol. This information may be located under the following titles: Census of Population and Housing—1980, Summary Tape File 3A—Oljeto and Red Mesa Divisions, San Juan County, on file in Office of State Planning Coordinator, State Capitol, Salt Lake City, Utah, 1–10, 229–40; Census—1990, File 1A and 3A County Subdivisions located in the Demographic and Economic Analysis Section, State Capitol, Salt Lake City, Utah.

5. See Gary Witherspoon, *Navajo Kinship and Marriage* (Chicago: University of Chicago Press, 1975).

6. Solon T. Kimball and John H. Provinse, "Navajo Social Organization in Land Use Planning," *Applied Anthropology* 1 (July–September 1942): 21.

7. Younger Navajo woman, interview by author, February 24, 1984, manuscript in possession of author.

8. Larry Rodgers, *1990 Census—Population and Housing Characteristics of the Navajo Nation* (Scottsdale, Ariz.: Printing Company, 1993): 42.

9. U.S. Congress, Senate, Public Law 90–306, United States Statutes at Large—1968, 82 (Washington, D.C.: Government Printing Office, 1968), 121.

10. "Annual Report of the Utah Navajo Development Council—1978–83," on file at UNDC's main office, Blanding, Utah.

11. Ibid., 10.

12. Kitty At'iinni, interview by Fern Charley and Dean Sundberg, July 13, 1977, OH 1224 Utah State Historical Society and California State–Fullerton Oral History Program—Southeastern Utah Project, 8.

13. Ann Metcalf, "From Schoolgirl to Mother: The Effects of Education on Navajo Women," *Social Problems* 23 (June 1976): 535.

14. Ibid., 543.

15. Alexander Leighton and Dorothea Leighton, *The Navajo Door* (Cambridge, Mass.: Harvard University Press, 1945), 46.

16. Kent D. Tibbits, "A Study of Parental Factors Affecting Success or Failure of Navajo Indian Students" (M.A. thesis, University of Utah, 1969), 25.

17. Rodgers, *1990 Census*, 48.

18. *Sinajini v. Board of Education* case materials on file at the DNA Office, Mexican Hat, Utah.

19. Ibid., "Agreement of Parties," Civil Number C-74-346, 7.

20. Ibid., 2.

21. Paul R. Platero, "Navajo Head Start Language Study," Final Report, First Draft, March 23, 1992, Navajo Division of Education, Navajo Nation, Window Rock, Arizona, 1.

22. Nedra Todich'iinii, interview by Fern Charley and Dean Sundberg, July 12, 1977, OH 1223, Utah State Historical Society and California State–Fullerton Oral History Program—Southeastern Utah Project, 12.

23. Older Navajo woman, interview by author, March 8, 1984, manuscript in possession of author.

24. Younger Navajo woman, interview by author, March 7, 1984, manuscript in possession of author.

25. Irene Fisher, Shirley Weathers, and Ann Kagie, "Report to the Governor: Poverty in Utah—1983," State Community Services Office, Department of Community and Economic Development, State Office Building, Salt Lake City, January, 1984, 10; Harold Lyman, Director of Job Service–Blanding, telephone conversation with author, July 29, 1992.

26. Fisher, Weathers, and Kagie, "Report to the Governor," 97.

27. Lyman, telephone conversation with author, July 29, 1992.

28. "Report on Minorities in Utah—San Juan County," Utah Department of Employment Security, August, 1980, n.p., in possession of author.

29. David C. Williams, "Spending Patterns of Navajo Families," *New Mexico Business* 28, no. 2 (March 1975): 4.

30. Younger Navajo woman, interview by author, February 24, 1984, manuscript in possession of author.

31. Younger Navajo woman, interview by author, March 19, 1984, manuscript in possession of author.

32. Younger Navajo woman, interview by author, March 12, 1984, manuscript in possession of author.

33. Middle-aged Navajo woman, conversation with author, March 30, 1994, manuscript in possession of author.

34. Nancy Belding, Tamara Sparks, and Guy Miles, "Perspectives of Adjustment: Rural Navajo and Papago Youth," *Report for the Manpower Administration* (Washington, D.C.: U.S. Department of Labor, 1974), 22.

35. Information on file in the Registrar's Office, College of Eastern Utah–San Juan Campus, Blanding.

36. Younger Navajo woman, interview by author, March 8, 1984, manuscript in possession of author.

37. This survey was part of the doctoral research project of William L. Olderog, "Variations in Value Orientations and Work-related Values: A Study of Navajo and Anglo-American College Students" (Ph.D. diss., Brigham Young University, 1991). The major focus of this study was to compare and contrast Navajo and Anglo values rather than explore gender differences. Olderog, however, was gracious enough to provide for me the rich raw data with which to

explore variations between Navajo males and females as well as Anglo males and females. What follows is a brief overview of what his survey indicates.

38. Older Navajo woman, interview by author, March 6, 1984, manuscript in possession of author.

39. See Clyde Kluckhohn, *Navajo Witchcraft* (Cambridge, Mass.: Beacon Press, 1944).

40. Younger Navajo woman, conversation with author, January 25, 1985.

41. Younger Navajo woman, interview by author, February 16, 1984, manuscript in possession of author.

42. Younger Navajo woman, interview by author, March 6, 1984, manuscript in possession of author.

43. Middle-aged Navajo woman, conversation with author, March 30, 1994, manuscript in possession of author.

CHAPTER 12

1. Wayne L. Welsh (Auditor General), "A Performance Review of the Utah Navajo Trust Fund" (Report 91–10), Office of the Legislative Auditor General, November 11, 1991, 7.

2. Ibid., ii.

3. Ibid., 14, 16–17, 34–45.

4. "Navajo Trust Fund Freeze Lifted," *San Juan Record*, June 3, 1992, 1; "Motion to Dismiss Trust Fund Class Action Lawsuit Made by State," *San Juan Record*, September 3, 1993, 1.

5. "Commissioners Discuss Trust Fund with Gov.," *San Juan Record*, October 21, 1993, 1.

6. "Utah not Liable for Trust Funds Lost, Judge Rules," *San Juan Record*, June 28, 1995, 1.

7. "Utah Navajo Trust," *Canyon Echo* (July–August 1995): 1.

8. *Pelt v. Utah*, Case #92-C-639 S, on file Utah Attorney General's Office, Salt Lake City, Utah, 17.

9. "Utah Gov. Would Rather Settle," *Navajo Times*, February 27, 1997, A8; "Utah Navajo Trust: Resolution at Last," *Canyon Echo* (April 1997): 3.

10. "Judge Orders Utah to Provide Data on Navajo Trust Fund," *Deseret News*, June 27, 1998; "Navajos Win Another Round on Trust-Fund Accounting," *Deseret News*, July 1, 1998; "Utah Ordered to Pay $2,450 for Withholding Navajo Records," *Deseret News*, October 20, 1998; "No State Statute of Limitations in Navajos' Case, Judge Rules," *Deseret News*, April 7, 1999.

11. Brochure, "Utah Navajo Trust Fund: Historical and Current Perspectives of the Trust Fund," State of Utah, January 1998; brochure, "Utah Navajo Trust Fund: Description of Program Activities," State of Utah, n.d.

12. "Lights at Last for a Remote Area," *Deseret News*, March 23, 1999.

13. "Miles Away from Health Care," *Deseret News*, May 30, 1999.

14. Telephone conversation with John Housekeeper, Fiscal Manager, Utah Navajo Trust Fund, July 1, 1999.

15. "Stakes Are High for Mobil Oil, Navajo Nation, and San Juan County," *San Juan Record*, January 15, 1997, 1; "Navajos Prevail as Mobil Closes Wells," *Salt Lake Tribune*, January 10, 1997, A1.

16. "Oil's Well That Ends Well as Tepee Talks Pay Off," *Salt Lake Tribune*, January 13, 1997, A1.

17. "U.S. Accuses Texaco of Polluting Utah River," *Deseret News*, March 28, 1998; "AEPA Files Lawsuit, Accuses Mobil of Polluting San Juan River," *Deseret News*, March 31, 1998.

18. "San Juan's Dirt Roads to Get Some Federal Help," *Deseret News*, June 12, 1999.

19. "Senate OKs $2 Million for Four Corners Center," *Deseret News*, September 20, 1998; "Utah, Arizona, Navajo Nation Join in Plans to Build State Visitor Center," *Deseret News*, June 27, 1999.

20. Chris LaMarr, "Free Exercise of Religion by Native American Prisoners: A Plan of Action," *NARF Legal Review* 1 (1996): 10–15.

21. "Indians Fight for Religious Freedom," *Navajo Times*, April 7, 1986, 1–2; "Utah Wardens Nix Use of Sweatbaths," *Navajo Times*, May 22, 1986, 1.

22. Attorney General Directive, "Providing for the Free Exercise of Religion by Native American Prisoners," 1995, in handout received from Leonard Foster, Director of Navajo Nation's Correctional Project, Navajo Studies Conference, Albuquerque, April 1996.

23. Utah Legislature, "Indian Worship at Correctional Facilities," *Utah Legislative Report 1996*, S.B. No. 128, February 27, 1996, 1025–26.

24. "Does Prison Stifle Indian Worship?" *Salt Lake Tribune*, November 12, 1996, B1, B4.

25. Leonard Foster, "Written Testimony of Len Foster, Director/Spiritual Advisor Navajo Nation Corrections Project, Window Rock, Arizona," given at the Missouri State Capitol in support of H.B. 325, March 4, 1997, 2, in possession of author.

26. "Bill Would Protect Inmate Rites," *Salt Lake Tribune*, February 8, 1996, B1.

27. "Does Prison Stifle Indian Worship?" *Salt Lake Tribune*, November 12, 1996, B4.

28. "Hale Working on Utah Agreement," *Navajo Times*, March 21, 1996, 1.

29. Utah Legislature, "Native American Legislative Liaison Committee," *Utah Legislative Report 1995*, H.B. 316, March 1, 1995, 458–59.

30. "Blue Ribbon Committee Meets to Study Creation of New County," *San Juan Record*, November 8, 1995, 1.

31. "New Study Investigates the Issues Involved in Splitting San Juan County," *San Juan Record*, July 1997, 1.

32. "Settlement Reached in Jury Selection Bias Case," *San Juan Record*, June 19, 1996, 1.

33. "San Juan Complying with Jury-List Decree," *Deseret News*, December 12, 1998.

34. "Another School Year Begins This Week," *San Juan Record*, August 20, 1997, 1; figure for fall 1997 enrollment from secretary, San Juan School District, telephone conversation with author, December 30, 1997.

35. "Voters Approve $5 Million Bond for School District," *San Juan Record*, May 14, 1997, 1.

36. "San Juan School Charged with Discrimination," *Navajo Times*, December 16, 1993, 6.

37. "School District Is Paying $58 per Student in Costly Legal Fees," *Blue Mountain Panorama*, October 16, 1996, 1.

38. "Settlements Reached on Host of School Lawsuits," *San Juan Record*, April 23, 1999, 1.

39. San Juan School District Language Development Program, 1998, available at the San Juan School District Office, Blanding, Utah, 1.

40. Appendix C, SAT-9 NCE, October 1997, San Juan School District Language Development Program, San Juan School District Office, Blanding, Utah, 76–78.

41. Ibid.

42. "Bilingual Proposal Gets Cold Reception from Educators and Parents," *Blue Mountain Panorama*, October 8, 1997, 2.

43. Carolyn M. Shields, *A Study of the Educational Perceptions and Attitudes of Four Stakeholder Groups in the San Juan School District in 1998* (Blanding, Utah: San Juan School District, 1999), 59–60.

44. Consensus Committee Report, April 1999, on file in the San Juan School District Office, Blanding, Utah, 4.

45. "1,000 March Against 'English-Only' Utah Bill," *Navajo Times*, January 29, 1998, 5; "English Only? House Says Nyet, Non, Nein," *Deseret News*, January 22, 1999.

46. "Utah House Rejects Controversial English-Only Initiative," *Deseret News*, January 22, 1999.

47. "1990 County Population by Race."

48. "Native Community Connections," Indian Walk-In Center Quarterly Newsletter, Spring 1996, 1.

49. Gail Russell, Executive Director, Indian Walk-In Center, conversation with author, November 13, 1997.

50. "Native American Connections," Indian Walk-In Center Quarterly Newsletters, Spring 1996 and Spring 1997.

51. Burton S. White and Robert D. Peterson, "Indian Training and Eduction Center Statistical Study 1989–1994," on file in the Indian Training and Eduction Center, Salt Lake City, Utah, n.p.

52. Robert D. Peterson to author, September 10, 1997, letter in possession of author.

53. "Hale Attends Signing Ceremony in Utah," *Navajo Times*, May 9, 1996, 9; "Leavitt, Hale Sign Historic Agreements during Blanding Visit," *Blue Mountain Panorama*, May 14, 1996, 1.

54. "County, Tribe Law Enforcement to Cooperate," *San Juan Record*, January 9, 1997, 1.

55. "Trackers from Navajo Nation Join Utah Hunt," *Deseret News*, June 7, 1998.

56. "Navajo Nation Seeks Aid to Pay for Manhunt," *Deseret News*, August 21, 1998; "Year Manhunt Yields Frustration, Few Clues," *Deseret News*, May 30, 1999.

57. "Navajos, State Sign Contract on Abused Kids," *Deseret News*, May 29, 1999; "Navajo Nation, Utah Team Up to Help Serve Abused Children," *Navajo Times*, June 3, 1999, 1.

58. "The Political Mark Maryboy," *Zephyr*, October–November 1998, 18–19.

59. "Maryboy Appointed by President Clinton," *San Juan Record*, June 15, 1994, 1.

BIBLIOGRAPHY

GOVERNMENT ARCHIVES

United States. Congressional Records, 1892–1990. Brigham Young University Library, Provo, Utah.

United States Census. Navajo Nation Census—1931, Microfilm #579,714, Genealogy Library, Harold B. Lee Library, Brigham Young University, Provo, Utah; 1960, 1970, 1980 Utah censuses, Government Publications Section, Harold B. Lee Library, Brigham Young University, Provo, Utah. 1980 and 1990 censuses, Utah State Capitol, Salt Lake City.

United States. Record Group 75. Consolidated Ute Agency Records, Bureau of Indian Affairs. Federal Records Center, Denver, Colorado.

United States. Record Group 75. Letters Received by Office of Indian Affairs, New Mexico Superintendency, 1858–1907. National Archives, Washington, D.C.

United States. Record Group 98. Letters Received by War Department, 1861. National Archives, Washington, D.C.

United States. Record Group 393. U.S. Army Continental Command, 1821–1920, National Archives, Washington, D.C.

United States. Record Group 75. Letters Received by Office of Indian Affairs, 1881–1907, Bureau of Indian Affairs, National Archives, Washington, D.C.

United States. Official Records of the War of the Rebellion. Brigham Young University Library, Provo, Utah.

United States. *Report of the Commissioner of Indian Affairs*, 1858–1905. Department of the Interior, Washington, D.C.

Utah, Legislature. *Utah Legislative Report*, 1995–96. Utah State Capitol, Salt Lake City, Utah.

MANUSCRIPTS, REPORTS, AND SPECIAL COLLECTIONS

"Annual Report of the Utah Navajo Development Council," 1978–83. On file at Utah Navajo Development Council, Bluff, Utah.

Brugge, David M. "Navajo Use and Occupation of the Area North of the San Juan River in Present-Day Utah." Unpublished manuscript in author's possession.

Correll, J. Lee. Collection. Navajo Nation Archives, Window Rock, Arizona.

Fisher, Irene, Shirley Weathers, and Ann Kagie. "Report to the Governor: Poverty in Utah–1983." State Community Services Office, Department of Community and Economic Development, Salt Lake City, Utah.

General History. Navajo Archives. Window Rock, Arizona.

Kelly, Charles. "Hoskaninni Begay." Interview, August 11–13, 1938. Charles Kelly Papers, Special Collections, Marriott Library, University of Utah, Salt Lake City.

Lyman, Albert R. "History of San Juan County, 1879–1917." Special Collections, Brigham Young University, Provo, Utah.

Minute Book, 1880–1914. "San Juan County Minutes." County Court House, Monticello, Utah.

Platero, Paul R. "Navajo Head Start Language Study." Final Report, First Draft, March 23, 1992. Navajo Division of Education, Navajo Nation, Window Rock, Arizona.

Pelt v. Utah, Case #92-C-639 S, on file Utah Attorney General's Office, Salt Lake City, Utah, 17.

Regan, Albert B. "Petrified Wood Myth." Albert B. Reagan Collection, Special Collections, Brigham Young University Library, Provo, Utah.

"Report on Minorities in Utah–San Juan County." Utah Department of Employment Security, August 1980, n.p., in author's possession.

Richardson, Gladwell. Collection. Special Collections, Northern Arizona University Library, Flagstaff, Arizona.

Registrar's Office, College of Eastern Utah—San Juan Campus, Blanding, Utah.

San Juan Stake History. Historical Archives, Church of Jesus Christ of Latter-day Saints, Salt Lake City.

Sherwood, J. M. "Notes Regarding Charles E. Walton." N.d. Utah State Historical Society, Salt Lake City, Utah.

Silvey, Frank. "History and Settlement of Northern San Juan County," n.p., n.d. Manuscript in Utah State Historical Society, Salt Lake City.

———. "Information on Indians," 1936. Manuscript in Utah State Historical Society, Salt Lake City.

———. "Stampede for Placer Gold." Unpublished manuscript, April 10, 1936, Utah State Historical Society, Salt Lake City.

Sinajini v. Board of Education. File at the Dinébe'iiná Náhiilna Be Agha'diít'ahii (DNA) Office, Mexican Hat, Utah.

Utah Navajo Development Council Historical Archives. Edge of the Cedars Museum, Blanding, Utah.

Welsh, Wayne L. (Auditor General). "A Performance Review of the Utah Navajo Trust Fund" (Report 9 1–10). Office of the Legislative Auditor General, November 11, 1991. State Capitol, Salt Lake City, Utah.

White, Burton S., and Robert D. Peterson. "Indian Training and Education Center Statistical Study 1989–1994." On file in the Indian Training and Education Center, Salt Lake City, Utah, n.p.

BOOKS AND PERIODICALS

Ambler, Marjane. *Breaking the Iron Bonds: Indian Control of Energy Development.* Lawrence: University Press of Kansas, 1990.

Amoss, Harold Lindsay, Jr. "The Ute Mountain Utes." Ph.D. diss., University of California, Berkeley, 1951.

Babbitt, James E., ed. *Rainbow Trails: Early-Day Adventures in Rainbow Bridge Country.* Page, Ariz.: Glen Canyon Natural History Association, 1990.

Bailey, Garrick, and Roberta Bailey. *A History of the Navajos: The Reservation Years.* Santa Fe, New Mex.: School of American Research, 1986.

Bailey, Lynn R. *If You Take My Sheep: The Evolution and Conflicts of Navajo Pastoralism, 1630–1868.* Los Angeles: Westernlore Press, 1980.

———. *The Long Walk.* Los Angeles: Westernlore Press, 1964.

———. *The Navajo Reconnaissance.* Los Angeles: Westernlore Press, 1964.

Belding, Nancy, Tamara Sparks, and Guy Miles. "Perspectives of Adjustment: Rural Navajo and Papago Youth." *Report for the Manpower Administration.* Washington, D.C.: U.S. Department of Labor, 1974.

Bingham, Sam, and Janet Bingham. *Between Sacred Mountains: Navajo Stories and Lessons from the Land.* Tucson: Sun Tracks and University of Arizona Press, 1982.

Blanchard, Kendall. "Changing Sex Roles and Protestantism among the Navajo Women in Ramah." *Journal for the Scientific Study of Religion* 14 (March 1975): 43–50.

Brightman, Robert A. *Grateful Prey: Rock Cree Human-Animal Relationships.* Berkeley: University of California Press, 1993.

Brough, R. Clayton, Dale L. Jones, and Dale J. Stevens. *Utah's Comprehensive Weather Almanac.* Salt Lake City: Publishers Press, 1987.

Brugge, David M. *A History of the Chaco Navajos.* Albuquerque: National Park Service, 1980.

———. "Navajo Prehistory and History to 1850." *Handbook of North American Indians* 10, ed. Alfonso Ortiz, 489–501. Washington, D.C.: Smithsonian Institution Press, 1983.

———. "Vizcarra's Navajo Campaign of 1823." *Arizona and the West* 6 (Autumn 1964): 223–44.

Budd, Michael N. "A Critical Analysis of Western Films Directed by John Ford from *Stagecoach* to *Cheyenne Autumn.*" Ph.D. diss., University of Iowa, 1975.

Bulow, Ernest L. *Navajo Taboos.* Gallup, New Mex.: Southwesterner Books, 1982.

Campbell, Joseph. *Myths to Live By.* New York: Bantam Press, 1984.

Charley, Fern, and Dean Sundberg. *The Navajo Stock Reduction Interviews of Fern Charley and Dean Sundberg*. Southern Utah Oral History Project. Fullerton: California State University and the Utah State Historical Society, 1984.

Chavez, Fray Angelico, and Ted J. Warner, *The Dominguez-Escalante Journal: Their Expedition through Colorado, Utah, Arizona, and New Mexico in 1776*. Provo: Brigham Young University Press, 1976.

Chenoweth, William. "Early Uranium-Vanadium Mining in Monument Valley, San Juan County, Utah." *Survey Notes* 18, no. 2 (Summer 1984): 1–20.

Chenowith, William, and Roger C. Malan. *Uranium Deposits of Northeastern Arizona*. Grand Junction, Colo.: U.S. Atomic Energy Commission, 1973.

Cole, Frank. *Well Spacing in the Aneth Reservoir*. Norman: University of Oklahoma Press, 1962.

Conte, Christine. "Ladies, Livestock, Land and Lucre: Women's Networks and Social Status on the Western Navajo Reservation." *American Indian Quarterly* 6 (Spring–Summer 1982): 105–23.

Correll, J. Lee. *Through White Men's Eyes: A Contribution to Navajo History* 1. Window Rock, Ariz.: Navajo Heritage Center, 1979.

Cronon, William. *Changes in the Land*. New York: Hill and Wang, 1983.

Day, Gordon M. "The Indian as an Ecological Factor in the Northeastern Forests." *Ecology* 34 (April 1953): 329–43.

Dixon, Winifred H. *Westward Hoboes: Ups and Downs of Frontier Motoring*. New York: Scribner's Sons, 1930.

Downs, James F. *Animal Husbandry in Navaho Society and Culture*. Berkeley: University of California Press, 1964.

Dunning, Charles H. "Arizona Uranium Rush." *Arizona Highways* 25, no. 8 (August 1949): 4–7.

Dyk, Walter. *A Navaho Autobiography*. New York: Viking Fund, 1947.

Dyk, Walter, and Ruth Dyk. *Left Handed: A Navajo Autobiography*. New York: Columbia University Press, 1980.

Ellis, Florence H. *An Anthropological Study of the Navajo Indians*. New York: Garland, 1974.

Elmore, Francis H. "The Deer and His Importance to the Navaho." *El Palacio* 60 (November 1953): 371–84.

Faunce, Hilda. *Desert Wife*. Lincoln: University of Nebraska Press, 1928.

Flader, Susan L. *Thinking Like a Mountain*. Lincoln: University of Nebraska Press, 1974.

Florence, William R."John Ford . . . The Duke . . . and Monument Valley." *Arizona Highways* (September 1981): 22–37.

Flores, Dan. "Bison Ecology and Bison Diplomacy: The Southern Plains from 1800–1850." *Journal of American History* 78 (September 1991): 465–85.

Fonaroff, L. Schuyler. "Conservation and Stock Reduction on the Navajo Tribal Range." *Geographical Review* 53 (April 1963): 200–23

Foster, Robert J. *General Geology*. Columbus: Merrill, 1988.

Frankl, Victor E. *Man's Search for Meaning*. New York: Washington Square Press, 1946.

Franciscan Friars. *An Ethnologic Dictionary of the Navajo Language*. Saint Michaels, Ariz.: Saint Michaels Press, 1910.

Frisbie, Charlotte J. "Traditional Navajo Women: Ethnographic and Life History Portrayals." *American Indian Quarterly* 6 (Spring–Summer 1982): 11–33.

Gilbreath, Kent. *Red Capitalism: An Analysis of the Navajo Economy*. Norman: University of Oklahoma Press, 1973.

Gillmor, Frances, and Louisa Wade Wetherill. *Traders to the Navajo*. Albuquerque: University of New Mexico Press, 1934.

Goulding, Harry. "The Navajos Hunt Big Game . . . Uranium." *Popular Mechanics* (June 1950): 89–92.

Goulding, Harry, and Joyce R. Muench. "When Tombstone Came to Monument Valley." *Desert Magazine* 11, no. 12 (October 1948): 6–10

Grey, Zane. *Tales of Lonely Trails*. New York: Harper and Brothers, 1922.

Haile, Father Berard. *The Upward Moving and Emergence Way: The Gishin Biyé Version*. Lincoln: University of Nebraska Press, 1981.

Hamamsy, Laila. "The Role of Women in a Changing Navajo Society." *American Anthropologist* 1 (February 1957): 101–11.

Hannum, Alberta. *Spin a Silver Dollar*. New York: Ballantine Books, 1944.

Hegemann, Elizabeth C. *Navaho Trading Days*. Albuquerque: University of New Mexico Press, 1963.

Henderson, Al. "The Aneth Community: Oil Crisis in Navajoland." *Indian Historian* (Winter 1979): 33–34.

Herrick, Genevieve. "Women in the News." *Country Gentleman* 46 (October 1939): 46.

Hill, W. W. *The Agricultural and Hunting Methods of the Navaho Indians*. New Haven: Yale University Press, 1938.

———. "Navaho Trading and Trading Ritual: A Study of Cultural Dynamics." *Southwestern Journal of Anthropology* 4 (Autumn 1948): 371–96.

Hobson, Richard. *Navaho Acquisitive Values*. Peabody Archaeology Papers 42, no. 3. Cambridge, Mass.: Harvard University Press, 1953.

Hoijier, Harry. "The Chronology of the Athapaskan Languages." *International Journal of American Linguistics* 22 (October 1956): 219–32.

Hyde, George E. *Indians of the High Plains*. Norman: University of Oklahoma Press, 1959.

Iverson, Peter. *The Navajo Nation*. Albuquerque: University of New Mexico Press, 1981.

———. "Peter MacDonald." In *American Indian Leaders: Studies in Diversity*, ed. R. David Edmunds, 222–41. Lincoln: University of Nebraska Press, 1980.

James, George Wharton. *Indian Blankets and Their Makers*. New York: Dover Publications, 1974.

Jensen, Bryant L. "An Historical Study of Bluff City, Utah, from 1878 to 1906." M.A. thesis, Brigham Young University, 1966.

Jett, Stephen C. "The Great 'Race' to 'Discover' Rainbow Natural Bridge." *Kiva* 58, no. 1 (Fall 1992): 3–66.

——. "Testimony of the Sacredness of Rainbow Natural Bridge to Puebloans, Navajos, and Paiutes." *Plateau* 45, no. 4 (Spring 1973): 133–42.

Johnson, Broderick H., ed. *Stories of the Long Walk Period.* Tsaile, Ariz.: Navajo Community College Press, 1973.

Jorgensen, Joseph G. "The Ethnohistory and Acculturation of the Northern Ute." Ph.D. diss., Brigham Young University, 1964.

Kappler, Charles J. *Indian Affairs—Laws and Treaties.* Vol. 3. Washington, D.C.: Government Printing Office, 1913.

Keele, Marsha. "Monument Valley Park Celebrates 25th Year." *San Juan Record,* July 28, 1983, 1.

Kelley, Klara B. *Navajo Land Use: An Ethnoarchaeological Study.* New York: Harcourt Brace Jovanovich, 1986.

Kelly, Lawrence C. *The Navajo Indians and Federal Indian Policy.* Tucson: University of Arizona Press, 1968.

——. *Navajo Roundup: Selected Correspondence of Kit Carson's Expedition against the Navajo, 1863–65.* Boulder, Colo.: Pruett, 1970.

Kildare, Maurice. "Builders to the Rainbow." *Frontier Times* 40 (June–July 1966): 14–17, 48–52.

Kimball, Solon T., and John H. Provinse. "Navajo Social Organization in Land Use Planning." *Applied Anthropology* 1 (July–September 1942): 18–25.

Klinck, Richard. *Land of Room Enough and Time Enough.* Layton, Utah: Gibbs M. Smith, 1984.

Kluckhohn, Clyde. *Navajo Witchcraft.* Cambridge, Mass.: Beacon Press, 1944.

——. *To the Foot of the Rainbow.* Glorieta, New Mex.: Rio Grande Press, 1967.

Kluckhohn, Clyde, and Dorothea Leighton. *The Navaho.* Rev. ed. Cambridge, Mass.: Harvard University Press, 1974.

Kneale, Albert H. *Indian Agent.* Caldwell: Caxton Printers, 1950.

Krech, Shepherd, III, ed., *Indians, Animals, and the Fur Trade: A Critique of Keepers of the Game.* Athens: University of Georgia Press, 1981.

Lamphere, Louise. "The Navajo Nation: A Case Study." Cited in *Economic Development in American Reservations,* ed. Roxanne Ortiz. Albuquerque: University of New Mexico Press, 1980.

——. *To Run after Them: Cultural and Social Bases of Cooperation in a Navajo Community.* Tucson: University of Arizona Press, 1977.

LaMarr, Chris. "Free Exercise of Religion by Native American Prisoners: A Plan of Action." *NARF Legal Review* 1 (1996): 10–15.

Leighton, Alexander, and Dorothea Leighton. *The Navajo Door.* Cambridge, Mass.: Harvard University Press, 1945.

Leighton, Dorothea C. "As I Knew Them: Navajo Women in 1940." *American Indian Quarterly* 6 (Spring–Summer 1982): 34–51.

León-Portilla, Miguel, ed. *The Broken Spears: The Aztec Account of the Conquest of Mexico.* Boston: Beacon Press, 1962.

Liebler, H. Baxter. "The Social and Cultural Patterns of the Navajo Indians." *Utah Historical Quarterly* 30 (Fall 1962): 298–325.

Luckert, Karl W. *A Navajo Bringing-Home Ceremony: The Claus Chee Sonny Version of Deerway Ajilee.* Flagstaff: Museum of Northern Arizona Press, 1978.

———. *The Navajo Hunter Tradition.* Tucson: University of Arizona Press, 1975.

———. *Navajo Mountain and Rainbow Bridge Religion.* Flagstaff: Museum of Northern Arizona Press, 1977.

Martin, Calvin. *Keepers of the Game: Indian-Animal Relationships and the Fur Trade.* Berkeley: University of California Press, 1978.

Matthews, Washington. *Navaho Legends.* New York: Houghton Mifflin, 1897.

McCarthy, Todd. "John Ford and Monument Valley." *American Film* 8, no. 7 (May 1978): 10–16.

McNitt, Frank. *The Indian Traders.* Norman: University of Oklahoma Press, 1962.

———. *Navajo Wars, Military Campaigns, Slave Raids and Reprisals.* Albuquerque: University of New Mexico Press, 1972.

———. *Richard Wetherill: Anasazi.* Albuquerque: University of New Mexico Press, 1957.

McPherson, Robert S. *A History of San Juan County: In the Palm of Time.* Salt Lake City: Utah State Historical Society, 1995.

———. *The Northern Navajo Frontier: Expansion through Adversity, 1860–1900.* Albuquerque: University of New Mexico Press, 1988.

———. *Sacred Land, Sacred View: Navajo Perceptions of the Four Corners Region.* Charles Redd Center Monograph Series, no. 19. Provo: Brigham Young University Press, 1992.

McPherson, Robert S., and Richard Kitchen. "Much Ado about Nothing: The San Juan River Gold Rush, 1892–1893." *Utah Historical Quarterly* 67 (Winter 1999): 68–87.

Metcalf, Ann. "From Schoolgirl to Mother: The Effects of Education on Navajo Women." *Social Problems* 23 (June 1976): 535–44.

Moon, Samuel. *Tall Sheep: Harry Goulding, Monument Valley Trader.* Norman: University of Oklahoma Press, 1992.

Moore, Harvey C. "Culture Change in a Navaho Community." In *American Historical Anthropology: Essays in Honor of Leslie Spier,* ed. Carroll L. Riley and Walter W. Taylor, 123–36. Carbondale: Southern Illinois University Press, 1967.

Morris, Ann Axtell. *Digging in the Southwest.* Chicago: Cadmus Books, 1933.

"Native Community Connections." Indian Walk-In Center Quarterly Newsletter, Spring 1996. In possession of author.

Navajo Nation. *1990 Census Population and Housing Characteristics of the Navajo Nation.* Scottsdale, Ariz.: Printing Company, 1993.

———. "Overall Economic Development Plan 1992–1993." Navajo Nation Division of Economic Development, Window Rock, Arizona, 1993.

Office of Program Development. *Navajo Nation Overall Economic Development Program*. Window Rock, Ariz.: Navajo Nation, 1974, 1980, 1983.

Oldendorph, O. F. "Monument Valley: A Navajo Tribal Park." *National Parks Magazine* 40 (August 1966): 4–8.

Olderog, William L. "Variations in Value Orientations and Work-related Values: A Study of Navajo and Anglo-American College Students." Ph.D. diss., Brigham Young University, 1991.

Opler, Morris E. "The Apachean Culture Pattern and Its Origins." In *Handbook of North American Indians* 10, ed. Alfonso Ortiz, 368–92. Washington, D.C.: Smithsonian Institution Press, 1983.

Palmer, Mildred. "Hanson Bayles: The Story." Published by the family, 1988.

Parman, Donald L. *The Navajos and the New Deal*. New Haven: Yale University Press, 1976.

Perkins, Cornelia, Marian Nielson, and Lenora Jones. *The Saga of San Juan*. Salt Lake City: Mercury, 1968.

Peterson, Charles S. *Look to the Mountains: Southeastern Utah and the La Sal National Forest*. Provo: Brigham Young University Press, 1975.

Philp, Kenneth R. *John Collier's Crusade for Indian Reform, 1920–54*. Tucson: University of Arizona Press, 1977.

Portilla, Miguel-Leon, ed.. *The Broken Spear: The Aztec Account of the Conquest of Mexico*. Boston: Beacon Press, 1962.

Preston, Don, ed. *A Symposium of the Oil and Gas Fields in Utah*. Salt Lake City: Intermountain Association of Petroleum Geologists, 1961.

Prudden, T. Mitchell. *On the Great American Plateau*. New York: G. P. Putnam's Sons, 1906.

Redd, Preston. *From Horseback to Cadillac, I'm Still a Cowboy*. Tempe, Ariz.: Tavas Cash Press, 1988.

Reed, Alan D., and Jonathan C. Horn. "Early Navajo Occupation of the American Southwest: Reexamination of the Dinetah Phase." *Kiva* 55, no. 4 (Fall 1990): 283–300.

Reichard, Gladys A. *Dezba: Woman of the Desert*. Glorieta, New Mex.: Rio Grande Press, 1939.

———. *Navajo Shepherd and Weaver*. Glorieta, New Mex.: Rio Grande Press, 1936.

———. *Spider Woman: A Story of Navajo Weavers*. Glorieta, New Mex.: Rio Grande Press, 1934.

Reno, Philip. *Mother Earth, Father Sky, and Economic Development: Navajo Resources and Their Use*. Albuquerque: University of New Mexico Press, 1981.

Richardson, Cecil. "The Navajo Way." *Arizona Highways* (July 1948): 20–25.

Richardson, Gladwell. *Navajo Trader*. Tucson: University of Arizona Press, 1986.

Ringholz, Raye C. *Uranium Frenzy: Boom and Bust on the Colorado Plateau*. Albuquerque: University of New Mexico Press, 1989.

Roberts, Willow. *Stokes Carson: Twentieth-Century Trading on the Navajo Reservation*. Albuquerque: University of New Mexico Press, 1987.

Robbins, Lynn Arnold. "Energy Development and the Navajo Nation." In *Native Americans and Energy Development*, ed. Joseph G. Jorgensen and Sally Swenson, 35–48. Cambridge, Mass.: Anthropology Resource Center, 1978.

———. "Navajo Energy Politics." *Social Science Journal* 16, no. 2 (April 1979): 93–119.

Rodee, Marian E. *One Hundred Years of Navajo Rugs*. Albuquerque: University of New Mexico Press, 1995.

Rodgers, Larry. *1990 Census—Population and Housing Characteristics of the Navajo Nation*. Scottsdale, Ariz.: Printing Company, 1993.

Roessel, Ruth, and Broderick Johnson, eds. *Navajo Livestock Reduction: A National Disgrace*. Tsaile, Ariz.: Navajo Community College Press, 1974.

Rounds, Michael. "Indian Sovereignty Issue Concerns Operators." *Western Oil Reporter*, June 1978, 19.

Sayle, W. D. *A Trip to the Rainbow Arch*. Cleveland, Ohio: Privately printed, 1920.

Shepardson, Mary. "The Status of Navajo Women." *American Indian Quarterly* 6 (Spring–Summer 1982): 149–69.

Shepardson, Mary, and Blodwen Hammond. "Change and Persistence in an Isolated Navajo Community." *American Anthropologist* 66 (Fall 1964): 1029–50.

———. *The Navajo Mountain Community*. Berkeley: University of California Press, 1970.

Shields, Carolyn M. *A Study of the Educational Perceptions and Attitudes of Four Stakeholder Groups in the San Juan School District in 1998*. Blanding, Utah: San Juan School District, 1999.

Silver, Timothy. *A New Face on the Countryside*. New York: Cambridge University Press, 1990.

Shumway, Gary L. "Uranium Mining on the Colorado Plateau." In *San Juan County, Utah*, ed. Allan Kent Powell, 265–98. Salt Lake City: Utah State Historical Society, 1983.

Smith, Chris, and Elizabeth Manning. "The Sacred and Profane Collide in the West." *High Country News* 29 (May 1997): 1, 8–11.

Stowe, Carlton. *Utah's Oil and Gas Industry: Past, Present, and Future*. Salt Lake City: Utah Engineering Experiment Station, University of Utah, 1979.

Thoene, Bodie, and Rona Stuck. "Navajo Nation Meets Hollywood." *American West* 20, no. 5 (September–October 1983): 38–44.

Tibbitts, Kent D. "A Study of Parental Factors affecting Success or Failure of Navajo Indian Students." M.A. thesis, University of Utah, 1969.

Trafzer, Clifford E. *The Kit Carson Campaign*. Norman: University of Oklahoma Press, 1982.

Treaty between the United States of America and the Navajo Tribe of Indians. Las Vegas: KC Publications, 1973.

Trigger, Bruce G. "Early Native North American Responses to European Contact; Romantic versus Rationalistic Interpretations." *Journal of American History* 77, no. 4 (March 1991): 1195–1215.

Tyler, S. Lyman. "The Yuta Indians before 1680," *Western Humanities Review* 5 (Spring, 1951): 153–63.

Udall, Stewart L. "More Tourists Please." *Cross Currents*, July 18, 1997, 11–14.

"Utah Navajo Trust Fund: Description of Program Activities." State of Utah, n.d.

"Utah Navajo Trust Fund: Historical and Current Perspectives of the Trust Fund." State of Utah, January 1998.

Valle, Doris. *Looking Back around the Hat: A History of Mexican Hat.* Mexican Hat, Utah: Privately published, 1986.

Weisberger, Bernard A. "You Press the Button, We Do the Rest." In *A Sense of History: The Best Writing from the Pages of American Heritage*, 521–36. New York: American Heritage, 1985.

West, W. Richard, Jr., and Kevin Gover. "The Struggle for Indian Civil Rights." In *Indians in American History*, ed. Frederick E. Hoxie, 275–93. Arlington Heights, Ill.: Harlan Davidson, 1988.

Wetherill, Hilda. "The Trading Post: Letters from a Primitive Land." *Atlantic Monthly* 142 (September 1928): 289–300.

White, Richard. "Indian Land Use and Environmental Change." *Arizona and the West* 17, no. 4 (Winter 1975): 327–38.

———. *The Roots of Dependency: Subsistence, Environment and Social Change among Choctaws, Pawnees, and Navajos*. Lincoln: University of Nebraska Press, 1983.

Williams, David C. "Spending Patterns of Navajo Families." *New Mexico Business* 28, no. 2 (March 1975): 3–10.

Witherspoon, Gary. *Navajo Kinship and Marriage*. Chicago: University of Chicago Press, 1975.

———. "Navajo Social Organization." In *Handbook of North American Indians— Southwest* 10, ed. Alfonso Ortiz, 524–35. Washington, D.C.: Smithsonian Institution Press, 1983.

———. "Sheep in Navajo Culture and Social Organization." *American Anthropologist* 75 (Winter 1973): 144–47.

Worth, Sol, and John Adair. *Through Navajo Eyes: An Exploration in Film Communication and Anthropology*. Bloomington: Indiana University Press, 1972.

Wyman, Leland C. "Navajo Ceremonial System." In *Handbook of North American Indians* 10, ed. Alfonso Ortiz, 536–57. Washington, D.C.: Smithsonian Institution Press, 1983.

Young, Robert W., ed. *The Navajo Yearbook, 1951–1961: A Decade of Progress.* Report no. 8. Window Rock, Ariz.: Bureau of Indian Affairs, 1961.

Young, Robert W., and William Morgan, Sr. *Analytical Lexicon of Navajo.* Albuquerque: University of New Mexico Press, 1992.

———. *The Navajo Language: A Grammar and Colloquial Dictionary.* 2d ed. Albuquerque: University of New Mexico Press, 1987.

Zahn, Curtis. "The Automobile Is Here to Stay." *Arizona Highways* 22, no. 6 (June 1946): 22–23.
Zolbrod, Paul G. *Dine Bahane: The Navajo Creation Story*. Albuquerque: University of New Mexico Press, 1984.

NEWSPAPERS

Arizona Republic, Phoenix.
Blue Mountain Panorama, Blanding, Utah.
Canyon Echo, Bluff, Utah.
Creede Candle, Creede, Colorado.
Cross Currents, Durango, Colorado.
Denver Post, Denver, Colorado.
Deseret News, Salt Lake City, Utah.
Durango Herald, Durango, Colorado.
Farmington Enterprise, Farmington, New Mexico.
High Country News, Paonia, Colorado.
Mancos Times-Tribune, Mancos, Colorado.
Montezuma Journal, Montezuma, Colorado.
Salt Lake Tribune, Salt Lake City, Utah.
San Juan Record, Monticello, Utah.
Times-Independent, Moab, Utah.
Zephyr, Moab, Utah.

INTERVIEWS

All interviews, unless otherwise noted, are in both tape and manuscript form in possession of the author. Interviews conducted with Navajo informants on the Navajo Reservation were performed under an ethnographic permit granted by the Navajo Nation.
Begay, Cyrus. Interview by author, May 14, 1991.
Begay, Jerry. Interview by author, January 16, 1991.
Begay, John Joe. Interview by author, September 18, 1990.
Begay, John Knot. Interview by author, May 7, 1991.
Begay, Mabel Jean. Interview by author, January 18, 1991.
Begay, Nakai. Interview by Bette Benally, February 24, 1991, used with permission.
Begay, Rose. Interview by Bertha Parrish, June 17, 1987, used with permission, manuscript in possession of author.
Ben, Joe. Interview by Lorraine Ben, March 16, 1986, used with permission, manuscript in possession of author.
Benally, Ada. Interview by author, February 6, 1991.
Benally, Clyde. Telephone conversation with author, April 30, 1992.
Benally, Slim. Interview by author, July 8, 1988.

Black, Ada and Harvey. Interview by author, October 11, 1991.

Blueeyes, Charlie. Interview by author, June 7, 1988.

Blueeyes, Mary. Interview by Bette Benally, March 10, 1991, used with permission.

Bluesalt, John. Interview by author, January 14, 1991.

Bradford, Cleal. Conversation with author, May 1, 1995.

Buck, Daisy. Conversation with author, August 18, 1989.

Chaffin, Arthur L. Interview by P. T. Reilly, December 24, 1966, Utah State Historical Society, Salt Lake City, Utah.

Chief, Robert. Interview by author, April 16, 1993.

Clitso, Seth. Interview by author, January 20, 1992.

Cly, Guy, and Stella Cly. Interview by author, August 7, 1991.

Dandy, Jim. Interview by author, December 4, 1989.

Dougi, Tom. Interview by author, April 8, 1992.

Dutchie, Edward. Interview by author, May 7, 1996.

Goldwater, Barry. Interview by author, December 12, 1993.

Hatch, Ira. Interview by author, May 30, 1991.

Haycock, Bud, and Sloan Haycock. Interview by author, October 10, 1991.

Holiday, John. Interview by author, September 9, 1991.

Holiday, Keith. Interview by author, April 9, 1992.

Holiday, Marilyn. Interview by author, February 14, 1992.

Holiday, Shone. Interview by author, September 10, 1991.

Housekeeper, John. Telephone conversation with author, July 1, 1999.

Howell, Kay. Interview by author, May 14, 1991.

Howell, Robert. Interview by author, May 14, 1991.

Hunt, Ray. Interview by author, January 21, 1991.

Hunter, Lyman P. Interview by Michael Hurst, February 21, 1973, Special Collections, Brigham Young University Library, Provo, Utah.

Hurst, William Riley. Interview by author, January 23, 1992.

Jay, Mary. Interview by author, February 27, 1991.

Katso. Interview by Samuel Moon, July 25, 1974, manuscript in possession of author.

Knight, Terry. Interview by author, December 19, 1994.

Lameman, Tully. Telephone conversation with author, August 13, 1996.

Laughter, Floyd. Interview by author, April 9, 1992.

Lee, Sally. Interview by author, February 13, 1991.

Luther, Velta. Interview by author, April 8, 1992.

Lyman, Harold. Telephone conversation with author, July 29, 1992.

Manygoats, Joe. Interview by author, December 18, 1991.

Meadows, John. Interview by author, May 30, 1991.

Moore, Catherine. Interview by Jessie Embry, April 23, 1979, Charles Redd Center, Brigham Young University, Provo, Utah.

Nakai, Hilda, and Tony Nakai. Interview by Bette Benally, March 3, 1991, used with permission.

Navajo, Buck. Interview by author, December 16, 1991.

Nez, Martha. Interview by author, August 10, 1988.

Nielson, Norman. Interview by author, May 1, 1991.

Norton, Florence. Interview by author, March 6, 1991.

Norton, John. Interview by author, January 16, 1991.

Oliver, Harvey. Interview by author, May 7, 1991.

Oshley, Navajo. Interview by Wesley Oshley and Winston Hurst, January 5, 1978, transcript in possession of author.

Parrish, Cecil. Interview by author, October 10, 1991.

Pehrson, Jack. Interview by author, June 20, 1992.

Philips, Pearl. Interview by Bertha Parrish, June 17, 1987, used with permission, manuscript in possession of author.

Redshaw, Helen. Interview by author, May 16, 1991.

Russell, Gail. Conversation with author, November 13, 1997.

Sakizzie, Ella. Interview by author, May 14, 1991.

Silas, Jane. Interview by author, January 27, 1991.

Smallcanyon, Walter. Interview by author, April 3, 1993.

Tom, George. Interview by author, August 7, 1991.

Wallace, Guy. Telephone conversation with author, January 27, 1992.

Weston, Margaret. Interview by author, February 13,1991.

Whitehorse, Ben. Interview by author, January 30, 1991.

Yazzie, Fred, and Suzie Yazzie. Interview by author, August 6, 1991.

Yellow, Billy. Interview by author, November 6, 1987.

INDEX

Aboriginal Uintah Nation of Utah, 225

Acculturation: trading posts and, 74, 82. *See also* Cultural change; Education

Acting: actors and, 142; criteria for Indian roles, 144; Navajos and, 154, 155–56

Adair, John, 155

Agriculture, 18, 117; government farmers, 48, 50, 51, 56, 57, 62; irrigation and, 44–46, 48–51, 54–55, 56–58, 61, 63

Ahkeah, Sam, 109

Airplanes, Navajos' early impressions of, 97–98

American Indian Movement (AIM), 188, 192, 193, 194, 196, 197, 198

American Indian Resource Center, 232

Anasazi, the, 7, 45; the earth and, 172; ruins of, 74, 75

Aneth, Utah, 17, 18; irrigation and, 50; Redshaw and, 56–61

Aneth Extension: part of Navajo Reservation, 20; oil and, 181, 220

Aneth oil field, 180; decline of production and, 183, 185; Navajo economy and, 196; Navajo occupation of Texaco pumping facility, 190–94; OPEC and, 183–84; various oil companies operating in (1978), 192; yield in first full year of production, 181

Aneth Trading Post, 52

Animals, 90; beaver hunting, 21–22; birds and, 179; as helpers and protectors in Navajo mythology, 13; the holy beings and, 4–5; horses, 88, 89, 91, 111, 113, 146–47; and hunting rituals, 25; and oil companies, 196; wage economy and, 201. *See also* Deer; Livestock; Sheep

Antes, Howard Ray, 17–18

Archaeology, 6–7; Navajos as laborers, 75–76

Arizona, 221

Arizona Dept. of Transportation, 225

Arizona Republic, 190, 192

Army, the (U.S.), 10–11, 14, 46

Arthur, Chester A., 16, 181

Artifacts, 74–75, 79

Ashcroft, Charley, 112

Atomic Energy Commission, 161, 174

Automobiles: cradle boards and, 90; first arrival of in Bluff, 86; the Franklin Camel, 93; gas and, 88,

Changing Woman, 5, 90, 158, 159, 178

Chantways, 6, 152, 156, 169; first Enemy Way ceremony, 159

Charley, Fern, 103

Charley, Perry, 176

Chee, Hastiin, 127–28

Chee, John, 110–11

Cheyenne Autumn (Ford film), 156

Chief, Robert, 133

Church of Jesus Christ of Latter-day Saints, 208, 232. *See also* Mormons

Chuska Energy Corporation, 195–96

Civilian Conservation Corps (CCC), 95, 117

Clansmen, Blind Salt, 124

Clarkson Tours, 131

Clinton, President Bill, 235

Cly, Guy, 140

Coalition for Navajo Liberation, 187–88, 190, 192, 193, 196, 198

Cody, Iron Eyes, 21

College of Eastern Utah, 215–16, 221

Collier, John, 103, 116–17

Colorado, 29

Colorado Club, 134

Colorado Plateau, the, 44; uranium and, 159, 161

Colorado River (Utah), 135

Colville, Clyde, 80, 129

Commerce. *See* Tourism; Trading posts

Conoco, 192

Construction, 129–31; canals and reservoirs, 48, 63; government station at Aneth Trading Post, 52; the holy beings and, 97; Lee's Ferry Bridge, 81–82; at mining sites, 164; movie companies and, 146, 148; oil companies and, 186; road from Aneth to Four Corners, 51–52; road from Gallup to Shiprock, 80; roads and uranium mining, 173–74;

schools, 228, 229; Vendor Village, 225. *See also* Irrigation

Correctional facilities: sweat lodges and, 225; tobacco and, 226

Cortés, Hernán, 83

Cortez Herald, 80

Council of Energy Resource Tribes (CERT), 184. *See also* MacDonald

Coyote, 5

Crank, Loren, 228

Crystal gazing, 162

Cultural change: cars and, 95; economic development and, 236; education and, 228; elders and, 202; livestock reduction and, 200; Navajo women and, 219; transportation and, 200. *See also* Acculturation

Culture: animals and, 4; cars and, 95; education and, 211; fear of the dead and, 73; Indian Walk-in Center and, 232; language and, 232; as matrilineal, 200; school curriculum and, 230; technology and, 98; wage economy and, 82–83. *See also* Education; Language; Navajo society; Song

Cummings, Dr. Byron, 125

Daw, John, 129

Dawes Act, 46

Deer: fawns and population of, 37, 41; Ford and, 150; grass and, 38–40; Hastiin Tso and, 24; hunting by Southern Utes, 28, 29, 30; hunting of, 22–24, 26, 32–33, 41–42; hunting of fawns, 27; population statistics, 36, 37; predation and, 38; vs. sheep in food preparation, 104–105; skinning, 25; slaughter of, 31, 34–35

Democratic National Convention (1992), 235

Printed in the USA
CPSIA information can be obtained
at www.ICGtesting.com
LVHW040215030224
770776LV00001B/42